PEACE LOVING NATIONS

PEACE LOVING NATIONS

Nilanjana Sanyal

KALPAZ

Peace Loving Nations

Rs. 850

ISBN: 978-81-7835-794-2

Published in 2010 in India by
Kalpaz Publications
C-30, Satyawati Nagar,
Delhi-110052
E-mail: kalpaz@hotmail.com
Phone : 9212729499

Laser Type Setting by: Quick Media, Delhi
Printed at : Chawla Offset Printers, Press, Delhi

Contents

Foreword

I consider this book on peace by Nilanjana, a young graduate in psychology from Delhi, a milestone for the youth. I wish all our young people are as passionately committed to peace as Nilanjana is. It is indeed a book worth reading by all those who care for peace. Though she is young but has very mature understanding of causes of conflict and violence. She very well understands that mere absence of war is not peace.

Violence is not mere disturbance of mind. There are deeper causes. It is mainly absence of justice and inequitable distribution of resources. It is not for nothing that in 19th and 20th centuries wars were fought mainly in Europe which emerged as continent of colonizers. The two World Wars of 20th century caused as much damage to human life and property as other wars in the past. Millions of people died. In Hiroshima and Nagasaki alone more than two hundred thousand lives were wiped out.

The European nations fought against each other for controlling the resources of Asia and Africa. And these two wars also brought about radical changes in the power equations, quite an unintende3d result and many colonies had to be released from yokes of slavery. Also, after these two wars, the balance of power shifted to America. America emerged as the most powerful nation on earth.

Now it was America which tried to dominate the whole world and disturb peace in African and Asian nations. The first major war fought by America was in Vietnam. There it killed thousands of unarmed peasants though it faced shameful defeat at their hands. But it hardly taught any

lesson to American ruling classes greedy for third world resources.

Its lates misadventures were in Afghanistan and Iraq. Thousands of innocent civilians perished in these wars and for America loss of these lives was nothing more than what it cynically described as 'collateral damage'. It waged war against Iraq in the name of 'weapons of mass destruction' but real reason, among others, was oil. Thousands are still dying in these two countries due to bomb blasts.

Nilanjana also points out double standards of American rulers when it comes to human rights and democratic norms. These beautiful terms are meant perhaps only for majority of while Americans, not even for its African minority or its Muslim citizens. For them it has Abu Gharib and Gontenamo or prisons in various East European countries where it could torture its helpless victims. Thankfully Barak Obama has brought some relief to these hapless victims of CIA wrath.

Nilanjana not only passionately pleads for world peace but throws adequate light on various factors which bring about war and destruction. She focuses on injustice as a main factor for absence of peace. In fact violence is directly proportional to degree of injustice in the world. A must read, I feel for lovers of peace.

Dr. Asghar Ali Engineer,

(Recipient of the Right Livelihood Honorary Award (also called the Alternate Nobel Award) for vision and work, Stockholm, Sweden, Dec.2004)

Preface

Differences between man and man have existed from the beginning of time. But it is only recently, in the process of fulfilling his own personal material desires, that man has not given any consideration to the consequences of his actions. The inevitable result: a world where an estimated 800 million go hungry; where children die of preventable causes (and treatable illnesses) on a daily basis and where even the international community struggles to put an end to wars/the threat of war and more bloodletting. 9/11, for instance, was a horrific thing to happen and should never have happened, but was war the answer?

This brings us to the Peace Debate: whether there is a 'Peace Gene' of sorts; whether Peace can be attained in our time and what are the mechanisms wherein the world can achieve peace?

I have not addressed these questions 'per se' in my book. A careful look at the questions will reveal to us that there are deeper complexities involved. Peace is not something that could be attained by mere wishful thinking: it would take us years to ever come to terms with the very essence of it. Indeed there are no ingredients in Peace; one has to look at it in totality. It is not within the capability of this young author to do complete justice to the debate.

There are some societies of the world where peace has been achieved largely due to an educated, enlightened populace. There are also certain primitive societies that value peace as an ideal to be lived and cherished by their populations. In the former case, I can cite Scandinavia, as for the latter; the Macuxi people in the Amazon are a peace-loving people for instance. I am reminded of Margaret Mead's famous Arapesh of Papua New Guinea. This brings us to the question of a 'Peace Gene'...

One thing is for sure: that peace is related to human development. There are indeed greater chances that warring societies/societies in conflict are those that are placed poorly on the Human Development Index (HDI) and vice-versa though this is not strictly the case. The Western world, for instance, lives in constant fear of terror attacks. This brings us to the question of global and regional insecurity.

PEACE IS NOT SIMPLY THE ABSENCE OF WAR/END OF WAR. To the deprived and vulnerable populations of South Asia and indeed Sub-Saharan Africa, a class we would call the "Poor", the terms G8 and nuclear non-proliferation and weapons of mass destruction would mean absolutely nothing. There are more important issues in their lives: just being able to put food on the tables for their families to eat; sending their children to school and renovating the leaking pipes/shacks/thatched hutments; and protecting themselves against eviction.

In a world overflowing with riches, this is the "Silent Holocaust". That 40,000 children die daily. More powerful than the Atomic Bomb. Than the Katrina. Than the Tsunami.

In recent years, global warming has assumed serious proportions. Our polar ice caps are melting, temperatures are rising and the Tsunami has grown fiercer. The poor are compelled by hardship to cut down trees for a livelihood; while on the other hand, the rich have chosen to indulge in more and greater wealth accumulation and limitless material consumption. This added to obscene speculation and a casino world economy have exacerbated the rich-poor divide, leading to greater global economic and social inequalities creating a wide chasm between the "haves" and the "have-nots". Unless poverty and inequality are addressed 'per se', climate change may go beyond our control.

Who am I to ever say this, but we ought to cut down on space exploration and set up a "child poverty consortium" in the developing/least-developed countries; divert a part of

world military spending to health and education, for instance. Participate in the day-to-day lives of the poor. Embrace their concerns as our own. Then and only then can Peace be achieved.

Personally I think that we cannot achieve peace and tolerance among the next generation as long as we have poor and uneducated people. The growing chasm between rich and poor will create a backlash that may destabilize the world further. Nations that are truly Peace-loving are the ones with the best spread of wealth. To build peace, we must increase the availability to information; and opportunities for literacy and education; and access to health and health reform.

Let us teach the fundamental values (liberties, humanitarianism, equality, peace, understanding, truth, justice and human rights) and a basic understanding of the things we either don't need/don't need much (ignorance, rudeness, bigotry, corruption, materialism).

I quote—Avatar Adi Da Samraj

Real Global Peace

It is now time to accept the political necessity for an end to confrontation-politics, and the establishment of a unified political entity to directly and truly and formally and accountably serve the right collective interests of mankind as a whole. Human beings must abandon their ancient egoic principles and renounce their political, social, and cultural provincialism.

Individuals within the collective order of mankind may yet suffer the un-Enlightened and immature disabilities of egocentric personality—but governments themselves, as well as institutions and leaders in every area of human endeavor, must abandon the egocentric, subhuman, merely materialistic, non-cooperative, and intolerant (or loveless) posture and style of life.

Indeed, humanity as a whole must demand that a new leadership of this kind come forward and accept responsibility, in a unified (and truly representative and accountable) manner, for the indivisible representation of its collective interests. . . .

I Call upon all the leaders and educators of mankind (now, and forever hereafter) to actively embrace, and to universally declare and promote, and to actively require and measure the universal real fulfillment of My simplest Law and Measure of Man: Cooperation + Tolerance = Peace.

(from "On Liberation from ego and egoic society, or, Cooperation + Tolerance = Peace")

A new world is emerging. A world that is moving towards compassion. A world that is moving towards greater tolerance. Towards Peace. There is now more demand for Equality than ever before.

A more tolerant generation is on the way. Conscientious of its duties and aware of its rights. Under these circumstances, it becomes necessary that we the 'Peace-loving Nations' of the world should facilitate the achievement of a more Egalitarian Global Order.

This is only a utopian dream. Until nations of the world strive to achieve this global order, we can have 'n' number of conferences and conventions and summits, but nothing much I guess would come out of them. We are responsible to our future generations, our children and it is to them that we are accountable (for indeed our actions). The decisions we take now shall determine the lives of the world's future, in the lifetimes of today's children.

There is simply no time. Our actions in war and peace and justice (as in applied notions of pre-emption and aggression/force) are affecting (nee ruining) the lives of innocent children worldwide who have done nothing to cause such actions. It is often difficult for children to recover from the horrors of war, indeed some are forced to relive the

trauma in times of war, fall victim to war crimes, genocide and crimes against humanity. Bosnia, Rwanda and in recent times, Darfur are a case in point.

Poverty and inequality is the worst scourge of our times, an era in which the rich have grown so rich that when they celebrate, their parties 'can be seen from space'. There is now a horrific trend towards mindless consumerism, food dumping and a 'Capitalistic temperament' and debt, all gifts supposedly of Capitalism, that are coming in the way of a more egalitarian global order.

'Born Free' that's what we are, and strive we must to put an end to the hegemonic systems/patterns of thinking that are not only causing irreversible damage to ourselves and our children, but harm to the environment as well. In the end, if we are successful, then 'the storms shall rage and the oceans roar', but we will have proudly established ourselves as "PEACE LOVING NATIONS"...

Nilanjana Sanyal

1

Excerpts from Remarks by ISMAIL SERAGELDIN at UTS Graduation Ceremony,

Sydney, Australia

(04 May 2004)

"..Today we are decoding the DNA blueprints of life, we are mobilizing bacteria to do our work, and we are manipulating the very building blocks of life...

Will these be the forces of homogenization or of diversity? Will they be used to crush the weak or to afford them new opportunities?

Much has been done much to make the world a better place for all. The twentieth century, was one of struggle for emancipation. The colonies were liberated, women got the franchise, racial, ethnic and religious minorities and non-conformists were all acknowledged to have political and civil rights that derive from their common humanity. Around the planet, more people than ever enjoy these freedoms. This has not come easily and the blood of millions was the price that was paid to reach where we have reached today.

On the socio-economic front, in the last forty years the developing countries have doubled school enrollments, halved infant mortality and adult illiteracy, and extended life expectancy at birth by an amazing twenty years. But despite that, much, so much, remains to be done. A global developmental agenda demands our efforts and our solidarity. This new world that has never been more promising or more perilous.

Consider the paradox of our times. We live in a world of plenty, of dazzling scientific advances and technological breakthroughs. Yet, our times are marred by conflict, violence,

economic uncertainty and tragic poverty. A sense of insecurity pervades even the most affluent societies. Nations are looking inward, and the rich turn their backs on the poor.

In this world so rapidly reinventing itself, where does ethical responsibility come in? The ruthless allocative efficiency of the market should be tempered by a caring and nurturing society. We cannot allow the gap between the rich and the poor continue to grow. We must recognize that we are all part of the same human family.

Abraham Lincoln once warned the American people that a house divided cannot stand, that a nation cannot live half slave and half free.

..a world divided cannot survive, that the human family cannot live partly rich and mostly poor.

We must change the world. The world can be changed, but only if we fight against the prevailing apathy and lack of caring.

..It is inconceivable that there should be some 800 million persons going hungry in a world that can provide for that most basic of all human needs. In the 19th century, some people looked at the condition of slavery and said that it was monstrous and unconscionable. That it must be abolished. They were known as the abolitionists. They did not argue from economic self interest, but from moral outrage.

Today the condition of hunger in a world of plenty is equally monstrous and unconscionable and must be abolished. We must become the "new abolitionists".

We must, with the same zeal and moral outrage, attack the complacency that would turn a blind eye to this silent holocaust which claims some 40,000 hunger-related deaths every day.

..The challenge is great, but it must be met...

Yes! We must change the world. We must ensure that the new millennium is indeed the millennium for all the wretched of the earth.

It can be done, it must be done.."

2

Space Exploration over Chronic Child Poverty Research

(Greater Global Accountability and Transparency Needed)

The year	:	1999 Anno Domini following the birth of Christ.
The place	:	Cape Canaveral, the United States of America.
The event	:	Preparing for the launch of a rocket into outer space.

The National Aeronautics and Space Administration (NASA) testing all controls and communication instruments, pressure testing the combustion chamber, testing the nozzle, testing the fuel.

Time: 10: 15: 03 GMT.

At this particular moment, something else is happening in another part of the world, called the **THIRD WORLD**, (may be), in Brazil or in India, **GOD** is trying to touch a trash can, yes, **A LITTLE FLOWER CALLED A CHILD** is picking subsistence ("food for thought") out of a trash can (actually, a garbage dump). And **GOD** wanted to warn policy-makers and environmentalists of the perils of neglecting a **CHILD** (hunger / malnutrition) and neglecting the environment, our beloved Eco-system. Yes, the policy-makers and environmentalists were sleeping and the two superpowers were vying with each other trying to build superior space shuttles. One underwent a series of reforms with Glasnost and Perestroika..as also a fall of its system

(Communism) ..Another power (may be star power) rose out of the ashes after President Harry Truman and Hiroshima and Nagasaki. Yes, the land of Zen Buddhism, 'Shinto' and beautiful Mt.Fujiyama and the Kamakura is now busy building fashionable cars, more comfortable cars. **PRAY, HOW MUCH MORE COMFORT DO WE NEED?** When, at this moment, a **CHILD** is being born as a cretin because his mother's diet lacked iodine.

[I MUST SAY THAT DISCRIMINATION BEGINS BEFORE BIRTH]

Did the ALMIGHTY want this kind of a world?

HE wanted **PEACE**.

Day by day, wars are increasing.

Have computers, technology been able to bring **PEACE**, solved **POVERTY**?

Has Science been able to bring **PEACE**, solve **POVERTY**? (I am, however, gradually coming to believe, that Science and Technology, well applied, can cure much of what ails mankind).

What is mankind coming to?

It may sound futuristic, but man is trying to act like the extra-terrestrial, create Jurassic Parks around himself. Man wants **PEACE**, "SHANTI". Man may be dreaming of **PEACE**, actually dinosaurs, which means life in the jungles (yes, man probably thinks he was at **PEACE** in the jungles, the beginning of civilization, so may be he wants to go back to the jungles).

There was **PEACE** in the past. There will hopefully be **PEACE** in the future, and the present is in turmoil. Before we discuss this turmoil, **LET US OBSERVE A MOMENT OF SILENCE:**

"OM SHANTI" (A salutation to the concept of **PEACE**)

"SILENT NIGHT, HOLY NIGHT" (A salutation to Lord Jesus, Christ the Lord)

"BUDDHAM SHARANAM GACHHAMI" (A salutation to Lord Buddha, the prince who renounced the world, let us put ourselves under his protection) **AND PRAY:**

- For those millions of **CHILDREN** who have been traumatized by mass violence (orphans of war, never again!) e.g. in Rwanda, Bosnia-
- For those suffering from the after-effects of the holocaust at Hiroshima and Nagasaki (never again should that happen!!)-
- For those in Asia, Africa and in the rest of the world suffering from (famine), disease and hunger-
- For those languishing under **POVERTY**-
- For those sleeping on the streets because of lack of adequate housing-
- For the rights of indigenous peoples-
- For those displaced by multinational projects-
- For those displaced from their homes as a result of civil war and social disintegration-
- For every plant, every flower, for every tree-
- For every animal or bird on the verge of extinction-
- For every man or every woman who has faced cross-cultural friction, community friction-
- For global refugees-
- For every man or woman or **CHILD** who has been denied the right to read and write-
- For all those who have suffered abuse of some kind-

WE BREAK OUR SILENCE, OUR PEACE, OUR "SADHANA" (meditation)

Time: 10: 20: 23 GMT.

The space rocket has taken off from the blast site, planning to go into a condition of ZERO gravity, weightlessness, perhaps carrying a cat (first there was a dog called "Laika" in outer space). At this moment, a man in a

country called Nepal in the Trans-Himalayas is FREEZING in the cold on the streets at night, when the temperatures have fallen below ZERO. (Be they in Nepal or in America, IMAGINE those having no homes to go back to?) At this time, in the Northern Hemisphere (GOD, why on Earth is everything on this planet so divided-including the hemispheres?) lakes have FROZEN at the North Pole. SO A MAN HAS FROZEN ON THE STREETS WHEN TEMPERATURES HAVE FALLEN BELOW ZERO? Yes, and the Earth is probably heading for FROZEN **PEACE**. So, let me tell myself, **my heart melts For a child (and it will any way, if not for other reasons, under present conditions of global warming!)**.

So, let me sacrifice my ice cream for a hungry **CHILD** on the street. **Let me look into my mirage and try to create an oasis in a desert**.

Let me, for once, sacrifice my meal for a hungry **CHILD**, and try to work to **green a desert.**

SILENCE PEACE
OM SHANTI A SALUTATION TO PEACE
PEACE PEACE
COMMONALITY TOGETHERNESS

At this moment, interballistic missiles are getting fired!!!!!

Think for a moment, while I pay homage to an American called Carl Sagan of "COSMOS" fame and a Frenchman called Jean Jacques Cousteau of "Secrets of the Sea" fame. With or without heresy, (remember Copernicus?), once again, take the plunge. GET A LITTLE DEEPER INTO SOMEONE ELSE'S WORLD. I know that in 1960, Bathyscape TRIESTE reached the deepest ocean bed- the Mariana Trench in the Pacific Ocean. But you do not have to build a "more fashionable" Bathyscape. I have better things to do- attending a "glamorous" 'International Convention' where policy-makers (and I am one of them) will discuss???????, the three most unfinished tasks on the global agenda-

POVERTY THE ENVIRONMENT
AND
GLOBAL HUMAN SECURITY
And ways to manage the events!!!!!!!

3

Jesus in our Time

Exploring the range of issues-dignity, development, poverty, genocide, sex and violence and DARFUR, where do we get our sense of right and wrong from? Are we born with a sense of moral reasoning? Is it inborn? Or is it imbibed from our environment?

For instance, how moral is it to starve children? How moral was it to invade Iraq? How moral will Abu Ghraib or Guantanamo ever be? How moral and indeed ethical is that we should go on consuming where half of humanity lives on $1 a day and where children die (of preventable causes) on a daily basis?

Existing quotients-intelligence, emotional, sex and social cannot simply serve our purpose, what we need now more than ever before is a 'moral quotient'. Morals, or the lack of them, appear to currently pervade even those societies that have apparently lost their sense of reason in the face of current global opinion!

Harvard University professor Marc Hauser has even written a book on the subject, 'Moral Minds: How Nature Designed Our Universal Sense of Right and Wrong'- and he puts a very relevant question-are we born with a sense of morality or do we biologically inherit it?

I trust different cultures have their own sense of morality, hence morality is an ethical question, but even in the so called civilized world, excesses do routinely occur.

One of these routine excesses is wealth accumulation, indeed man's greed, which has unfortunately, in recent

years, become a horrific trend. There is more and more material consumption or patterns of consumerism, sadly, in the developing world; one in every fifth child does not live to see its fifth birthday. These figures are not absolute.

That amounts to murder but not heresy or treason. The inevitable consequence, those that have committed the genocides in Darfur and Bosnia and Rwanda have gotten away; those that have tortured and abused in Abu Ghraib and Afghanistan and Guantanamo have gotten away; and those that have forced, raped, plundered and looted millions of innocents in Africa have also gotten away. Sometimes, the notion of pre-emption or pre-emptive reasoning has so long been forsaken in search of greater aggression and gore and our leaders have more often than not chosen to look the other way.

Looking at torture, we find and you would agree that torturing a war criminal, for instance, could also be wrong. But can it be morally permissible to torture a man who can tell you where a bomb has been planted? What if the torture saves a 100 lives?

All we need now is a JESUS IN OUR TIME.

4

An Elixir for Justice?

"Now the trumpet summons us again...

..a call to bear the burden of a long twilight struggle, year in and year out, rejoicing in hope, patient in tribulation's struggle against the common enemies of man : tyranny, POVERTY, disease and war itself. Can we forge against these enemies a grand and global alliance, North and South, East and West, that can assure a more fruitful life for all mankind?"

-President J F Kennedy, USA,
in an address to the nation

I often feel concerned that we do not live in a just world. Lopsided development and rampant consumerism have widened the chasm between the world's rich and the world's poor. We have witnessed a gross violation of human rights across the globe. Millions of the world's **CHILDREN** still cling precariously to life. About 40,000 of them die every day due to preventable causes-hunger, disease, war and neglect. Women in the developing world face gross inequities in food and nutrition, income(s) and opportunity. Terrorism is devastating large parts of the globe. Millions of the world's people lack access to safe drinking water, decent health care, shelter, education, and means of communication and jobs. The task of ending world hunger remains formidable. Increasing population pressures, deforestation and desertification are eating away our precious natural resources. Many countries face the 'darker' side of development, "Debt". War and disease are forcing millions to flee their home countries. And, indigenous people all over

the world are becoming fast endangered under pressure from the forces of global expansion. Also, there are those innocent people being sexually abused, raped or mutilated (as in war). Drugs, alcohol, poor mental health, juvenile delinquency and HIV/AIDS are taking a heavy toll. Pollution is now a major health hazard. The ozone layers are getting depleted. And the Earth is warming up...

How does one respond to the crises? What do we, the inhabitants of the planet, owe to one another? What institutions should we recognize? What ethical standards apply throughout the world?

There is no concept of "distributive justice". What a strange anomaly, that 1.1 billion people-18% of humanity, should have to live below $2/day while on the other hand, the Canadian government provides farmers with $3/per cattle for food. So the food we consume, is eating better than the people in the Third World countries. I ask you, is this distribution of wealth JUST?

I often wonder if there could be an elixir for justice. To me, the end of inequality is a utopian dream that we must all strive to achieve. We could for instance achieve a violence-free world. There would be no need for wars on terror. However, there are some questions to examine in the process.

What is the root cause of poverty? Is it the systemic injustices of the world economy? Don't the rich have an obligation to help the poor, or is aid simply a matter of charity, and therefore to be admired but not morally needed? If the poor should be helped, how much help is required – just enough that they can fulfill their basic needs, enough that they can flourish as humans, or until THEY ARE NO LONGER WORSE OFF THAN THE RICH?

Perhaps more than any other institution- the state, communes, federal entities, global financial institutions like the World Bank, international NGOs, multinational corporations, international courts, what we need today

perhaps is "A WORLD GOVERNMENT"..to best achieve the ideal of global justice. But whose responsibility would it be to create and sustain such an institution?

Possibly the answer lies in the EYES OF THE POOR. Or in diverting a part of global spending on arms to the social sector. Or in possibly introducing an international insolvency law.

There is the problem of "Debt"...We are examining the darker side of development... And there arises a need to re-orient national and international plans and policies in favor of the poor...

The UN has brought relief from under-nourishment to many millions (in the Third World) and saved many more, by providing vaccination and treatment...from disease...has delivered many small farmers in developing countries from struggling on poor or unirrigated soil...our world is changing...We have achieved a victory over smallpox..new vistas of communication have opened up...The risk of nuclear war has receded..or has it? A vast number of people are living in inhuman and degrading conditions...

Talk cannot prevent a CHILD from dying...cannot produce enough food for a single family...or sink wells or dig irrigation channels to produce better crops...it cannot provide medical care for families that have never seen a doctor in their lives...all "Unfinished Business of our 'Beloved" Planet.. So much to be done..so much that can be done...

The time has come in the history of nations to liberate their peoples from centuries of illiteracy, ignorance, poverty, disease and war, centuries of inequality. The poor are often reduced to the harsh realities of survival in their daily lives, be they are lying below the poverty line, or be they displaced, or be they stand infected with TB/HIV/AIDS...

I do not understand much of fiscal policy or bulls and bears. What I do understand is the language of the poor

and the marginalized, or the language of the harsh realities of staying alive till the next moment, the next day, the language of survival...

More than ever before, issues of food production are directly tied to national security. There could be no greater catastrophe than the vulnerability of our food supply in the post 9/11 era..of confronting malnutrition and hunger in the developing world...

In the post 9/11 world, where the fight against terrorism has changed the political landscape, people are hungrier than ever. On that same fateful day (September 11), around 16000 children worldwide died from hunger-related causes. By the time you finish reading this book; a few more children will have died. Talking about challenging the systems that feed hunger...

What will happen (social ferment, discontent, civil strife, chaos) if global inequality is not addressed?

We are facing a time of ferment, if not crisis, in the existing global order..from the global inequality gap between the haves and the have-nots. I feel that the ferment rippling across the global neighborhood is indeed a consequence of gross inequalities, and where these inequalities are not addressed, discontent is inevitable and conflict likely.

I am convinced (as an Indian citizen) that Inequality is what threatens our economic stability. We might call ourselves a stable nation, but judging from the recent Mumbai terror attacks, we are certainly not. In fact, such conditions are the ones that have bred Maoist insurgency; indeed we must solve the problems of inequality, discrimination, poverty, corruption, and injustice, before we would ever think of calling in the police or anti-insurgency laws to deal with the Naxalite movement.

Income inequalities within nations breed insurgency and conflict, and can give rise to the situation we see in India today.

Inequality also breeds contempt. And contempt breeds terror. Poverty may be an underlying cause of terrorism, and so could grievances of the past (rooted in the history of man) and unfair trade practices, though I am not too sure. It makes more sense to address the root causes of inequality than to carry on with a so-called war on terror. Have we at any rate wiped out terror or tried to address the root causes?

Now is a world apart. A growing number of ecologists, ethicists and economists believe that the needs of the 'have-nots' will one day become too powerful to ignore. We live in a world of vast disparities between the living standards of developed and underdeveloped nations and it would be unwise to look the other way. A social ferment is building up, somewhere, strong enough to blow away the Statue of Liberty sometime. Why would those whose habitats have been displaced look the other way? Why would those whose forests were being cut down by powerful Western corporations? Why would a refugee continue to suffer in silence? These problems are linked to global economic issues, such as a lack of access to capital markets and dependence on foreign aid.

Time is running out. We MUST start today-to address the root causes of inequality both between and within nations..Chasing Weapons of Mass Destruction will not help. Staging and attending 'glamorous' conventions, conferences and workshops THAT UNFORTUNATELY DO NOT REACH THE POOR will not help either. A 'WAR ON TERROR' WILL ONLY TAKE AWAY MORE LIVES, BUT WILL NOT HELP...

WE MUST START WITH THE POOR. With those that are too poor to buy essentials. Too poor to send their children to school. To have access to health, education, clean drinking water and sanitation, and means of communication and jobs. To those that are at THE END OF INEQUALITY.

It is to the poor, the most unfortunate, the most wretched and the ugliest on the planet that I dedicate my work...

5

A Very Sick World

Another World is Not Only Necessary But Possible

The Earth is now wealthier than ever before, but the majority continues to suffer more injustice, more cruelty and death. A majority of the world's population lives on $1 a day, and 25,000 people die of hunger daily. Desertification threatens the lives of millions and so do pests, locusts, crop failure and disease.

It is sometimes heard that in this our globalised world, the poor often may get new life chances, through MIGRATION. While this is true to a limited extent, it is also true that migration is more often a matter of compulsion. Today, migration is not simply readjusting the human species, but a process rooted in the very history of man and extremely painful a process.

More and more people are forced to suffer in silence, as global spending on ARMS and ARMIES reaches unprecedented levels. This is more than what the world spends on food and agriculture, and ought to be a major cause of contemporary global concern. The trade in arms continues to be high on the agenda and indeed a source of profit for many states. Amnesty International estimates that at least half a million people are decimated annually by small arms.

"The aim of globalisation is to dominate the rest of us, any other country, any other world. Globalisation is simply westernisation. The West wants to be the centre of the world."

(Aminata Traore: World Social Forum, Mali)

Hunger, weapons and forced migrations through lack of land, water and soil, decimate on a regular basis. Diseases, like HIV, TB and malaria decimate as well, what with the multinational pharmaceutical companies seeking to protect their own patents by lobbying against much cheaper life-saving generic treatments available. Experience tells us that the fundamental cause is CAPITALISM.

According to L. de Sebastian:

"Real capitalism" is responsible for the organisation of the world economy that is ethically and morally wrong, for the shameful and absurd coexistence in an even more integrated world of appalling poverty with unprecedented wealth.

In a world of sin and greed, it often takes a Tsunami to take notice of immoralities. Human beings in the contemporary era have not only become wealth-producing machines, but wealth-worshipping as well. The principle of human dignity is then applied only to those that are able to produce more and more wealth adding to the oppression of those who cannot. The inevitable result, a widened chasm between the so-called HAVES and the so-called HAVE-NOTS.

We live in a cruel society of sorts. Cruel, because it comes down heavily on the oppressed, and also because those intoxicated by abundance simply refuse to feel for those suffering.

Someone has aptly put it:

"When future generations judge our time, they will call us barbarians, inhuman and pitiless, because of our heartlessness towards the sufferings of our brothers and sisters."

"If human beings had even a little humanity, just 4% of the 225 largest fortunes in the world would be enough to

give food, water, health and education to all." That is obscene.

We could go on and on. This is the "serious illness" of an entire civilization. As a Colombian missionary put it, 'Statistics don't bleed, people do.'

And indeed. Man has often failed to apply his moral reasoning with disastrous consequences. Afghanistan was wrong, Iraq ran contrary to moral pre-emption, and Somalia and Darfur were excesses that morally outraged the international community.

That leaves our mortal human beings with a sense of DEHUMANIZATION. We are dehumanized by our own selfish morals, indeed our heartlessness towards the dramatic facts of cruel poverty, obscene inequality, social exclusion, discrimination and AIDS. We are often dehumanized by our own utter contempt for the poor and the wretched of the earth, and our utter disrespect for Mother Nature.

Ignoring HUMAN DIGNITY often carries a price. An often slow rate of progress. The Millennium Goals will often not reach their targets and will do little to diminish poverty if the poor are not treated with 'human respect' or included in the achievement of these goals. Reducing by half the 'number of people suffering from hunger will take 145 years, and not be achieved by 2015' as 189 heads of state had guaranteed.

'Political Will' is needed. Hunger continues to decimate on an unprecedented scale, this means human will to eliminate hunger is lacking. One might blatantly ask: do we human beings want to eliminate hunger?

The EMPIRES OF GLOBALIZATION simply do not. Therein arises the QUESTION OF IMPERIALISM.

I am glad I am giving up imperialism for 'globalization'.

LET THERE BE WORLD PEACE.

Actually, WHY TALK OF OTHER USELESS THINGS WHEN THERE IS SO MUCH INEQUALITY IN THE WORLD? ARE OUR HEADS OF STATE SERIOUS ABOUT GLOBAL INEQUALITY?

I agree that there is so much unbearable injustice and suffering in our world. Sadly, most people I talk to runaway from the subject, things are determined in a way where even thinking becomes futile, and inequality, chaos and suffering of our brethren continue on a daily basis.

THERE ARE WESTERN DOUBLE STANDARDS.

I hope that Western governments do not observe double standards on the question of human rights as happened in Afghanistan, in Iraq. SANCTIONS are most undesirable and at the best obscene. The standards should be the same- be they for the world's major powers or for the world's despots. Western governments often turn a blind eye to the extensive violation of human rights and the rules of democracy by their allies, but they show great sensitivity to human rights violations committed by their enemies.

We must not forget that in nearly every instance, Western governments have played a significant role in the emergence of poverty and wretchedness in peripheral societies through their direct or indirect support for incompetent and unworthy rulers. They, therefore, bear their share of the responsibility for the terrible conditions in the South.

INCLUDING NUCLEAR WEAPONS..?

I am opposed to an arms race, the proliferation of nuclear weapons and imposing unilateral policies on the strength of nuclear threats absolutely and whenever they occur. Strict adherence to the NPT is a good starting point for all the nations of the world; it will allow them to prevent new nuclear weapons from emerging and to destroy existing nuclear weapons.

6

I am Opposed to the Arms Race and the Proliferation of Nuclear Weapons

JOHAN GALTUNG, THE DALAI LAMA

and DAISAKU IKEDA

(WEAPONS OF MASS DESTRUCTION/A PEACE UNIVERSITY IN EVERY CONTINENT!)

"OURS IS A WORLD OF NUCLEAR GIANTS AND ETHICAL INFANTS. WE KNOW MORE ABOUT WAR THAN WE KNOW ABOUT PEACE, MORE ABOUT KILLING THAN WE KNOW ABOUT LIVING. WE HAVE GRASPED THE MYSTERY OF THE ATOM AND REJECTED THE SERMON ON THE MOUNT."

-OMAR N. BRADLEY

(WHY ON EARTH DOES EVERY THING HAVE TO COME DOWN TO CONFRONTATION?)

(Dreaming! Actually, not everything. A Lot of it does come down to **"Synergy"**...

Dreaming as usual...! *Celebrating the Human Species! The assassination of Kennedy, the landing of man on the moon, the Berlin Wall fell and in more recent times, the twin towers of the World Trade Center were struck down!)*

FROM NUREMBERG TO BOSNIA and RWANDA, AND ISRAEL AND PALESTINE – WAR CRIMES, GENOCIDE AND CRIMES AGAINST HUMANITY - HOW TO STOP HATING AND START LOVING?

On a somewhat cold winter morning, I happened to be thinking of what would happen to ordinary people in Iraq if the United States attacked the country; sanctions had already done so much of harm... Besides, war could destabilize the entire Arab World, in the words of the Arab League, and thwart the Middle-East by usage of the Suez Canal, so very crucial for any invasion Logistics...Then, something else caught my attention, and it went like this:

> "..Leading German officials were tried before the International Military Tribunal (IMT) in Nuremberg, Germany. The IMT consisted of judges from Great Britain, France, the Soviet Union, and the United States. The overwhelming majority of post 1945 war crimes trials, however, involved lower-level officials and officers. Among them were concentration camp guards and commandants, police officers, members of the mobile killing squads, and doctors who participated in medical experiments. These war criminals were tried by military courts in the British, American, French, and Soviet zones of occupied Germany and Austria; and in Italy. Others were tried by the courts of those countries where they had committed their crimes. Many war criminals were never brought to trial or punished.."

I was actually reading an account of the "Trials of War Criminals in Europe" of the Jewish Virtual Library, a Division of The American-Israeli Cooperative Enterprise (2002)...

So, Slobodan Milosevic was NOT the only one, I thought..It had been carried down the ages by people as ruthless as Klaus Barbie and Adolf Eichmann..and the Khmer Rouge's Cambodia..When the Khmer Rouge ruled the country in the 1970's, more than a million people died of Starvation, Disease, Torture, and Execution..It has been reported that Cambodians have still not recovered from the horrors of the slaughter that were perpetrated on them...

But the story did not end with Cambodia...

In the autumn of 1991, (a scene captured by a BBC Reporter), marching through the ruins of destroyed Croatian town Vukovar, were gangs of blood-thirsty Serb Chetniks singing..Slobodane, Slobodane, salji nam salate; bi'ce mesa, bi'ce mesa klat cemo Hrvate! ...

In other words, calling up their leader Slobodan Milosevic:

> "Slobodane, Slobodane, send us some salad; It's gonna be a lot of meat, a lot of meat- we will slaughter Croats!"

Bosnian Serbs were massacring Bosnian Muslim civilians near Srebrenica, and raping innocent civilians (including children), the total figure being placed at 60,000 according to the Final Report of the UN Commission of Experts on the **Former Yugoslavia**, which concluded that about 16 rape camps existed, in addition to numerous concentration camps and death camps, forcing at least 1.5 million women and children from their homes and villages to overcrowded and primitive refugee camps...

Rwanda in Africa was at least as bad if not worse..In Spring-Summer of 1994, within a matter of weeks, every Hutu (in a majority) was exhorted to kill Tutsis, or face dire consequences. What followed was perhaps one of the greatest "Genocides" ever committed in the history of civilization, or, lack of it rather. In three months time, between 500,000 and a million people were killed..Prior to 1994, Rwanda was the most densely populated country in continental Africa..Between April and August 1994, Rwanda lost about 20% to 40% of its population to slaughter and exile..Among the accused were two Roman Catholic Nuns and a Professor of the National University of Rwanda. This left the International Community in a state of utter disbelief and shock..Ironically, this very Community was, following the carnage, debating whether trials were to be carried out by an International Tribunal or by Rwandan courts..But then, have conditions ever been better?

The answer is an emphatic NO. Not in South African Apartheid, and more recently, as I would call it, **White Farmers and 'Reverse-Apartheid'** in Robert Mugabe's Zimbabwe...We are already into the 21st Century, but war and ethnic violence continues on a sustained basis. In many societies of the world today, for people (and children???), violence and conflict have become daily realities..as common as perhaps the daily struggle for food, clothing, education, medical care, shelter and safe drinking water..However, there is optimism about the fact that Nations of the World have started sensitizing themselves to Crimes Against Humanity, like trying out War Persecutors and Criminal perpetrators..Indeed, Human Rights have come a long way...

I dare quote a CASE IN POINT: 'The Forensics of Genocide':

> "Chris Joyce reports that creating a sense of normalcy in the former Yugoslavia after a decade of war has been a slow and laborious task. While aid agencies can provide money and advice, there remains an enduring wound that is slowest to heal-the disappearance of thousands of civilians. One group, Physicians for Human Rights, has focused on closing that wound by creating a system for identifying bodies from mass graves and counseling the survivors. It has become perhaps the world's most comprehensive forensic project designed for the survivors of war crimes, rather than for those seeking to prosecute the perpetrators."
>
> ***- Jeff Rogers and Eric Stover (website: www.crimesofwar.org)***

So, is Collective Violence an aberration from Social Norms, or an inherited trait? No one would know for sure..Even then, one could safely predict that very often, Violence would be the direct or indirect way to deal (not cope) with **FRUSTRATION CAUSED BY BAD REGIMES AND FAULTY OR POOR LEADERSHIP..**This factor, apart from **CHILD POVERTY**, would, undoubtedly, be the

single most important cause of Crime, Violence and Conflict in the contemporary era...

Take the case of **Iraq**, which is in constant fear of war, in addition to an economy that is in tatters...We have begun to hear voices, of Iraqi dissidents, to those strongly opposed to a forced regime change in Iraq by US military intervention..Someone in Iraq feels strongly that the extent of the burden of its leader makes the forced removal of Saddam Hussein the only ethical solution, and that, although the use of force may by itself be unethical, the rigorous demands of the situation in Iraq are enough to justify the use of force..Someone else, in the same tone that I do, feels that "Saddam Hussein has used the complex social and political landscape of Iraq to create a system of rule highly resistant to peaceful change..". He goes on to add that militarism wouldn't be the right answer, and that we must follow an intelligent strategy of novel creativity and careful thought-something like offering exile to Saddam and his clan on the one hand, and Economic Reforms on the other..At the same time, the anti-war Lobby is growing by the day, around the globe and in America alike, there is now more than ever before, genuine talk of the interests of the Iraqi people, the justice and Morality of War, US Power and the Role of the UN...

It wouldn't be out of place or context to mention the traumatic effects of US Sanctions against Iraq. On the 6th of August 1990, the UN Security Council imposed Economic Sanctions on Iraq in response to its invasion of Kuwait. All imports into Iraq (excluding medical supplies) and all exports from Iraq were forbidden, unless the Security Council allowed exceptions..what followed was a nightmare for the people of Iraq - Low birth-weight babies, maternal and child malnutrition, a horrific rise in prices according to a UN World Food Programme Report, an intense deterioration in infrastructure and standards of living, a breakdown in health care and hospitals, the return of communicable diseases, child labor, as well as adverse effects

on Iraqi Society and Economy, which can all be summed up in the words of one man, Denis Halliday, the former UN Humanitarian Co-ordinator in Iraq, who resigned in protest : "we are in the process of destroying an entire society. It is as simple and terrifying as that. It is illegal and immoral..."

We can only hope that nothing of this sort will happen again in the history of civilization..No prizes for guessing, ..but don't you think we can do something **POSITIVE AND CONSTRUCTIVE** about not only Iraq, but also the tension in the Middle East, and the relentless standoff between India and Pakistan, the War against Terror, and every other bitterness that exists in the world today?

Look at the **Middle East** first. A serious crisis looms large over the global horizon with Israel and Palestine locked in Violent Hatred. There is more to this crisis than simply violence. There are lacunae in the political set-up as well. People in this troubled region have lost all hope. Having to endure the circumstances has been accepted as pre-ordained. An American Lady tells us that she was engaged to an Israeli, whose brother-in-law was murdered by Palestinians. Yet, she believes that "we need more than a token Palestinian state..." She is perhaps not the only one who dreams of peace in the Middle-East region. An Israeli, Yossi Alpher, former Director of the Jaffee Center for Strategic Studies at the University of Tel Aviv and once advisor to Prime Minister Barak (2000), and Palestinian Ghassan Khatib *together* run "Bitterlemons", a website for a more comprehensive understanding of the Middle East situation. Although they have somewhat different views, by and large they advocate **PEACE**..While Alpher feels "escalation of the search for a solution to the international level must be seen as a welcome development", Khatib, a Palestinian analyst, sees evidence of genuine Arab and Palestinian interest in achieving **PEACE,** as well as an end to the occupation. Further, he reiterates the role played by the "Saudi Peace initiative" in the past, which offered Israel "not only Palestinian, but Arab willingness to bring about a

comprehensive final peace and normalization in return for an Israeli withdrawal to UN-sanctioned borders in Resolution 242, as well as a solution to the refugee problem, according to UN Security Council Resolution 194.." Unfortunately, not only did Israel maintain that this was an unacceptable proposition, but also, "timed its reoccupation of Palestinian territories for the very same day of the Arab Summit's approval of its peace initiative.."

SAD, VERY SAD, BUT THIS IS HAPPENING THE WORLD OVER..Take the case of the two "belligerent" South Asian neighbors, **India and Pakistan**..Their perpetual conflict lies deep-rooted in the circumstances under which they (Pakistan and India) were created. It started with the "*Two-nation* Theory" justifying Partition, but even after Partition is long-dead, factors such as raunchy Nationalism, Pseudo-politics and Falsified history remain..in fact, **Children in the two Nations are growing up on a diet of "obscene" hatred..they really have no choice..both of these South Asian Societies have provided absolutely no scope to their citizens to think independently**..In fact, we have, in the midst of our constant bickering, forgotten about issues such as the Plight of Child Laborers in the Carpet and Fireworks Factories in India, and those in the Football-stitching industry in Pakistan..Future South Asian leaders, especially those in the two countries, should actually start working on collaborative programs towards Socio-economic Development (as some sort of an "Indo-Pak Consortium")..particularly, in as much as they relate to KASHMIR..The time has come in the history of India and Pakistan, to **GIVE UP HATRED AND START LOVING...**

October 12th, 2002, is a date that will go down in history as a day on which some 180-odd innocent people (largely, Australian) were massacred in the bomb attacks on **Bali**. This was a massive blow to Indonesia's large tourism industry..I'm saying this although I'm a Hindu myself, that, many Muslims in Indonesia are themselves suffering the evil

repercussions of extremism, for which they are not to be blamed..Even today, Mohammad Asep, a student, and other local Muslims are to be seen making some provisions for the Poor outside a mosque in Indonesia..and yet, there is still more hatred in our world than there is love. How else would you justify the steady nuclear build-up in countries as diverse as Pakistan, India and North Korea..?

It has come to our hearing that two weapons inspectors have recently been expelled from **North Korea** in an escalating row over Pyongyang's nuclear complex..this means, a Nuclear Arms buildup in North Korea...

I wonder how we can get to the root causes of Crime, Violence, Conflict and Hatred..in other words, the Psychology of Belligerence or Aggressive Behaviour. Military Interventions would only aggravate such behaviour. International Courts of Justice wouldn't do much better. Any aggravation could be curtailed only through harnessing of that one most important Resource, **PEACE**, **PEACE**, and only, **PEACE**..I have just come to know that the European Union is sending a Special Police Mission to Bosnia. I may be wrong, but this is what has come to my hearing...

The ONLY way to counter War or Ethnic Paranoia, Death and Destruction would be to START LOVING, BECAUSE **LOVE** IS THE MOST POWERFUL TRUTH ON THIS OUR BELOVED PLANET..Conflicts, be they National, Political, Religious or Ethnic, "urgently need to be explained, their causes clarified, and creative solutions explored", according to Rosemary Bechler of 'Open Democracy Ltd', London..To this, I have to add that the International Community (particularly, the United Nations and the United States) has to ensure that **every CHILD,** no matter what the race, ethnic origin, religion, caste, creed, class, etc, **gets his/her share of Food, decent shelter, health care, education, and LOVE AND AFFECTION ..**Every human being on this our Beloved Planet is entitled to certain Basic Human Rights as promised by the "Universal Declaration

of Human Rights", which was adopted by the United Nations on the 10th of December, 1948..Currently, such rights remain the prerogative of a few only (the 'Haves')..Democracy has to function well, and future Global Leadership has to be made stable as well as accountable...

David Loyn, BBC Correspondent for 'Developing World' (a programme I watch regularly) in his critique of "**Afghanistan**, "One Year On", had this to say about the rebuilding of the country, "..There is progress, but is it too little, too late? Civil servants in Afghanistan are unpaid, roads impassable, and justice undone..Where there is..more money being spent on warfare than development aid..The centre of Kabul is now awash with gleaming white Toyotas, and the only visible reconstruction in the city has involved the refurbishment of their offices..The main problem is that Afghanistan has not received enough cash..each of these refugees who have come to have a look, and then gone back again, represents a failure of international policy..However, it would be wrong to say that international development is making no difference. The sight of just one girls' school open would make it all worthwhile. The thousands of girls now getting their first formal education will create a social revolution in time..." **(quoted from "Afghanistan, One Year On"-Copyright of David Loyn, 2002)**

There is a similar resonance from **West Africa**, and we hear what the Chairman of the African Commission on Human and Peoples' Rights, Mr. Kamel Rezag Bara, has to say, "..It is true that there have been positive development in certain states..This is the cases of Sierra Leone, Madagascar and Angola where wars and internal tensions have recently come to an end and new chance is being given to Peace and national reconciliation..." He, however, expressed his concern over the internal crisis in **Ivory Coast** which according to him, "has claimed the lives of hundreds of people and forced many more to move within or outside the country..." Mr. Bara also added that the Commission recognized the high rates of human rights violations

(including, among others, amputation, stoning, lashing and other cruel inhuman and degrading treatments that still existed in some African countries), which in my opinion as well, would seriously undermine Africa's Social progress...

One of Africa's longest civil wars, the one in **Angola**, finally came to an end after 27 years. Angola is famous for its grinding Poverty and Systemic Corruption. It is rich in oil; however, Angola's elite has always cited War as an excuse for the poor record of the country's progress..although no one can deny that War definitely did extract a terrible price. In some towns, whole sections of populations starved to death..and it was common to stumble upon landmines. Actually, what are we passing on to the Children of Angola's 21st Century?

We come to the final question, that is, "what **can we do to help bring Peace to the world**, prevent the manufacture and sale of Arms (excluding those required at the minimum towards Defense), and diverting to human development..or, something else?" Article 26 of the UN Charter talks of reducing "diversion for armaments of the world's human and economic resources" by a set percentage per year. Even a reduction of one percent can be utilized on Poverty Reduction, Education, Medical care, Sustainable Development, work on the Environment as well as Conflict Resolution..According to a UN Survey, 500 million small arms and light weapons are in circulation worldwide, with a sizeable number being used by **CHILDREN** below the age of 18. This is a Humanitarian problem of mammoth proportions..Then, there are Nuclear, Chemical and Biological weapons, but actually, who needs them and for which purpose, is the big question..In recent times, organizations such as Oxfam, Greenpeace, Abolition 2000 and Safer World have been doing some very good work in this direction. We have to Lobby World Governments to discourage arms manufacturers from the production and supply of arms, and civil society from using them..we must, also, Campaign in Schools and colleges towards spreading

the message of the Harmful Consequences of Arms-usage as well as the Rich dividends of Peace..These issues should be raised in the Media..Perhaps, we can encourage people all over the world to hand over their arms in exchange for Food, Education, Health care, agricultural tools (for farmers) and other basic necessities..If we can stop the source..then we shall have won half the battle, too many of our world's gun bearers are unsure as to why they are doing what they are (senselessly) doing...

I wish to wind up with the words of Stephen Jay Gould, writing in The New York Times following 9/11: "Good and kind people outnumber all others by thousands to one. The tragedy of human history lies in the enormous potential for destruction in rare acts of evil, not in the high frequency of evil people. Complex systems can only be built step by step, whereas destruction requires but an instant. Thus, in what I like to call the Great Asymmetry, every spectacular incident of evil will be balanced by 10,000 acts of kindness, too often unnoted and invisible as the 'ordinary' efforts of a vast majority."

Let us all work towards a Peaceful World... because, we all want Peace..NOW!!!

7

Is World Peace a Guarantee of Security between and Within Nations?

A Sense of Insecurity Pervades Even the Most Affluent Societies

In contemporary society, almost everyone claims to be a peace-lover. But the real meaning of "PEACE" eludes us, indeed eluding efforts to arrive at an unequivocal answer: Peace is a 'State free of war'...

One inherent characteristic is that peace is non-violent, but not necessarily secure or eternal. Peace exists as a phenomenon of human society.

NON-VIOLENCE is that state in which there is no armed violence. The Norwegian scholar Johan Galtung even claims that the meaning of peace ought include what he calls "STRUCTURAL VIOLENCE", such as combating SOCIAL INEQUALITIES like poverty, political oppression, racial discrimination indeed starvation.

Peace and War do not necessarily define security. There are periods in which all-round war is not waged, nor complete peace achieved.

Peace is not always secure. Indeed, during a relatively peaceful period, threats, dangers and incidents may arise. For the same reason, a sense of insecurity often pervades even the most affluent societies.

There may be peace with no security, partial security or fair security. In the real world, absolute security does not exist because every danger, threat and incident cannot be

removed. To illustrate, America, the world's sole superpower in the post Cold-War era had a defense budget of $250.5 billion in 1998, one-third of the entire world's defense expenditure that year. By 2002 the defense budget had grown to $328.9 billion, further increasing the chasm with other nations in this respect. But these mammoth expenditures do not guarantee absolute security, as shown by an increase in terrorist attacks against America, the most serious of which as we all know destroyed the World Trade Center and killed 3000 people.

Peace and security differ by nature. Peace is only one state of security and by itself is no guarantee of the absence of threat or danger. Peace is only the non- existence of armed conflicts, the international community or nations indeed do face threat, armed conflicts or war even under conditions of peace. Peace does not mean or is no guarantee of international or national security especially in the post Cold-War era.

After World War I, peace was achieved when Germany accepted all the terms of the Treaty of Versailles insisted upon by the victorious Allied powers, including restraints on German armaments and on other matters of national sovereignty.

Peace has never been a Natural criterion of justice. Indeed, peace can be achieved through power politics in which case it becomes an injustice. For the same reason, peace is no guarantee of dignity but may reinforce the humiliation process.

Mao Zedong believed that "War is the highest form of struggle".

The UN adopted the Declaration of the International Year of Peace in 1985, declaring 1986 the International Year of Peace.

8

The Silent Holocaust

IN A WORLD OVERFLOWING WITH RICHES, 40,000 CHILDREN DIE ON A DAILY BASIS MAKING FUTILE DECLARATIONS and FALSE PROMISES AS FREE NATIONS A WORLD GOVERNMENT-MAKING FREEDOM FROM HUNGER A REALITY

"Progress in reducing world hunger has virtually come to a halt. The number of undernourished people around the world has increased to 840 million. More than two billion people worldwide suffer from "hidden hunger," or micronutrient deficiencies, meaning, for instance, that children fail to grow and develop normally, their bodies are stunted and sometimes deformed, as are their intellectual capacities and immune systems. Every day, every seven seconds, another child under the age of 10 dies from hunger or hunger-related diseases...

Hunger also has effects through the generations as undernourished mothers give birth to children that will never fully develop..."

- Excerpts from *the report of the U. N. special rapporteur on the right to food to the 59th session of the United Nations Commission on Human Rights (UNCHR) in Geneva, Switzerland, that is dated Jan. 10, 2003.*

"Universal Declaration on the Eradication of Hunger and Malnutrition": This was adopted on 16 November 1974 by the World Food Conference convened by the United Nations and was oriented towards developing

ways and means whereby the international community, as a whole, could take specific action to resolve the world food problem within the broader context of development and international economic cooperation.

Despite the fact that the right to food is recognized directly or indirectly by all countries in the world, hunger, whether caused by war, drought, natural disaster or poverty, continues to cause widespread suffering. And poverty, one of the causes of hunger, is also a consequence of it.

Hunger dulls intellect and thwarts productivity, thereby prevents reaching the full potential of any society. Added to this, for poor families, hunger-related illness adds to household costs and increases the burden of care for healthy family members often already struggling for survival. When this hardship is multiplied by millions of families worldwide, it creates a devastating ripple effect globally. And finally, hunger leads to character with value erosion and eventually tears apart the moral fabric of any society.

At one World Food Summit, leaders from 185 countries and the European Community reaffirmed, "the right of everyone to have access to safe and nutritious food, consistent with the right to adequate food and the fundamental right of everyone to be free from hunger." They further pledged to cut the number of the world's hungry people by half by 2015.

Eradicating hunger should not be the only goal. Ensuring the right to adequate food and the fundamental right to be free from hunger is a matter of international law, which policy and decision makers /social activists of countries around the world have committed themselves to and have worked out ambitious plans and targets.

There is a difference between ***"the right to be free from hunger and the right to adequate food"*** The first one is a fundamental right and the country must ensure that people do not starve. The country should also do everything possible to promote adequate food availability for everyone

within the territory. This means that people should have moral, ethical, physical and economic access at all times to food that is adequate in quantity and quality. Production must not only be environmentally and socially sustainable but the acquisition also must be cheap and reasonable within moral, ethical and dignified human rights.

The global issue of HUNGER of FOOD ***"...of the people..."*** need to be solved "***...By the people, for the people...***" and is a fundamental right to human dignity.

FOOD, HUNGER and THE RIGHT TO HUMAN DIGNITY

Photograph of a poor undernourished boy and a dog inhumanly cramped inside a dustbin, each one trying to find food for itself gets the best photography award in a photographic competition...

At least 20,000 persons, mostly the old and children, are in urgent need of help in Kashipur block of Rayagada district, Orissa, India; even as the death toll has risen to 23 with two more persons succumbing to mango kernel paste in Tikri...Government denies starvation deaths...

We have to fill our stomach with something or other to survive. Does the government give us proper food? Does anybody think of feeding us? There is nobody for us...

Out of extreme poverty and hunger, the parents of a child had no option but to sell him off for a paltry sum of Rs 160/ - to a childless couple...

After the death of husband, widow arrested from a red light area >reason, she had to feed four siblings and finding no honorable work, had decided to enter flesh trade...

...I needed money for food... I was picking pockets during the day and sell myself during the night.....I was going with anyone who asked... Nothing was important for me....I just wanted to live but....

Millions of rupees squandered from grants on "mid day meal" ...children are beaten when ask for food, which was promised...

Police lathi charge villagers to control mob violence thronging Government godowns to collect rice and wheat, which was rotting for years without a proper distribution system and was in the process of being transported to a trader elsewhere..

These are not cases for academic interest. These are ruthless pictures and the hard core reality of the society we live in, the world to which we all belong...

«In a world overflowing with riches, it is a outrageous scandal that more than 826 million people suffer hunger and malnutrition and that every year over 36 million die of starvation and related causes. We must take urgent action now.»——-**Jean Ziegler, April 2001, UN Special Rapporteur on the Right to Food.**

"...At a time of widespread hunger in drought-affected areas, the government was busy hoarding food on an unprecedented scale and striving to keep prices up, making it that much harder for drought-affected people to buy food on the market..." ————*Jean Drèze in Hunger Amidst Plenty.*

Concerns leading to this global issue (>>as to why there is food insecurity, why such state of affairs, "Garibi Hatao" (REMOVE POVERTY) changes sarcastically to "Garib Hatao" (REMOVE THE POOR), why **INEQUALITY** is growing complemented with wider eliticism, why there is economic inequality and rural poverty, is population explosion the only reason, what is the responsibility of the Government., why there is a discrimination between a boy child and a girl child, why female infanticides are rampant in some parts of our country, why there is under nutrition and high death rate among children, what is poverty line and endemic hunger, is shortage of food produced- a cause or an effect, why store food grains and allow food to rot or get eaten away by rodents, who controls the pricing, is the public distribution system ineffective and corrupt because

of connivance, why major initiatives like "food for work", "mid day meal" fail, what are the employment opportunities amongst the rural poor, why social awareness thru media coverage is not made mandatory, what are the current challenges facing mankind, what legal experts and social activists have to say on these etc. etc. >>) is endless.

SIMPLY A MATTER OF POLICY?

"**POST-IRAQ:** Would shifting UN HQ's from New York to Africa, say, Sub-Saharan (child micronutrient-deficiency) and/or South Asia (India has some 40 Million Children out of school, of which a substantial number work in hazardous occupations) create for a more tolerant society that respects the needs of its young lives, both in the South as well as in the North, away from the primarily "Materialistic" (NOT WESTERN, why are we always blaming the West?) Culture of Sex and Violence....?

NO ONE CAN SAY FOR SURE!

....No more in-country Flights only (lavish!) trains, to facilitate greater interaction between the Official Elite and grassroots-inhabitants! 'La-Palace-on Wheels', the cosmetic Indian train that travels through rural Rajasthan, where women walk a mile each day in parched heat to fetch water, a sad reflection of our times!...

Rampant consumerism, mindless waste-dumping in the likes of China, and Global Climate Change are likely to be a major cause of discomfiture ('nee disconcert') among **poor children** in developing nations and the most likely cause(s) of Global **Instability**, including Ethnic Conflict...

AND I TOLD YOU (YOU WHO?) BUT YOU SIMPLY WOULDN'T LISTEN. "GREW UP WATCHING SEVERAL BRANDS OF CHEESE ON TV, MY HEART YEARNED FOR THEIR LIKES, WHEN I WOULDN'T EVEN GET MY SHARE OF FOOD TODAY...

MAY GOD BLESS HIROSHIMA, YANGON AND VIETNAM, MAY GOD BLESS THE WORLD...."

9

Out of the Ashes – Celebrating the Human Species

(HIROSHIMA, NAGASAKI, PEARL HARBOR, VIETNAM and THE GESTAPO)

Are they also likely to mete out similar treatment to the Jews?

Maybe..maybe not...

VIKTOR FRANKL WAS A JEW..who was 'imprisoned' by the Nazis, when he went through experiences that were so repugnant to our sense of decency that one can't describe them..torture, indignities and humiliation..but his captors could not take away his "last of the human freedoms", more freedom than perhaps those to his captors! He soon became an inspiration to those around him, his guards included! He helped others find meaning in their suffering and dignity in their prison existence. In the midst of the most degrading circumstances imaginable, Man is endowed with the freedom to choose..a uniquely human ability, something that lifts him well above the animal world...

'Frankl is one of many who have been able to develop the personal freedom in difficult circumstances to lift and inspire others. The autobiographical accounts of Vietnam prisoners of war provide additional persuasive testimony of the transforming power of such personal freedom and the effect of the responsible use of that freedom on the prison culture and on the prisoners, both then and now...

We have all known individuals in very difficult circumstances perhaps with a terminal illness or a severe

physical handicap who maintain magnificent emotional strength. How inspired we are by their integrity! Nothing has a greater, longer lasting impression upon another person than the awareness that some one has transcended suffering, has transcended circumstance, and is embodying and expressing a value that inspires and ennobles and lifts life..'.

(Covey et al, Simon and Schuster, 1992)

It's all about..tremendous intrinsic worth...(Lives of) character, contribution, service, love, concern and appreciation..dedicating us to..!

It's about..magnificent attitude and communicated love and compassion and courage..yes, it takes courage!

We're coming to the real issues..humility and humiliation and human dignity...

Look at **Gandhi**. During the time that his accusers were in the legislative chambers criticizing him for having refused to join them in their condemnation of the British Empire, Gandhi was out in the paddy fields slowly and steadily expanding his base among the laborers..thus being able to build up a swell of support in the countryside...Gandhi had no office or position to fall back upon, but he had ensured that that extra support was to go a long way in bringing England to its knees, most certainly an exemplary in compassion, courage, fasting and moral integrity...

Consider the words of Joseph Addison:

"When I look upon the tombs of the great, every emotion of envy dies in me; when I read the epitaphs of the beautiful, every inordinate desire goes out; when I meet with the grief of parents upon a tombstone, my heart melts with compassion..when I see kings lying by those who deposed them..or the holy men that divided the world with their contests and disputes, I reflect with sorrow and astonishment on the little competitions, factions, and debates of mankind..I consider that great Day when we shall all of us be Contemporaries, and make our appearance together.."

'But how do you love when you don't love?'

In the great literature of all progressive societies, love is a verb..trust Hollywood! Love is something you do: the sacrifices you make, the giving of self, like a mother bringing a newborn into the world. If you want to study love, study those who sacrifice for others, even for **PEOPLE WHO OFFEND OR DO NOT LOVE IN RETURN...**

We Must LOVE and DEDICATE and RE-DEDICATE OURSELVES..to..well, I understand I am writing for elite, enlightened readership!

"We are dedicated to ending humiliating practices and breaking cycles of humiliation throughout the world.

We believe that through this, space is opened for mutual respect and esteem to take root and grow. We believe that a mindset of connection and a spirit of shared humility is necessary and not a mindset of humiliation.

Great deposits in the 'Emotional Bank Account' come in these sincere words:

"I was wrong...
That was unkind of me...
I showed you no respect...
I gave you no dignity, and I'm deeply sorry..."

Previously intractable conflicts may thus become amenable to dignified resolution.

I was just thinking I should tell you the story of **Anwar Sadat**, past Egyptian President..one of the most inspiring accounts I have read during my little lifetime. Sadat had actually been reared, nurtured, and deeply 'scripted' in a hatred for Israel. He made huge crowds chant, 'Never, never, never!' And realized it was rather foolish of him..So he rescripted himself through a continuous process of meditation and prayer..They did not understand him...

'And when that time came, when he became President of Egypt and confronted the political realities, he rescripted

himself towards Israel. He visited the Knesset in Jerusalem and opened up one of the most precedent-breaking peace movements in the history of the world, a bold initiative that eventually brought about the Camp David Accords...'

(Covey et al, 1992)

(I remember such major traumas as the Civil War, Vietnam, Hiroshima, or Watergate, and in more recent times, ***IRAQ, ALL EXERCISES IN 'SELF-GRATIFICATION'****, what Pascal called, 'licking the earth'!)*

SO SAID MAHATMA GANDHI: "It has always been a mystery to me how men can feel themselves honored by the humiliation of their fellow beings."

AND, VICTOR ZURBEL (2004) STRONGLY THOUGHT:

Humility is Grace

Humiliation is Disgrace

"If you're going to bow, low," says Eastern wisdom. 'Pay the uttermost farthing', says the Christian ethic...

Leo Roskin taught, "It is the weak who are cruel. Gentleness can only be expected from the strong."

So, what are the "principles of empathic communication"?

One had to ask Auschwitz survivor, 2004, Evelin Lindner and Jo L., what they felt like: "Pessimism is a luxury we can afford only in good times, in difficult times it easily represents a self-inflicted, self-fulfilling death sentence..."

We believe that by eliminating these harmful cycles, a space is opened for **mutual respect** and esteem to take root and grow, thereby leading to the **resolution** of previously intractable **conflicts**. We believe that both **global sustainability** of ***social cohesion*** and ***ecological survival*** require a **mindset** of connection and a spirit of shared humility - and not a mindset of humiliation.

"The very way that a man and a woman bring a child into the world is synergistic. The essence of **Synergy** *is to value differences- to respect them..as in the case of* **Sir Winston Churchill** *who when called upon to head up the war effort for Great Britain, is said to have famously remarked that all his life had prepared him for this hour..."*

N. Eldon Tanner has remarked: 'Service is the rent we pay for the privilege of living on this earth.' And there could be so many ways to serve, irrespective of and/or lack of church or organizational affiliation, and ought not a day go by without serving one other human being by making deposits of **Unconditional love and conditional hatred (makes sense?)...**

In the words of **DAG HAMMARSKJOLD:**

"You cannot play with the animal in you without becoming wholly animal, play with falsehood without forfeiting your right to truth, play with cruelty without losing your sensitivity of mind..."

As researchers we study the dynamics of humiliation, the antecedents and consequences of humiliating behaviors, and interventions that can help break the cycle of humiliation and restore human dignity. As practitioners we attempt to bring ***incidents of humiliation in international affairs*** to the attention of people across the globe, to create public awareness of the destructive effects of such humiliation, and to promote ways of dealing with tensions in human affairs that generate ***human dignity and respect***.

Many reject research on "**evil**" as naïve appeasement. This is not our view. We believe that "**understanding**" and "**condoning**" ought not be conflated. **Nelson Mandela** showed the world that humiliation does not automatically lead to mayhem. His example attests to the constructive ways out of humiliation that merit to be studied and

promoted. We wish to learn from those constructive elements in Mandela-like or **Gandhi**-like approaches - for example, Mandela could have instigated genocide of the white elite, yet he did not.

What is our aim?

We wish to help discontinue humiliating practices wherever they occur, globally and locally. In order to do this we aim at ***building bridges...*** between research and practice. We wish to... **"change the world"** more directly through interventions. (Nancy Fraser (2000) discusses this in Rethinking Recognition).

Human rights ideals emphasize that each human being is born with equal dignity that ought not be humiliated..human rights are universal, or not, and whether their **advocates** are arrogant Western imperialists, or not, accompany this ***debate*** on all sides. We wish to contribute to building a ***future world society*** that includes all humankind in constructive and dignified ways.

OUR VISION: With NEW, INNOVATIVE INITIATIVES we wish to promote a new level of **consciousness** that is characterized by caring, mutual respect and sensitivity to dignity, thereby fertilizing new and constructive community action.

WE HOPE TO REMAIN INDEPENDENT OF ANY RELIGIOUS OR POLITICAL AGENDA...We are committed to a wide range of ***knowledge creation*** and dissemination, from shifts in awareness and practice at the ***local micro-level*** to larger changes at the level of the global community.

..To be PASSIONATE ABOUT **PEACE** without losing analytical rigor; to be moved by what is just while conceding that no one has a monopoly on **JUSTICE** ..To live our **values...**

..COMMITTED to creating a better future for our world, for our **CHILDREN AND GRANDCHILDREN** ..dedicated to providing effective and creative platforms for building

bridges in situations of disagreement and conflict and for generating a program of future-oriented activities that result in a viable global community...

Some have reflected:

"Pessimism is a luxury we can only afford in good times, in difficult times it easily represents a self-inflicted, self-fulfilling death sentence. This insight, to me, is real Realism or real Realpolitik, far from blue-eyed Idealism. We have to courageously resist the current tendency to suspect those who work for a better world to be hopeless idealists. This would mean Realpolitik letting disaster happen (by deepening fault lines instead of transcending them), and us not at least attempting to prevent this. Strange real Realpolitik!"

Evelin Lindner, 2004.

AND AGAIN!

"To be hopeful in bad times is not just foolishly romantic. It is based on the fact that human history is a history not only of cruelty, but also of compassion, sacrifice, courage, kindness. What we choose to emphasize in this complex history will determine our lives. If we see only the worst, it destroys our capacity to do something. If we remember those times and places - and there are so many - where people have behaved magnificently, this gives us the energy to act, and at least the possibility of sending this spinning top of a world in a different direction. And if we do act, in however small a way, we don't have to wait for some grand utopian future. The future is an infinite succession of presents, and to live now as we think human beings should live, in defiance of all that is bad around us, is itself a marvelous victory." Howard Zinn (You Can't Be Neutral on a Moving Train: A Personal History of Our Times, 2004, p. 208)

10
A Beautiful Mind

(THE "PROGRESS OF NATIONS" CAN BE ACHIEVED!)
PROGRESS CAN BE ACHIEVED!!!

Writes Pierre Zanre, a 18 year old girl student from Burkina Faso, Africa-

"When people no longer buy weapons,
When people no longer sell weapons,
When society parties are no longer held,
When hospitals are less full,
When school attendance rises,
When children know the joy of living,
When parents can procreate without worrying,
When people give to receive,
When people receive to give,
When people work for other people...
Then I can say that I am in a humane society."

(And, there was that girl - *who used to wake me up each lovely day! And say, "Good morning! Wake up!"As I prepared for prayer; and come and chant with me every single day that the sun rose, and the flowers looked even more beautiful because of her* ***love****! She was, is and will continue to be my best* ***friend****! My precious* ***friend****! My heart goes out to you!!!)*

I have my *dreams*, and *I dare* say:

"I want to work to erase ***inequality****"-*

"**Some day**, *however distant..."*

(And, I have received some peace cards already!)

Because it is in the '*mysterious equations of love*' (with

a bit of hugly, cuddly affection thrown in between!) that I have *rediscovered myself...*

That I have realized that there is a world beyond me..a world crying for attention..a world so unimportant yet so important..a world of children..all with dreams...

Young ***children****, Oh! Children! Driven by* ***poverty*** *to* ***sheer desperation*** *to* ***losing*** *(channelized)* ***direction-these 'unimportant' members of our 'civilized world'*** *(our 'elitist', so-very enlightened lauded socialites, applauded poets, galleried artists and Booker/Pulitzer writers)- those very children (of* ***the world's future****!) lynching and cycle-thieving and body-assaulting and mugging and jewellery-hiesting and country-liquor consuming and smuggling and killing- are (perhaps) the* ***only ones that make sense to me****-does **anyone** have the right to send them to the gallows, or even fine or imprison them?

((“Lord! Forgive them! For they know not what they do))” **courtesy Jesus for Freedom (Tim Rice and Andrew Lloyd Webber cryin' Christ Superstar))**

“..They don't really care about us!”

- Crooning and cryin' Jackson! (Married to the mob and to Memphis Presley's daughter!)

As though we're all peace-loving nations, we're just **obliged** to love peace...

My Mind takes me to Cambridge, MA, Princeton, to Albert Einsteins (and Dreamy Ones!) and MATHEMATICIANS and Decipher(ing) Codes and “Intelligence Quotients”, The PENTAGON and..finally OSLO... a Prolific Rioting of Ideas, A Story of Immense Courage in the face of Adversity and Ultimate Triumph following a life of harrowing Struggle, a Triumph not through War, Conflict and Gore (and Talk of Pre-Conflict and Post-traumatic Disorders and Resolution and Reconstruction and/or Transformation!), but through the

POWER OF THE HUMAN SPIRIT TO EVER make POSSIBLE the Near-I'M'POSSIBLE CONVERSION of Lives and Pasts of DARKNESS into PATHWAYS OF LIGHT-(nee BEACON LIGHT)...

(Dreaming..!)

But this beauty queen didn't say she would work for world peace and a drug-free world if she won the title. Angelica Mazua, the statuesque Angolan serving five years on international drug smuggling charges, was voted 'Miss Penitentiary 2005' after a six-hour contest that pitted 40 women inmates from 10 prisons in Sao Paulo, Brazil. The contest, say the organizers, instills confidence in the inmates, besides providing a break from the dull routine and a prize worth $ 160...

(Information Courtesy: DNA Magazines, Dec. 2005, Mumbai, INDIA)

OF GOODWILL AMBASSADORS AND YOUTH EMISSARIES

[Our dear Angie (Jolie) is now WORKING STEADFASTLY TO MAKE THE WORLD A BETTER PLACE TO LIVE IN through her MISSION as 'GOODWILL AMBASSADOR' with the UN High Commissioner for REFUGEES, NY OR GENEVA or Whatever]

'Dreaming..'.

Jolie and Pitt, if I remember correct, were in earthquake-ravaged Pakistan quite some time back, where she is said to have remarked that promises of help for Pakistan's earthquake survivors must be kept, and quickly, else many people could freeze to death as a bitter Himalayan winter gripped the region..Aid donors had promised Pakistan about $6 billion in help (all that 'Big Money from the Western World' Rhetoric!) but most of it was for medium and long-term reconstruction..('Yes! Western World..do please allow them, 'those unimportant people' to live in the long-term, and their children do not get **ORPHANED**! Thanks very much indeed').

11

Fast Food Nations, Rich-Nation Double Standards

(THE POOR CREATE JOBS – SO KEEP THEM WHERE THEY ARE!)

The **TRUTH** (AND A STARK ONE, THAT TOO!) IS:

Our Gods and Seers and Saints

Have prescribed certain Medications for the Health, Good, Wellness and Welfare of MANKIND...

And We are All Writing Our Own Prescriptions...

Without ever **caring to reflect** on the likely consequences of such our personal interventions on people other than our very own...

(And that would be the penultimate lesson in **international understanding**, the ultimate being **love**)

Without ever **caring to share information/ knowledge**

(And that would be the penultimate scourge on the developing world, the ultimate being **hatred**)

I have to ask **Mr. Shashi Tharoor** though!

Without ever **caring to dare** incorporate (O! They are all in the corporate sector!) **change(s)** in the way most of us think and act on these our very issues!

(And that would be the penultimate impediment to the "**progress of nations**", the ultimate being mindset!)

At this moment, I am reminded of Dr. Carol Bellamy!

So, what are these our very issues?

(These are, I guess, the state of the world's children!)

These are the, if I may (I dare worth a try!) universities, the world's most democratic institutions (our universal cities of the future, sorry! There are no global villages, what a tragedy!)...

"And there is no shortcut in developing them. The law of the harvest governs; we will always reap what we sow- no more, no less. The law of justice is immutable, and the closer we align ourselves with correct principles, the better our judgment will be about how the world operates..."

(Covey et al, 1992)

These are the ones (these principles) that Promise to teach you:

(1) How (best) to Exploit the Poor-

(2) How to Keep People Where They Are (FEED THEM NOT FOOD, BUT RELIGION)-

(3) How to Ensure that Children Die of Malnutrition-

(4) That Innocent people are killed-

(5) How to practice Genocide, War Crimes and Crimes against Humanity-

(6) U's of Child Conscription and Landmine Instruction-

(7) U's to teach how the West can rule the world-

(8) How the US can ensure nuclear reactors, enriched uranium, weapons of mass destruction, Iraq and vast reserves of oil, Iran, North Korea (Pyongyang), the whole wide world and another Abu Ghraib for herself-

(9) How to infringe upon the rights and freedoms of other religious and racial groups-

(10) How to be 'more global' at the risk/cost of those 'less global' like the world's poor-

(11) How to compromise with ***human dignity***: Reduce earthly men to man-days and brick-kilns and innocent flowers called **children** to out-of-school 24-hr low-pay (nimble fingers) workdays-

(12) How to ensure that the night-soil picker, scavenger and sex-worker is made to keep 'scavenging for justice'-

(13) How to stop respecting the morals, perceptions and values of others-

(14) How to teach our children lessons in disrespect, inequality and oppression- that ***we are born and must remain unequal***-

(15) How we must rule at the expense of another-

(16) How the West (Western nations) can wine and dine (away) while the developing world is made to struggle in debt, HIV/AIDS, poverty and sheer desperation-

The poor create jobs

(17) How 'jobs'out of the Poor and Poverty are to be made, how to relegate the underprivileged to tortuous misery and sheer desperation, call such 'mortal' beings *poor and their condition poverty and ensure that "we", the civilized nations of the world, can "ever manage to manage" fat pay-checks out of, well, I understand that I am writing for an "enlightened, elite" readership-*

(18) How "we" must, for the betterment of the world and as 'free-thinking nations' *conform to certain 'global' "codes of conduct"* like rolling out red carpets for those with *villas, ranches, crafts and copters, estates and private farms* (and Michael Douglas and Tom Cruise and Ethan Hawke and Hugh Grant and Catherine Zeta-Jones and Naomi Campbell and Robbie Williams and Shakira!) while a *vast majority are made to eke out a living on less than $1 in 24 hours-*

(19) How Kate Moss and Linda Evangelista and Cindy Crawford and Christy Turlington can compete for *brand ambassadorship of fur-coats in Milan* (O! I forgot! That was

the fashion capital of our brutally-civilized world!) while *the very same people(s) strut and stupefy* (in all their finery and finesse!) *with some exotic voice-overs and voice-talks on whale, seal and polar bear skinning-*

(20) From gender to danger-from engendered to endangered species-

I am woman, and frailty my name-

But I would personally love to be appointed "Dean" of my 20-point '*dream secretariat*' of the U's that impart 'lessons' (nee instruction') in indignity (that may not be a word, though), disrespect, inequality and oppression- wow! That would be ..tremendous! What a feeling?

Robert Mugabe slams "global inequality"

Zimbabwe's President Robert Mugabe once attacked global inequality and what he described as the imperious attitudes of the US and Britain.

He was speaking at a UN conference on internet technology in the Swiss city of Geneva in the early part of the century.

There could be no just information society without more social inequality. He said there was no point in providing poor people with computers unless they were also given electricity and a phone network to run them.

He then attacked the general world order, saying digital technology was being used by some to dominate the globe.

'The deadly televised spectacle of an unjust war of occupation in Iraq based on blatant lies was a dramatic example of a false and failed global information society founded on the twin aggressive impulses of shock and awe', he said.

12

Washington D.C. and War as Business

PEACE IN IRAQ! NOTHING CAN JUSTIFY FURTHER BLOODSHED!!

Some of the most celebrated "pacifists"/spiritual leaders/peace-lovers the world has ever known have spoken about the importance of peace on earth, and I quote, beginning with the Dalai Lama: **"Anger or hatred is like a fisherman's hook. It is very important for us to ensure that we are not caught by it."**

Five environmental scientists on a remote island can create renewable energy using bones..convert sea water into pure distilled water using solar energy..the developing world can invite Mr. Bill Gates to visit the poorest of the poor..or, invite a larger number of foreign journalists to capture lackadaisical attitudes...and cinema can go on portraying increasing amounts of sex and violence, thereby adding to the already-existing crime-rates... But..nothing, I say nothing, could justify the war on Iraq...

Let us begin on this premise: that the major factors in youth frustration are less likely to be religious fundamentalism and ethnic sentiment, and are more likely to be child poverty, raunchy nationalism, poor leadership and bad regimes, among others...

Every year, 11 million children die of preventable diseases...

And others either go hungry or miss out on school...

Food for Thought Really?

Actually, what kind of a World is it that we are passing on to our Children? A World filled with war, violence, deep perversions, murder, mayhem, looting, arson, sexual assault, plunder and child abuse including paedophilia.

Before you read on, please beware that what you are about to read might shock you...

We are talking about the war on Iraq.

But "war would have devastating human and environmental consequences", said Greenpeace. The last Gulf War killed two hundred thousand people. Many of the war's survivors were left hungry, diseased and dying. The war left in its wake as well damage to the immediate environment years after it ended. Could we afford to have another war? Greenpeace further opined: "War is an ineffective way to deal with weapons of mass destruction..there is a need for global disarmament..that must be achieved through peaceful diplomatic negotiations..."and, as Nelson Mandela said, and, as we all understood, an attack on Iraq would be clearly motivated by President George W. Bush's desire to gain control of Iraq's oil reserves. Further, this war would be illegal and would set a dangerous precedent. Even Henry Kissinger argued that "the notion of justified pre-emption runs counter to modern international law, which sanctions the use of force in self-defense only against *actual,* not potential threats." Finally, it should be noted that it was hypocritical to single out Iraq. Other countries such as India, Pakistan and Israel, all possess weapons of mass destruction...

So, first of all, there were the grave humanitarian consequences of potential military intervention on civilians, and these eventually led to serious humanitarian crises. Moreover, a military strike on Iraq could not be justified. Millions of Iraqis were highly vulnerable to any military action, which could increase civilian suffering and fuel regional instability. Up to 16 million people already relied on a fragile system of food aid for their survival.

OXFAM, a leading international NGO, had assessed that over 15 million people of Iraq's 22 million people were already on World Food Program (WFP) rations- a consequence of the last war, over 10 years of Sanctions, and the policies of the Iraqi Government- there were huge risks to millions, especially, vulnerable groups such as children, and the Elderly. "Air strikes", as during the last Gulf War, posed a grave risk- of targeting and destroying power stations. If that happened, the Iraqi Water and Sanitation system, which depended on electricity, would collapse, leaving millions of people vulnerable to diseases and epidemics, malnutrition and child mortality. Other serious consequences included possible internal displacement and even refugee movements of over 1.62 million people, as well as major political destabilization in the region. According to Oxfam International Executive-director, Mr. Jeremy Hobbs, "This could be from huge refugee movements but also from the anger that is already evident in many parts of the region, whether in the Middle East or in countries with significant Moslem populations such as India..." Perhaps, the only solution was to negotiate through the United Nations.

"..We cannot see..how such an attack could be waged without violating international humanitarian law", said Director of Oxfam Great Britain, Barbara Stocking. Here, there were three major considerations: (i) War could lead to an increase in the suffering of ordinary people in Iraq and the rest of the Middle East; (ii) It would be likely to aggravate instability in the region, and hinder progress towards a just solution of the Israeli-Palestinian Conflict; and, (iii) It would diminish respect for international humanitarian law- and of the role of the UN as the genuine voice of world opinion.

We are again talking about the war on Iraq.

But, pray you, what about innocent civilians in Iraq? What had they done to deserve this? And, what if the reverse were to happen? What if, Iraq and /or someone else were to

"invade the United States", despite its mammoth size? President George W. Bush called it "war", but I should say that there is a difference between the term "war" and the events of 9/11. 9/11, undoubtedly, was a horrific thing to happen, it should never have happened, and should never again happen. It involved the loss of innocent people. I do indeed condemn 9/11. But war was not the answer. I will not say much beyond this, except for the fact that Iraqi children (as well as all others likely to be affected by this war) will grow up on a diet of obscene hatred in the event that there should be war...Children cannot forget the horrors of war??? And, Iraq's children, her "innocent flowers", are simply no exception to the rule.

The Pope had asked Catholics to fast for the cause of Peace (Feb. 23, 2003, the Vatican City, AP) in the light of impending war against Iraq. He had said that he was worried a U.S.-led war against Iraq could unsettle the entire Middle East. He had denounced war as a way to resolve the conflict.

"We Christians in particular are called upon to be sentinels of peace," John Paul said, calling on Catholics to dedicate their fasting on Ash Wednesday, March 5, for the cause of peace. On that day, the Pope said, faithful will pray for "the conversion of hearts and the long-range vision of just decisions to resolve disputes with adequate and peaceful means." He also reiterated that the fast is an "expression of penitence for the hate and violence which pollute human relations."

We MUST learn to FORGIVE. FORGIVENESS can be the most long-lasting "War" on EVIL.

In fact, there are people who believe we shouldn't torture suspected terrorists. Dr. Orlando Tizon, himself a survivor of torture, and now Assistant Director of the Washington D.C.-based "Torture Abolition and Survivors Support Coalition International", feels that we can't possibly practice the terrorism that is torture in order to fight terrorism..This,

he further adds, would run in contravention to the UN Convention against Torture which was adopted in 1986 and signed by the U.S. and hundred other nations. Every man (or woman) is entitled to certain basic rights, and acting contrary to international law, human rights, and democracy, according to Tizon, would mean "winning one battle, but not winning the war.." I should add here, that torture would further, be unjust to our children, our future...

I wish to wind up with what one group of Canadian, American, and other "Christian Peacemaker Team Volunteers" posted in Iraq had to say (Monday, Mar 17, 2003), "..we write to clarify our presence..We accompany civilians who are suffering, largely due to the combined effects of the U.N. sanctions and the Gulf War..We have [visited] important humanitarian sites because of relationships we have built with people, and because of the death that sanctions has caused them, and because of the horror that would be caused by the further attacks..We are convinced that..non-violence is more life-sustaining than violence..friendship is more sustainable than enmity.." They further went on to point out that war was criminal, and that they would respond non-violently and respectfully to all people, including those with whom they disagreed or even those who used violence against them. Finally, they said "..we hope for peace for all of us and for all of our children.."

I personally feel, as do many others like Peggy Gish, one of the volunteers, "it is especially important that people of conscience and faith act strongly and boldly to declare a gospel of peace..or we lose our very soul.."

"LOVE WHOLEHEARTEDLY" should be our motto.

13

World Leaders (Connect to Love)

THE IMPORTANCE OF GLOBAL COOPERATION

Perhaps it wouldn't be out of place to see what some of our greatest "leaders of humanist thought", truly men and women of faith have had to say on the matter, perspectives, if I may, "wonderful people of a wonderful world", our principles of creative cooperation:

"I take as my guide the hope of a saint:
in crucial things, unity—
in important things, diversity-
in all things, generosity."

Aldous Huxley (1894-1963), British novelist and essayist thought that "it is a bit embarrassing to have been concerned with the human problem all one's life and find at the end that one has no more to offer by way of advice than 'try to be a little kinder..'."

Seneca (4? BC-65 AD), Spanish-born Roman statesman, philosopher, and dramatist said "all my life I have been seeking to climb out of the pit of my besetting sins, and I cannot do it and I never will unless a hand is let down to draw me up..."

In fact, there are those like POPE BENEDICT XVI that feel that "Having a clear faith..is labeled as fundamentalism. Yet relativism- that is, letting oneself be carried here and there by any wind of doctrine-appears as the sole attitude good enough for modern times..."

(If you use the internet..instead of trekking to a library to locate and pore over stacks of books and other printed material, you can have a whole world of information at your fingertips! All you need to do is access an internet search engine, type a few key words, and click "search"! Within seconds, links to numerous Web sites related to whatever it is you're looking for appear on your computer screen..Wouldn't it be great, though, if instead of merely supplying you with information, the Internet could actually solve your problems, answer your really deep questions, help organize and direct your daily life, and satisfy your emotional and spiritual needs? The Net will never be able to do all those things, of course, but God can..You can reach Him anytime, from anywhere, for free..He always knows exactly what you need...

All you need to power up all that hardware and software within you is faith! Look at all the people in the Bible who had to learn to hear from God, and to wait for Him to work-David, Moses, Noah, Abraham, the apostle John, and Jesus Himself, to name a few...

Pray! God has all the answers..Prayer is not just getting down on your knees...Study His Word, and put His principles of love into practice in your daily life! Turn on the power and connect to His love today! He is full of words of comfort and advice that can help see you through life's problems. He is the author. And He loves you! So tap into the greatest creative energy there is, or ever will be-the power of prayer! The Power of **LOVE**!

-(Literature Courtesy "God Online..From Jesus With Love", www.activated.org)

Finally, it certainly wouldn't be out of place to quote Theodore Roosevelt (1858-1919), 26th President of the United States: "There are those who believe that a new modernity demands a new morality. What they fail to consider is the harsh reality that there is no such thing as a new morality. There is only one morality. All else is immorality.."

Are the presidents and the prime ministers and the chancellors of our respectable nations of the world listening?

Are they? Or, for that matter, are you?

So, what are we driving at? Human emotions; human rights; human dignity; human everything; just being human!

HUMAN NATURE!

"The Lord works from the inside out. The world works from the outside in. The world would take people out of the slums. Christ takes the slums out of people, and then they take themselves out of the slums. The world would mold men by changing their environment. Christ changes men, who then change their environment. The world would shape human behavior, but Christ can change human nature.."

- EZRA TAFT BENSON

THE DESIRE TO GIVE BACK EXISTS DEEP WITHIN EACH OF US.

Don't Wait! You can start now! Sacrifice, sensitivity, empathy, caring, sharing and understanding..are integral to your innate human nature..Don't just reserve these traits to your family..There is a world outside that neither demands nor expects anything from you! But rewards even the most minute step you would take selfless service..Most certainly, you will feel great satisfaction and true happiness..So, give back to the society you live in. Be responsible, and concerned!

Introspect! What bothers you? What matters to you? What do you truly care about even if it is unrelated to your family? Can there be a solution? Is this what you would like to do? Suddenly, there will be too many issues, too many **DREAMS** *and too little time..You can and will make a difference! Say it! Do it! You have the power, initiate it! Take one step towards it. Write about it, against it. Make your voice heard! And embark on that special journey..Just listen to your heart!*

(Dreaming..as always! I am ***Practicing Humanity***.*.)*

14

Born Free (The Universal Declaration of Human Rights, 1948)

On December 10, 1948 the General Assembly of the United Nations adopted and proclaimed the Universal Declaration of Human Rights..Following this historic act the Assembly called upon all Member countries to publicize the text of the Declaration and "to cause it to be disseminated, displayed, read and expounded principally in schools and other educational institutions, without distinction based on the political status of countries or territories."

Article 1.

All human beings are born free ("the spirit of freedom") and equal in *dignity* and rights. They are endowed with reason and conscience and should act towards one another in a spirit of brotherhood...

I shall not keep myself from quoting our two great Alberts:

Einstein said: "Nothing truly valuable arises from ambition or from a mere sense of duty; it stems rather from **love** and devotion towards men..."

Schweitzer said: "Life becomes harder for us when we **live for others**, but it also becomes richer and happier..."

Please would you note the common threads of thought running through the great Albert mind?

Thanks very much indeed!

My mind takes me to ***'Emergent Africa'***, "live-aid";

"famine-relief"; (not "band-aid" strategies); Oh! All these 'aids': Hearing aids, prosthetic aids, HIV/AIDS, I remember there's a film of the kind, a "war-n-peace" film,

But first, before I FLY YOU to "**BEYOND BORDERS**",
a Little Prayer:

"SPEAK TO ME
Speak to me of faith.
Help me to believe
In what I cannot touch,
In Someone whom I do not
fully understand,
And yet,
Help me to put my faith
In Him
For now and forever."

15

Darfur – All Empty Rhetoric

THE PLIGHT OF THE WORLD'S REFUGEES, ASYLUM SEEKERS and INDIGENOUS PEOPLES

(EMERGENT AFRICA NEEDS A NEW DIRECTION)

"Beyond Borders" (let there be none save those that have in our minds existed through a brief history of time!)-

Thought i, scene i, action: I only sincerely wish I could be the one to have made this film but my friends in the West (my wonderful whatever!) have outrun me to the core! Martin (director) Campbell! And James (music/score) Horner!!

-CUT-

Thought ii, scene ii, take i, action: Exotic banquets, some exquisite cuisine, some crooning!, AIDS charity dinners, and Africa goes on, so does South Asia, Latin America, Eastern Europe and Western homelessness and ghettos!

In comes "girl-(un) interrupted", "Gia", Angie (Angelina) Jolie, our very own UN Goodwill Ambassador for Refugees (and, asylum seekers/ displaced persons: God alone knows whereto they all get displaced!)...

-CUT-

Thought iii, scene iii, action: "Since when did the CIA start giving a shit about the starving in Africa?"- Asked a relief-worker (originally, an English med professional) based in Ethiopia...

-CUT-

Thought iv, scene iv, action: Africa for you, 3 years, no rain, not a drop, and war camps, disease, measles, typhoid, kala-azar, yellow fever, hay fever, locusts, HIV+AIDS, debt, Geldof and Bono?

-CUT-

On the sets of Africa, a live experience of famine-relief for you!

"Full bag? I take one truck (of food)..." that's meaningful cinema for you 'celebrating' the politics of food in starving Ethiopia!

While the Western world celebrates AIDS charity (nee Sotheby's and Christie's!) with bottles of wine! And plates of dine!!

The pain of surgery vs. The pain of hunger

"She's beyond pain" (while operating) - an English doctor in Ethiopia (a Westerner)...

"Have you asked her that?"- Our brave Angie Jolie (also a Westerner) asks him...

I guess it takes oceans! Of courage and will to survive..in the face of war and persecution!

-CUT-

Thought v, scene v, take i, action: One more 'child of Millennium Development Goals Africa' in the grave, being buried by his family members..calling it 'divine intervention'...

And camps and refugees ('of food on the tables, child conscription, of Western splendor and war, angels in America and (suffragette) Alice Paul 'iron-jawed angels', of inmates and death rows, Rwandan genocides, Milosevic war crimes and Abu Ghraib crimes against humanity: It is our marathon, we ought run..')...

And 'Medecins-sans-Frontieres' (physicians/doctors without borders)..and they have indeed done a very good job..kudos!

-CUT-

'I dream of childhood...

I dream of love...'} the English doctor

While Africans have run out of food,

Our Westerners have run out of love..narcotics and carjackers and high-octane nightlife and Philadelphia AIDS...

Oh! No! They haven't! Who ever said so? They're such lovely people (with resources at their command) with lovely relationships and children and grandchildren!! The little Kevins and Ethans and Heathers and Catherines and St. Pauls and St. Peters! Working in/for Africa...

-N.B. (It would seem) not a single dollar changes hands without authorization-

- (It would also seem) the death of a child is grave offence and amounts to investigation-

Well, children... in South Asia and Sub-Saharan Africa die anyway... daily...preventable deaths so as to say..a few dollars and cents per child...

-CUT-

Finally, the doc from London (wow! To most people!) talks of "my courageous Africa"...

And, the UNHCR-later, later, later; children chasing a truck full of Westerners and presumably, goodies! As well!

And, Angie answers a call for UNHCR...

-CUT-

Thought vi, scene vi, action: Ethiopia's and Pakistan's and Cambodians and (the) United Nations!

"What do you know about Cambodia? There's a civil war going on, the Khmer Rouge and measles/pneumonia and no vaccines, no prosthetics, corruption and landmines (mine fields) and Angkor Vat (not the vat question!)...

Maybe if I jump (not Murdoch, Rupert!), maybe if I find a rock to match my weight, but nothing can be done against the landmine..."

The politics of boxes (for whom?) (artificial limbs) meant for women and children in war-torn (Khmer Rouge) Cambodia (vs Moulin Rouge France!)...

Chechnya, Somalia, Cambodia, Ethiopia, it's the same shit all the time- what language!

What kind of (a) (life) lives is the developing world leading?

-Food! Mines!! And emaciated child corpses!!! Being buried in rich African sands by their (birth) fathers-

And Chechnya is a dangerous place!

Soldier: "He doesn't give a shit to other people..he just want to fire.."

-CUT-

Vietnam

Thought vii, scene vii, take i, action: "Your CIA agent working for Vietnam..one of you must die.." (and mysterious disappearances of aid workers?)

A child loses his mother in the bargain...

Coke anorexia diet coke diet pepsi and bulimia hot dog western world vs developing world food stamps and stampedes...

(Lovely film score though!)

The plight of the world's refugees and asylum seekers

There are over 50 million refugees and displaced persons and asylum seekers in the world today..unfortunately, closed minds and funding shortfalls add to an already existing global dilemma!

16

Africa Underprivileged: A Global Dilemma

Africa's landscape still remains marred by poverty and violence.

INTERNATIONAL SUMMIT ON CHILDREN, POVERTY AND VIOLENCE

(OCT 22 AND 23, 2004, MONTREAL, QUEBEC, CANADA))

A MAMMOTH TASK REALIZING THE AFRICAN DREAM

Despite the fact that the countries of Africa have ratified the UN Convention on the Rights of the Child and even implemented the regional treaty African Charter on the Rights and Welfare of the Child, a number of glaring issues concerning the rights and welfare of children remain unresolved in the national laws of many African states.

Although not restricted to Africa, the phenomena of child soldiers, child refugees and displaced children tend to recur on the African continent. In addition, drought, famine and disease affect children. The greatest threat that children face at birth is the risk of HIV infection from infected mothers..Estimates say that by 2010, a couple of million children will be orphaned by this pandemic in South Africa alone.

Children also suffer at the hands of family, friends and strangers and abuse, especially sexual abuse can be scourging.

African children still need protection. A mammoth task awaits us as the world sets out to realize the African dream.

MESSAGE FROM THE CHAIRPERSON OF THE INTERNATIONAL SUMMIT

"..Children continue to suffer and die needlessly everywhere in the world. In the developing countries, a large number of children suffer from poverty, hunger, and the destruction of the environment. Exploitation through child labour remains prevalent...

Statistical data from the Unicef indicates that nearly 650 million children worldwide live in extreme poverty- victims of social abuse, child labour, the sex trade and health disorders. Every year about 11 million children die of preventable causes..Everyday, more than 30,000 children around the world die of preventable diseases. Globally, more than 104 million children between the ages of 6 and 11 are not in school, 59 million of them girls.

We live in a violent world. More money and resources have been spent on war activities during the last 50 years than in the entire millennium. We must recognize that, since 1990, almost 80% of the victims of war and conflict have been civilians, mostly women and children...

The proliferation of small arms, in particular, has caused children to become killers as well as victims of these deadly weapons of destruction.."

Riccardo Di Done

Founding President of the O.P.C.R.

17

Peacekeeping Requires A New Approach

Poverty and peace: The role of hunger and deprivation among children in situations of conflict, with a brief reference to South Asia. War children have difficulty turning into peace children: The vicious cycle.

I hope this wouldn't be treated as audacity on my part, but I would like to quote **Sen. John Kerry from "Foreign Policy: If I Were President"**: "Foreign aid must be increased and reformed to focus on education. We must give countries in the Middle East a reason to want peace. In the next few years, if changes aren't made, the potential for violence in that region will only increase. If we fail to reach the children and the families wrecked by the violence of poverty and seclusion, the growing population of unemployed and unemployable kids will find in fanaticism a tragic answer to its problems..."

PEACEKEEPING REQUIRES A NEW APPROACH.

In developing countries of Asia, child protection laws such as the Juvenile Justice Act of 1986 (India), the Employment of Children Act of 1991 (Pakistan) and others like the Regional Working Group on Child Labour are firmly in place and amended from time to time. India which has 68% of the child population of South Asia spends a meager 2% on health and education as against 16% on defense. Economic globalization and structural adjustment programs have been largely responsible towards the

development of such lop-sided development models...

The issues involved here are extremely complex...

Speaking the language of peace, changing the lives of the world's children

(Much of this write-up derives from an article by Gordon Conway, dated April 2002, courtesy "the Rockefeller Foundation-Mission and Vision")

"I thought my life had come to a sudden standstill after that gunshot. Today, I see a ray of hope."

- A child victim of terrorism, being currently supported by the Rajiv Gandhi Foundation, New Delhi, India. Yes, there is hope as long as there are people working to convert hopes into reality.......

I do not believe in any religion...

I am not a Hindu. I am not a Sikh. I am not a Jew. I am not a Christian...

I do not have a religion called Hinduism. I do not have a religion called Islam. I do not have a religion called Jainism. I do not have a religion called Christianity...

I do not believe in hatred (post-Sept. 11, 2001 on the World Trade Center, the Pentagon)...

I believe in only one ism...and one ity- **this is the religion of humanism and the religion of humanity...**

My religion has a simple alphabet "e" embedded in it...

This is the religion of peace and love...

I do not know whose quote it was but this bit is worth noting.

"Love is the greatest force in the world,
And the word of God the most powerful truth on earth"

- Anonymous

The 20th Century has come and gone, and now, as never

before, we have a rare and distinct opportunity to assess its most significant events. This is a time for introspection not only for policy makers but also for each one of us for the world as a whole. The task is especially urgent now. Terrorist strikes against the United States and others, the resurgence of ethnic nationalism, the rise and spread of Islamic fundamentalism, the spread of Westernization in the East, the expanding rights of women and minorities, the collapse of Communism in the Soviet Union (meaning the loss of an important ideology for the world), Nazism and Fascism, the two World Wars, the Cold War, the Bretton Woods Conference and the birth of the United Nations, the rise and spread of technology, and man in space are some of the most significant events that have left an indelible impression on the human psyche...

Far too many mind-boggling problems, issues those, if you will...

A recent Gallup International-TNS Poll (Sept. 2002) indicated the following:

The biggest problems today are...

Problem	**Opinion Poll**
Terrorism	20
Unemployment	17
Corruption	15
Poverty	14
Overpopulation	6
Global Recession	6
Crime	5
Lack of Education/Illiteracy	5
War and Conflict	3
Others	Rest

There is this "big game"; of Peace; Security and Developnient..Painful disparities in how people live, among and within nations, generate plenty of fissionable material..International Peace and Security rest as much on

human well being as on law and order..there is therefore a need to realize the **enormous scope of this important correlation and the potential impact of poverty, especially child poverty (hunger and deprivation) on peace and conflict...**

Countries like India, Pakistan, Afghanistan, Nepal, Bangladesh and Sri Lanka have millions of impoverished people without basic services such as food, clothing, shelter, sanitation and hygiene, clean drinking water, jobs, education and health care, among others. As the World Development Report 2000 / 2001 has pointed out, the world has deep poverty amidst plenty...of the world's 6 billion-odd people, 2.8 billion, almost half, live on less than two dollars a day, and 1.2 billion, a fifth, live on less than one dollar a day, with a majority living in South Asia and Sub-Saharan Africa. According to latest reports (Sept, 2002), Southern Africa is in the grip of a starvation crisis, sooner, and worse than anticipated. And of those living on less than one dollar a day, 44% are in South Asia alone...

I wish, at times, that our children could lead better lives, and that the rich, industrialized countries could cut down on their extravagant consumption patterns, waste dumping, greenhouse gas emissions, etc, to help children in the south (as well as those in the north) enjoy better lives. I wish the rules of trade could be fairer and that the dividends accruing therein could be channelized into education ('feeding minds, fighting hunger')...

Remember John Lennon's 'Imagine', "you may say I'm a dreamer, but I'm not the only one.."

We pause for a moment...and dare to stimulate our minds to think..of those millions of children **caught up in situations of** deprivation and conflict..**all over the world, thousands of these "innocent flowers"(getting trampled as they are under the forces of globalization), die of** poverty **daily..**this is, according to John Pilger, the "true terrorism" of our times..**and what**

better example to give than South Asia, where, in the lives of children, deprivation and conflict occur on a common platform...

It is a fact that most of us would be able to visualize the recurring image of smoke rising from the ruins of the World Trade Center...just as we could (or, should I say: Could not?) the image of a little flower called a "child" working on a Shikara (houseboat) on the Dal Lake in war-torn Kashmir. This child should have been in school instead...and there are still many South Asians (particularly, innocent women and children) who are suffering silently the backlash based on religion...

It is but natural that this question should arise: What can we do to help prevent future acts of terrorism and restore **peace** and normalcy? The answers can never be simple, and yet these answers lie in the lives of our children..the "real victims" (of terrorism)..let us examine, in brief, the impact of conflict/terrorism on the lives of a few such children:

Imkong Sema lost his father to unidentified assailants, in Nagaland, India, when he was 16 years old, an age when most children need to be guided for their future;

Ajay Kumar is a very quiet and withdrawn child. His father and uncles were killed before his eyes while he stood helplessly on the terrace of his house. He has been unable to get over this trauma in life and feels scared of the terrace. This happened in the state of Punjab in India.

Little Anjali lived with her five sisters and parents in Srinagar, where they had a well-established carpet business. One unfortunate day, Anjali's father was kidnapped and later killed. The family then lost most of its assets as a direct result of the death of the father and was forced to leave their home..the ordeal had just begun...

- Case studies, (courtesy of the) Rajiv Gandhi Foundation online, New Delhi, India.

There is, I believe, a bit of a link between terrorism/war/(ethnic) conflict on the one hand, and childhood poverty and exclusion on the other. It is evident that those involved in conflict have themselves either grown up in poverty (with much needed love and attention being denied to them as children) or that they draw much of their support and justification from those who are, or perceive themselves as, unjustly impoverished. Surely, no one individual or group of individuals would want to become "scavengers of peace", as I would call them. They sure deserve better lives, but circumstances in childhood have been somewhat unkind to them...

More precisely, appreciating the reversible correlation between deprivation and conflict, it can be safely asserted that children growing up in conflict situations are particularly vulnerable, as they get exposed to familial destruction, forcible displacement, child conscription, long-term physical and psychological wounds and abandonment, among others. **For one who has known only violence, the faculty of adaptation to peace and social solidarity will be impaired in adulthood..and the vicious cycle continues...**

Let us learn to speak the language of peace in a world filled with violence..and hatred..it's high time we started working for a more peaceful world for our children, our future...

18

The Day Will Come when Nations will be Judged

Not by their military or economic strength

Nor by the splendour of their capital cities and public buildings...

Child injury deaths – Unicef Innocenti Report Card

> ***"Injury has become the number-one killer of children ages one to fourteen in developed countries and accounts for almost 40 percent of deaths in that age group"***

> **"We are all God's children...**
>
> **(Are we not)?"**

It was only today that I was thinking about this, and I deemed it fit, at the very outset, that I should, share a statement made by the 'greatest man to have ever walked the length of this planet': **Gandhi**:

> "If we are to reach ***real peace*** in this world, and if we are to carry on a real war against war, we shall have to begin with children. And if they will grow up in their natural innocence, we won't have to struggle, we won't have to pass fruitless, idle resolutions, but we shall go from love to love and peace to peace, until at last all the corners of the world are covered with that peace and love for which, consciously or unconsciously, the whole world is hungering."

Commitment to the Child: Convention on the Rights of the Child

Adopted by the General Assembly of the United Nations on 20 November 1989...

Preamble

The States Parties to the present Convention,

..in the Universal Declaration of Human Rights, the United Nations has proclaimed that childhood is entitled to special care and assistance,

..Recognising that the child, for the full and harmonious development of his or her personality, should grow up in a family environment, in an atmosphere of happiness, love and understanding,

..Bearing in mind that, as indicated in the Declaration of the Rights of the Child, "the child, by reason of his physical and mental immaturity, needs special safeguards and care, including appropriate legal protection, before as well as after birth",

..Recognising that, in all countries in the world, there are children living in exceptionally difficult conditions, and that such children need special consideration, taking due account of the importance of the traditions and cultural values of each people for the protection and harmonious development of the child,

Recognising the importance of international co-operation for improving the living conditions of children in every country, in particular in the developing countries...

Further to this, "the Progress of Nations" published annually by Unicef, states:

"The day will come

When nations will be judged

Not by their military or economic strength,

Nor by the splendour of their capital cities and public buildings,

But by the well-being of their peoples'

By their levels of health, nutrition and education...

..And by the protection that is afforded to the growing minds and bodies of their children."

(O.K. So there is something called the) "Convention on the Rights of the Child.."

(And), the Government of India acceded to this Convention on 11 December 1992...

The state shall, in particular, direct its policy towards securing:

(.) That the health and strength of workers, men and women, and the tender age of children are not abused and that citizens are not forced by economic necessity to enter avocations unsuited to their age or strength;

(..) That children are given opportunities and facilities to develop in a healthy manner and in conditions of freedom and dignity and that childhood and youth are protected against exploitation against moral and material abandonment.

Excerpt from Article 39,

Directive Principles of State Policy

But what has really happened, let us see for ourselves...

Indeed (f) actually, something very unfortunate...

"Ek Din Achanak (suddenly one day) the branches of the beautiful tree are cut down, what a tragedy.." we start with a narration:

Nandita, the protagonist, a 26-year-old woman, unmarried, stays with her widow mother in a small flat her father had purchased years back. She is convent-educated and currently a teacher (**"feeding minds, fighting hunger"**) of an English medium school. She has a dream – a dream that "the world shall be a better place to live in for our children, citizens of tomorrow's world" and feels that one day she would start an NGO working with 'underprivileged children' and embark on a mission of the kind she should

already be having in mind for them. She is associated as well with quite a few voluntary organizations in the city. She firmly believes that children are the future of any society and that all of us need to do 'some thing' or the other for them and that "we must give back to society a part of what we, as individuals, have got from it..."

In a 'lighter' perspective, "Newton would wake up from his grave if I said that 'every action **ought to** have an equal and opposite reaction'..."

"Anyway..back to the future..nee our children"...

Today she (Nandita) comes home late at night, has already had dinner with friends. Doorbell rings. Mother answers the door; Nandita tells her that she wouldn't have dinner tonight and straight moves to her room.

She changes into her nightgown in a hurry and drops into bed like a hog. In the evening, while with her friends, and munching on snacks and coffee, she has had a debate, amongst others, on Ms Medha Patkar and politics and the "**Narmada Bachao Andolan**" (Save the River Narmada movement)... however, amongst others, this discussion was also inconclusive...

She being tired puts off the night lamp and retires for the night...

Suddenly she hears the cries of a child "didi mujhe bachao, didi mujhe bacha lo, didi mujhe jine do"(dear sister-referring to an elder one, please save me; dear sister please would you save me; dear sister please help me live (survive)...

She is deep asleep, however, she still tries to get up, tries to listen to, and finds, much to her amazement, that from every corner of the room, there is a soft groan emanating from within: "Didi mujhe bachao, didi mujhe bacha lao, didi muje jine do".

Shrieking voices from children of all ages, some as young as seven, some nine, some are eleven, and for some it would be difficult to imagine their age. Some are boys, some are

girls but one thing is for sure: (the) 'commonality of attribute' on all these faces: **poor, 'wrinkled' ('scars of a difficult childhood'),** haggard looking. Tattered clothes, semi-nudity (this shouldn't at all sound 'glamorous' to you), tearful eyes expecting hope, space, solace, shelter, mercy, pity, compassion and love....

For a moment, she is dumbfounded. She goes to the one who is close by, others rush to her from every corner. She tries to comfort one, others jostle to get a share of love and comfort. She hears only the reverberations of the same monologue. She asks one, then another, then the third one and listens to each story, in the background the others keep sobbing and saying "didi mujhe bachao, didi mujhe bacha lao, didi mujhe jine do".

These are known faces ... of Aarti, of Raju, of Savita, of Ramu and of Zubeida to name a few...

Aarti starts her story : (Any resemblance to actual characters purely coincidental):

Aarti lives in the slums of Mukherjee Nagar, Delhi. One day, the Mathematics teacher of her school, almost broke the upper portion of Aarti's left hand as punishment for not completing her homework. It was only after she started complaining of excruciating pain that she asked her teacher, who after much persuasion took a closer look at the arm. Aarti had been severely injured. He informed the authorities who took her to the local hospital. She was administered first aid after which she felt better. This case was clearly medico-legal.

So, "What exactly does our Centers for Human Rights alternate reports for the UN Committee on the Rights of the Child" have to say on the issue of "children are being rendered **corporal Punishment in Schools**?"

Raju starts his story: Raju too comes from a very poor family. His father is an alcoholic, does not have any work to do, sleeps the whole day, mother works as domestic help

in the apartments nearby and in the evening, his father comes home drunk, takes another heavy dose of alcohol, beats Raju and his mother, and that's Raju's daily story. One day his father sells Raju to a middle class working couple from the city for a paltry Rs 100 and (Raju comes to know about this only much later on) misleads him (Raju) about his future, talking about the so-called comforts in the city: car, TV, good food and entertainment. Raju feels that this should be somewhat better than getting beaten on empty stomachs literally every single day and goes with the couple. The dust raised by the moving car causes blurred vision between Raju and his parents. The last time he saw his mother, she was crying helplessly, and father waving. In the city as well, there is no respite with the couple.18 hours of work both as domestic as well as external help, inadequate food, no food on some days, constant scolding and beating was to become a part of his life, no rhyme no reason. The rebel in Raju wakes up...This is too much. He has seen the commercial on TV of a man in elegant suit flying like a bird. Raju wanted to be a bird, to fly, to be free. He throws a padlock on the TV, which breaks into pieces, and flees the house one day leaving all the "comforts" in the city: car, TV, good food, entertainment. Raju now feels that flying like a bird is better than **18 hours of work, scanty food, scolding and beating from the master**. He lands up on the railway platform and meets Aarti, Savita, Ramu, Zubeida and others. Life here is worser than that was expected but was still 'sans' ("bereft of") beating...**when, Oh when! Would we be able to assure a 'life of dignity' to the "equally-vulnerable" boy-child, in an era in which everybody seems to be talking of the girl-child**, now that's something that we would touch upon later...

Savita starts her story:

Savita comes from a very poor family. **Her father works as a farmer but the 'rain-Gods' have betrayed them**, and thereby, food grown for the family of four (father, mother, 2 year old brother and she) is far from sufficient...

No proper meals during the day, toiling hard to get wood from the jungle, taking care of household chores from dusk to midnight. One day she comes to know that her father has decided to sell her off for Rs 2500/- (in the name of marriage) to an old man aged about 60. She had a dream of life, marriage to her "prince-charming", children and a closely-knit 'decent' family and certainly the realities were far away from the dream. She dreamt of a small hut, her own home but what was this? As the d-day (**dooms**!!!) day drew near, she ran away, ran and ran and finally came to the railway station; she landed up at the railway platform where she (refers to Savita) met Raju, Ramu, Zubeida, Aarti and others. Life here turned out to be worse than what was expected.

Ramu starts his story: (Any resemblance to actual characters purely coincidental):

Ramu comes from a very poor family (of Dharavi, Asia's largest slum area) where he was mercilessly beaten and then driven out by his step-mother (his father's second wife, whom he had married after the sudden death of his first wife, Ramu's biological mother, **a sad reflection of the status of "India's girl-child"**). What was Ramu's crime? He was extremely hungry and had asked for some food from his stepmother when she was feeding her own son. He ran away from the house (when could we ensure that every child had a 'home' in the true sense of the word) and since then, did a lot of odd jobs **and managed to just about sustain his own life**, (and I am referring to the '**scars of a difficult childhood'**and **the marauding evil called "child labour"**) until finally one day he landed up at the station and became friendly with the rest of his peer-group... on the railway platform he met Aarti, Savita, Raju, Zubeida and others. Life here was undoubtedly worse than that was expected.

Zubeida starts her story:

Zubeida happened to be a victim of the Gujarat Carnage. She had seen in front of her eyes her eldest

married sister Marzina being killed by the rioters, when she was 6 months pregnant. The pilferers had split her abdomen and flung her foetus into the burning inferno and split her (Marzina's) throat to ensure that no remnant was visible of this family. Zubeida started running along the darkness, not knowing where to go but only to save herself. She did not know after that, as she fell unconscious. Later on she found herself in a camp. She couldn't find any known faces neither did she want to go back to her native place nor could she recall where she was staying prior to the trauma. She ran away one day and landed up at the railway station, where she is now since then, some how managing **"to live"**. She has also often been sexually abused by **the "juveniles"** (**society's term for such children**) at the shacks along the railway lines and has accepted her life as it is...

Life goes on for Aarti, Raju, Savita, Ramu, and Zubeida..the protagonist has been listening to a number of stories. But she knows that there are thousands of Aartis, Rajus, Savitas, Ramus, and Zubeidas **in this poor nation called "India" (which spends more on cricket than on...well, we all know, do we actually?)...** It might be that the names are different, might be that the stories are different but all of them have one thing to say... They want to live, they want to "jinha chahata" (want to live)...they might not be living like John and Bobby and Sheena and Ashita and Sameer and Rohan Sen and Salim Khan from among **the elite, who can afford to gorge on the most-expensive 7-star lamb goulash and their favourite liquor: either white, sparkling wine or a 'Bloody Mary', drive a Mercedes/Limo and purchase aircraft and real estate..and organize and be a part of "fairytale-like weddings"...**

An indeed sad reflection of our times: The deep "chasm", I should say, between "have" (children) and "have-not" (children).

But they (these underprivileged children) have the right

to live, nutrition, have access to a decent education, basic health care, a family who cares; they want love, attention, affection, peace...

At this point, Nandita, the protagonist, starts riding a horse and gallops to the distant horizon when the sun is rising in the east. The sound of the galloping horse mixes with the reverberating sounds of "didi mujhe bachao, didi mujhe bacha lao, didi mujhe jine do".

The sun really gets up early in the east. It is morning. Nandita wakes up at the wake up call of her mother:

> " Nandu, wake up beta. It's already seven past. You are getting late for school".

Nandita's dreams: Are these realities? Can she really start a "**Bachpan Bachao Andolan**" (Save The Childhood movement)? Who shall help her? **India** with her economic liberalization, multinationals, mergers and acquisitions, high-octane life style, excellence in software skills, LPG (liberalisation, privatisation and globalization), MTV and ZEE English and Home Box Office (HBO) and how could one forget, the Mumbai bash of 'Sex and the City' ("Sarah: Would you marry me?") Though not quite $ billion worth Billy Crystal at the "Academy Awards", correct?), would anyone believe that these are stark realities?

Actually, what kind of a World Are We Passing On to our Children? A world filled with "atrocious" hunger, war, violence, deep perversions, murder, mayhem, looting, arson, sexual assault, plunder, (child) abuse including Paedophilia, raunchy Nationalism, Ethnicity, religious fundamentalism, added to poor leadership and bad regimes, amongst others...

Before you read on, beware that what you are about to read might shock you..This deals with **War** (Global Instability), but what about innocent civilians? War is that period during which innocent children would most likely grow up on a diet of "obscene hatred"...Because **Children** cannot forget the "horrors of war"... "hungry children", moreover...

Because rural children in Haryana and Rajasthan are being married off..meaning innocent, **Child Brides**..and consequent, Female Morbidity and Child and Female Mortality...

Because "**Female Foeticide**" in the states of Uttar Pradesh and 'Elitist' Delhi would actually mean nothing to the perpetrators...

Because rural children in Maharashtra, Bihar, Jharkhand and West Bengal trek long distances on foot to attend "**School**" (and, most likely, on empty stomachs)..and both rural as well as urban ones have to put up with Corporal Punishment...

Because little girls in Orissa are being sold off into the hands of '**pimps'**...

She (Nandita) does not get any answer. She has a nasty headache.

No answer would be ordinarily given, no reasoning could be found out, since each one of us is responsible for this situation- **the society**, the economy, the ecology, and what not. Because it would be our moral responsibility, for you, for me, politicians, policy-makers, social workers and thinkers to at least make an attempt to change ourselves, our immediate environments and finally, this beautiful World, to bring hopes to everyone, to bring smiles on the faces of the millions of downtrodden, poor, suffering, marginalized, "Have-not" Children, "our truly suffering Humanity". Simply "Imagine..A Better World" for "our Children, our future"! May God Bless The World!!!

Mama's lovely daughter, Nandu tells her: "Mamma, I will not go to school today. Tell Ruchika that I am not well and wouldn't really feel like going to school. Let her inform Sister Desouza..."

The story ends with a song at the background being played on either TV or radio "Hum Honge Kamiyabb." "Hum Honge Kamiyabb..." "Hum Honge Kamiyabb Ek Din..." (We

shall Overcome...We shall Overcome..**We shall Overcome some day..**)

Remember, before we talk of War (or, National, Regional and Global Instability)..Weapons Of Mass Destruction, Disarmament, Ceasefires, Peace Talks/Diplomatic Negotiations, Bilateral Trade...

Let me Warn You..We could have 'n' number of such 'discussions' (although I wouldn't say that all of these might be irrelevant), forgetting at the same time all the promises we had made to work for a better future for our children... But nothing much I guess should come out of them...

The **'implications'** would be enormous..well-fed; well-cared-for and loved; and healthier as well as more-educated children, and, as a consequence, **no more child poverty..and sustainable peace...**

19

The World Summit on Sustainable Development-From Children of Rio (1992) to Children of Johannesburg (2002)...and Beyond...A Revolution in Kindness Needed

"The central idea of sustainable development is to seek both efficiency in the use of natural and environmental resources and equity within and among generations. Sustainable development provides a significant bridge between the aspirations of environmentalists for conservation and the efforts of traditional development specialists to reduce poverty. It is relevant to both industrial and developing countries. However, history demonstrates that sustainable development does not arise spontaneously but must be carefully defined, crafted, and nurtured by many agents working together..."

-Quoted from "Intellectual Exchange", The Japan Foundation Center for Global Partnership.

The concept of "**sustainable development**" was first popularized by the World Commission on Environment and Development (the Brundtland Commission) in the 1987 report, "Our Common Future". Since then, governments, international organizations and non-governmental organizations (NGOs) have adopted the concept as a new paradigm for development.

Between August 26th and September 4th 2002, world leaders, world governments, country representatives, the United Nations as well as grassroots organizations and

business leaders were meeting in **Johannesburg (South Africa)** to discuss key issues: **Poverty alleviation, trade (more aid and fairer trade), water and sanitation (clean water), protection of the environment (like, saving rainforests), promoting solar power and fighting AIDS**.

Prior to the Summit, some delegates said that although there was less acrimony between the rich and the poor then that during the last preparatory talks in Asia in June 2002, there existed a fundamental rift between the developing countries demanding more aid and **fairer trade** on the one hand, and the Western powers trying to keep those vital issues off the agenda in Johannesburg. Eighteen months of bargaining had produced only a 77-page Draft Plan for easing Poverty and protecting the Environment. The attending 100 World Leaders were to approve this plan.

In the Year **1992**, 10 Years prior to the Johannesburg Summit, nations of the World had gathered in **Rio de Janeiro (Brazil),** at the **"Earth Summit"**, with the aim of discussing efforts for a greener, fairer world, and hope of realizing the same. The "Rio Declaration", Agenda 21, the Forest Principles and the "Biodiversity Convention", embodied general principles for action to protect the Environment and laid the basis for specific goals and plans of action. Only the "Convention on Climate Change" set out a specific goal: the reduction of greenhouse gases to "earlier levels" by the year 2000.In addition, through UNICEF and WHO, two specific goals were established, universal access to safe drinking water, and to sanitary means of excreta disposal.

Many of Rio's promises to narrow the yawning wealth gap without the environmental damage that accompanied prosperity in the West, have been broken, or, at best, remain unfulfilled.

Since the Rio Summit, we have witnessed growing Global Inequalities as well as more Migration, Epidemics, Conflicts and Instability. Rio was all talk and no action...

The Rocket gets launched: 1st Day (Aug 26): The South African President, (who was also Summit President), H.E. Mr. Thabo Mbeki, called for **an end to "Global Apartheid" between rich and poor**, and the creation of a New Global Society based on Care and Humanity. At this juncture, there would be a need to state the priorities of the Developed Countries at the Summit, namely, issues such as the Environment, and those of the Developing Countries, Economic Development and **Poverty**. Health was to be a major, key issue, with a focus on HIV/AIDS. Efforts were to be made towards the Creation of an environmentally sustainable future, with Protection of the Environment and Poverty Reduction foremost on the agenda. Water and Renewable Energy were other important issues to be discussed (actually, debated?). The poor called for more aid and **fairer trade rules**, while the rich were reluctant to pay more cash, and at the same time, seemed to be concentrating on the Protection of the Environment.

For Summit President, H.E. Mr. Mbeki, it was a precarious position. On the one hand, he had to speak on behalf of the developing world (example, Africa), on the other; he had to ensure that the Summit succeeded as far as its objectives were concerned.

For this was a Summit worth $50Million, in a country where people remain deprived of essentials like food and clean drinking water, and especially vulnerable to disease and **Poverty**, and in a world in which there are "Islands of Prosperity" surrounded by a "Sea of **Poverty"**.

A major issue at the Summit was the "Asian Haze", smog enveloping the Environment. It was evident that the world's most populous country, China, is the largest producer of greenhouse gases after the United States.

At about the same time, Business leaders were meeting Politicians at the Summit. It was felt that Environmental Responsibilities and good Corporate Social Responsibility could help make business more "Sustainable", as well as

raise the value of the Company in the eyes of its shareholders. The following two facts deserve special mention, namely, that the Poorest Nations attract only a tiny fraction of private investment, as well as that firms were pushing for (more) "Earth-friendly" Credentials.

The three main aspects of Sustainable Development, Social, Economic and Environmental, remained much in the spotlight, with **Poverty** being seen as potentially harmful to the Ecological System. Indeed, the Poor, out of desperation, are often driven to destroy the biodiversity and the Environment. Poverty and Environment are, thus, inextricably linked. There cannot be any Sustainable Development without Development i.e. putting it mildly, a genuine relief from **Poverty**, and consequently, much hardship and suffering...why is it that the poor always have to suffer, and very often, at the hands of faulty government policies?

2nd Day (Aug. 27.): Farming and **Agriculture** topped the agenda on the 2nd Day. Developing Nations wanted an end to "Subsidies" for farmers in Developed Countries. No consensus was reached. The Europeans were busy criticizing the Americans of intense discussions "behind closed doors", as well as for opposing the setting of Specific Targets on critical issues. Farming **Subsidies** and **Trade** dominated the day. It was strongly felt that the Developing Worlds' Farmers were at a big disadvantage compared to Farmers in the Developed World. The US Farm Bill had actually increased subsidies to farmers. And the Governments of the advanced countries were imposing high tariff barriers on Developing Worlds' Produce. Summit Participants were concerned that these policies could actually ruin farmers in the Third World. There were also some discussions on Pollutants, Consumption Patterns and Waste Dumping that the Developed countries force on the Developing countries. It was also felt that Aid should be diverted to Education, Health Care and **jobs**, among others.

3rd Day (Aug. 28): Clean Water, Sanitation and Energy were the major topics of discussion. 2.2 Million people die each year from diseases caused by the lack of Clean Water. A third of the world's population has no access to clean water or Sanitation. This trend was noticed on the outskirts of Johannesburg itself. The discussions centered on "Achievable Goals", such as, for instance, Self-help programs run by Self-help groups, National Governments using all the Resources at their disposal, and, Support from the International Community. Participants struck a deal involving fish stocks, more precisely, a deal to replenish rapidly decreasing fish stocks in our oceans. The US announced an Aid Package to promote Clean Water Initiatives. However, EU Delegates were questioning US commitment. They were criticizing the US for opposing the setting of specific targets. **Trade** was another issue that dominated the 3rd Day. The big power Blocks (the US and Western Europe) were reluctant to commit, with the Developing Countries demanding more Commitment as necessary for Sustainable Development. Participants were now talking about "Renewable Energy", or the kind of Energy that does not hurt the Planet's Ecology.

There was much to agree about, but much disagreement, too...

4th Day (Aug. 29): Economic Development and the Environment dominated the 4th Day. One major success centered on the Plan to replenish dwindling **fish stocks** in our oceans by the year 2015. It was being expected that the US would announce plans along with the Developing World towards **Poverty** and Environmental Protection. The main question that occurred to most participants was that how much Aid would the Developed Countries actually give the Developing Countries and how?

5th Day (Aug 30): Large parts of the agenda over **Poverty and the Environment** were agreed upon, and everybody seemed to be getting ready for a Plan of Action. Yet, there was still a deadlock over major issues like subsidizing farmers in rich countries. 101 Heads of State were being expected for the coming week.

6th Day (Aug 31): The 6th Day started with protests from several thousand protesters hailing from the poor black township of Alexandria. Alexandria township lies right in the heart of Johannesburg, marked by conditions such as water polluted by human waste, and squatter settlements. These people were reiterating their need for land, clean water and sanitation. They were also protesting against the **power of corporations**, and an utter failure of governments to address the central issue of **poverty**. Protesters included landless workers, AIDS activists, and, ordinary people relegated to the background by an **unequal society**, so much characteristic of Africa. Let me add something to this question: Delegates had unlimited access to mineral water, whereas ordinary people in Johannesburg have relatively little or no access to clean water for drinking and other purposes. **We can have 'n' number of conferences, conventions and glamorous summits, but I guess nothing much will come out of them.** At this moment in Johannesburg, a man's water supply (a basic human right) is being cut off because he cannot afford it. We talk of "justice for all"? A major fear in developing countries concerns the issue of **liberalization in human services**, which can lead to unquestioned control over resources, including water. Ever heard of the "water wars" in regions of conflict, this includes the rivers, the Tiger, the Euphrates and the Nile, etc in Africa? Ever heard of selling one's body to ensure for one's children a decent supply of water fit for consumption??

WHAT HAVE THE POOR DONE TO DESERVE THIS?

This was a question that remained unanswered.

In between proceedings (sessions), delegates were attending debates on critical issues. **"Earth summit: The debate"** centered on the crucial issues. The question that came to everyone's mind was: "What do we have in store for our planet, not just for our species?"

Debate participants were discussing "the most pressing problems facing the world today": Participants included South African Nobel laureate

Nadine Gordimer; **Dr. Bjorn Lomborg**, author of "The Skeptical Environmentalist"; **Dr. Vandana Shiva** from India; **Prof. Jeffrey Sachs**, Director of the Earth Institute at Columbia University, New York; **Dr. Ricardo Navarro,** Chairman of the "Friends of the Earth International"; **Martin Khor**, Director of the "Third World Network", Malaysia; and **Ms. Penny Fowler** of "Oxfam International", among other dignitaries. Water, AIDS, climate change, power of international corporations, clean water and sanitation, privatization of all aspects of life, survival of the species, etc were issues that came up in the course of the discussion.

It was with immense concern that participants noted that following RIO, Green Fields had become Barren Deserts; Natural jungles had become barren jungles; the number of Global Corporations had risen from 35,000 (in 1992) to 50,000 in 2002; Global Warming (meaning Disease, Agricultural Slump, Economic Decline, Rising Sea Levels, Drought, Floods, etc. among other repercussions) was touching Mammoth Proportions; and that Globalization had adversely affected a large number of people, most of whom have no decision-making power, leading to a situation in which a third of the world's people were living in extreme deprivation. It was recognized that all issues were interlinked.

HOW TO LIFT PEOPLE OUT OF POVERTY WITHOUT DESTROYING THE ENVIRONMENT?

(a) This was a question that was being discussed at the Debate. There was talk of increasing Food Production, including production of "Genetically-modified Food". But, how many of these Elitist Delegates were actually bothered about the fact that across Southern Africa, just a few hundred miles from the venue of the Summit, people were dying of Hunger? It was recognized that as far as Trade was concerned, rich countries gave more in subsidies to their own farmers than they gave in aid to developing countries, and that, in poor countries, crops would at times die from pesticides and viruses. Hunger, Poverty and Malnutrition were seen as the chief issues in Africa. Radical Solutions

included Proper Governance and Appropriate Technology. Biotechnology could help. The issue of "Genetically-modified Food" raised quite a few eyebrows. (b) There was talk of the "Global Politics of Food", dumping of heavily subsidized food by the US and Europe in Developing Countries. Land Reform could be a probable solution. (c) It was also noted that Farmers in Developing Countries were desperately vulnerable to Climatic Shocks and Low Productivity. The solution lay in Intercropping for Better species. (d) Participants recognized that Developing Countries were trying to ape Consumption Patterns, and that the Solution lay in investing more in Education and Awareness. It was obvious that educated people would be more sustainable in their Attitudes and Ways of Life. Finally, there was recognition of the importance of Appropriate and Better Technology.

7th Day (Sept 1): Nelson Mandela, while addressing the World at the Summit, said that nations should provide clean drinking water to the billions of people who were going without safe water for consumption. There was widespread disagreement over energy sources at the end of this week. The UN reiterated that it felt that **Water** would dominate the Agenda (with its implications for health, sanitation and hygiene) over this Century.

8th Day (Sept 2): The final stage had begun. UN Chief **Kofi Annan** warned of disaster if adequate steps were not taken to combat **Poverty** and Environmental degradation. He called on the world to be responsible for the Poor and the oppressed. By then, a deal on **Climate Change** had been ratified. However, Targets for use of **Renewable energy** were still not agreed on. By then, World leaders had gathered for the Summit's final conference. The EU and the United States were locked over energy.

Meanwhile, delegates had been working throughout the night for an outline agreement. A possible agreement would deal with COMBATING **POVERTY** AND ENDING OF HUMAN MISERY.

There was hardly any commitment on foreign aid. Britain promised to raise its Aid to Africa to $1.5 billion p.a. by 2006, and by 50% to all countries in general.

Mr. Kofi Annan advised business leaders at the Summit that they must invest in Developing countries.

9th Day (Sept 3): There was no clear consensus on Renewable Energy. The immediate discussion centered on the impending War between the US and Iraq. China and Poland, had, by then, ratified the **"Kyoto Protocol"**. The World bank Chief, Mr. James Wolfensohn, asked the **Developed Nations to cut their Agricultural (Farm) Subsidies (which could be harmful for Trade) to help THE POOR**. Delegates committed to restoring fish stocks and improving access to Sanitation. It was commonly agreed that leaders would have to sell summit ideals to voters in their countries.

10th Day (Sept 4): Mr. Colin Powell was to speak at the Plenary Session on the Final Day. Environmental groups had staged a walkout (such as, over Renewable, cleaner Energy) to protest, at compromises in the action Plan, which according to them, "failed to recognize primacy of human dignity". By then, however, negotiations had finalized the draft for an action plan for sustainable development. Mr. Colin Powell's speech was, meanwhile, disrupted by disturbances in the hall.

The US unveiled **New "Partnerships" on Energy, Water and Agriculture**. This was clearly stated by Mr. Colin Powell. Mr. Kofi Annan and Mr. Thabo Mbeki gave a joint news conference.

New targets were set for sanitation in poor countries and restoration of fish stocks. World leaders were expected to adopt the Action Plan during the Final Session on Wednesday. UN Secretary-General Kofi Annan gave the final press conference of the summit. Environmentalists present at the Summit said that the action plan would strengthen the economic system, which in turn would harm the environment.

ATLEAST THESE ISSUES WERE BEING TALKED ABOUT AT THE SUMMIT.

People were only talking about environmental vulnerability, actually, the "vulnerability of the poor" and poverty. They were talking about the impact of policy and practice in the north and "pro-poor" policy change.

To conclude, I would like to quote some extracts from the draft declaration submitted at the Johannesburg Summit on Sustainable Development, September 2002:

"Sustainable development" requires a long-term perspective and broad-based participation in policy formulation, decision-making and implementation at all levels. As governments we will continue to work for stable partnerships with the private sector; labour; civil society, and all major groups, respecting the independent and important roles of these social partners...

We recognize that the process of globalization is accompanied by the emergence of leading private sector corporations which have a responsibility to contribute to the evolution of equitable and sustainable communities and societies...

We undertake to strengthen and improve governance at the local level, for the effective implementation of Agenda 21, the Millennium Development Goals and the Johannesburg Commitment...

We agree that women's emancipation and gender equality should be integrated in all activities...

We urge the promotion of dialogue and cooperation among all the world's peoples and civilizations, irrespective of race, disabilities, religion, language, culture and tradition.

We affirm that armed conflict and warfare are inherently inimical to sustainable development.

To achieve our goals of sustainable development, we need a democratic system of global governance with enhanced and accountable international and multilateral institutions.

We further commit ourselves to monitor progress towards the achievement of our sustainable development goals and objectives at regular intervals.

We commit ourselves to act at all levels that are required to save our planet, promote human development and achieve universal prosperity and peace...

From the African continent, the cradle of humankind, we declare to the peoples of the world that we are determined to ensure that our collective hope for sustainable development is realized." Adieu, Sommet De Johannesburg!!!

20

Michel Adam Fashion-TV in Johannesburg and Falsified Notions of Progress

GLOBAL WARMING, RAVE PARTIES AND DARFUR

MORE WINE WILL FLOW, JESUS

September 19, 2002: Civil war starts in Cote d' Ivoire.

October 12, 2002: Militants detonate bombs in two nightclubs in Kuta, Bali, killing 202 people and injuring over 300.

(WHY NIGHTCLUBS AND A LARGELY EXPATRIATE POPULATION?)

March 19, 2003: The first American bombs drop on Baghdad.

March 22, 2003: America and Britain begin their 'shock and awe campaign' with a massive air strike on military targets in Baghdad.

BY SHARP CONTRAST (SANE WAS IT?)

The 75th Academy Awards ceremony takes place at the Kodak Theatre in Hollywood. 'Chicago' wins Best Picture.

As American forces seize control of Baghdad, President George W Bush lands on the aircraft carrier "USS Abraham Lincoln", where he gives a speech announcing the end of major combat in the 2003 invasion of Iraq. "Mission Accomplished".

April 2004: Darfur. And still more bloodletting...

December 26, 2004: The Tsunami hits South East Asia when the strongest earthquake in 40 years hits the entire Indian Ocean region. The official death toll in the affected

countries stands at 186,983. More than 40,000 people reported missing.

December 31, 2009: As the rich and the famous party in Jo'burg, yet another child dies of hunger.

Nina Ricci, Yves Saint Laurent, Dolce & Gabbana, Christian Dior and Giorgio Armani, F Parties: Fashion Bar Party (Singapore), exotic Jaguars on display.

Paris and Milan fashion weeks, the Rio Carnival, an American Idol pervades our senses as the developing world struggles to survive.

The poor boy eyes the D'damas diamond collection. Diamonds are forever.

All that Western music, Western culture, all those bare abs, all that topless nudity.

All that white skin vs. Sheer native desperation...

Sprawling mansions in Malibu, and personal private golfing estates and dream fairytale-like weddings..pray, how much more does the rich man need beyond his bread?

Paris-the fashion capital of the world; Kalahandi-the desperation capital, actually, how much more comfort do we need?

As the rich of the world celebrate Christmas party on the Black Diamond in Genoa (25 December, 2008 22:00 hours), the poor of the world will die on the streets on these cold wintry nights...

As Woody Allen arrives in his Red Ferrari and Penelope Cruz in her black Limousine...

A nation will lose yet another child of hunger.

That big is beautiful; these are our falsified notions of progress...

The greatest unfinished task on the global agenda is managing an event called time. An event is happening and we on Planet Earth are running out of time. At this moment, someone's expectations are rising. Can we predict the

consequences of a rising expectation? A man in a remote village expects an e-mail facility in his village at subsidized rates so that his wife can send a message to him during his lunchtime in the field. But think, a heavy metal group slashes innocent pigeons on stage and a big group of people watch. Is Interpol sleeping? Come to think of it, such a thing happening at the turn of the century?

Actually, how humane are we? Glaring inequalities in society exist. Those wallowing in luxury and privileges beware. Unrestrained open displays of wealth and privileges and indifference to the poor might one day arouse such rage as to cause a bloody revolution as happened in France.

We still have a long way to go to call ourselves civilized or humane or compassionate or sufficiently tolerant.

It's a world of stark injustices. Righteous indignation often focuses on violence, sin and pornography, rather than on macro-ethical issues like poverty, inequality, race, war and injustice. By the same token, the Favelas in Rio, those festering piles of people separated by bits of cardboard and corrugated iron are not very important. At any rate, the poor are lazy and stupid, aren't they?

The middle classes have a choice-to identify with the rich and influential, or with the poor, who have very few choices (Paulo Freire). The income-gap is meanwhile not 'trickling down' to the poor, whose numbers are going up.

The earth was given to all, not just to the rich. (There is enough food to go around-for every man's need, but not every man's greed. It is not God's will that a quarter us lives in luxury while the rest struggle to survive).

National and international systems revolve around greed and power: "The international imperialism of money". It's all about a flawed distribution system.

Former US President Richard Nixon once said in a moment of candor: "The main purpose of American aid is not to help other nations, but to help ourselves."

Selling powdered milk to the poor (who often cannot read the directions) makes money, so why not, never mind the babies dying?

Growing coffee in the Third World, where people are desperate for food, is often a political gimmick. The rich can definitely afford coffee, while the poor in the Favelas of Sao Paulo cannot afford food. So why wouldn't I as a plantation owner grow coffee for the rich, let's just leave alone black beans to fill the poor man's belly?

Multinational corporations exist to make money for their stockholders, a job they are doing very well. Dom Helder Camara has been saying for years that if rich nations paid fair prices to developing countries for their natural resources there would no longer be any need for aid and relief projects.

Poverty creates jobs-like development professionals, line and staff ministries, social welfare workers, the police and corrective services, so keep them where they are.

The poor have their own particular cultural, ethnic and political distinctives that ought to be respected. First World models may often not suit developing countries.

Albert Einstein once famously remarked: "The problems of the world cannot be solved with mechanisms, but only by changing the hearts and minds of man and speaking courageously."

But one must remember that there's no point in bearing a cross if you don't believe in resurrection...

"The aim of globalisation is to dominate the rest of us, any other country, any other world.

Globalisation is simply Westernisation. The West wants to be the centre of the world."

There are simply no rules for the West. The West wants to be the centre of the world.

21

US of A, The United States of America

(Our white European Western free Nations!)

And Donald Trump and Trump Plaza, rave and the city, sleaze and cyber-pornography and Paris Hilton – the obsession with celebrity lives

Yes, the US of A, my right-honorable!

The world's richest nation,

A nation of limousines and ghettos,

(Of "**liberty, equality and fraternity**")...

Of rhythm and 'blues' (and Prozac to drive them away for an estimated several million of them!), some soul-searching (over nuclear reactors, enriched uranium and the world's oil reserves!), 'soul music',

Of U's of the poor and 50-cents,

Of Taylors and Fortenskys and Jackson (villas) and pedophilic slaps!

(Of Spielberg and Lucas and Air Force One! And Jesus 2000 and Chicago and Erin-effluent-sewage treatment-million dollar lawsuit Brockovich!)

Of hot dogs, pizza, pepsi coke! Broccoli and spaghetti,

Of (Las) Vegas Casino Culture-

AND DONALD TRUMP PLAZAS

Of Hugh Hefners

RAVE AND THE CITY
SLEAZE AND CYBER-PORNOGRAPHY

AND PARIS HILTONS – THE OBSESSION WITH CELEBRITY LIVES

(What about the Miltons!)

In all their 'Anorexic' finery (ies)!

(And, medical investigations and false allegations and ER!)

Of Mt. Sinai, John Hopkins and (what they don't teach you at) Harvard Medical School, Cambridge, MA!

Of 'video-camera societies'; national ID cards, global positioning satellites (GPS); the 'verichip' (unveiled by Florida-based Applied Digital Solutions- ADS in Dec 2001): Microchips implanted under the skin..the latest sci-fi (and lifesavers for Alzheimer's patients and godsends for emergency room medical personnel and peace of mind through enhanced personal security) ..and civil liberties advocates who worry that the device will someday come under the control of big brother...

Of bureaucrats, high-handed (White House) administrations and Third World (as if one never existed!) HIV+, debt, poverty, (and sheer desperation) and empty war rhetoric..straight out of Washington's suave 'closets'!-

Of Columbia's Earth Institute and Presidential advisors and Prof. Jeffrey Sachs,

Of Mark Malloch Browns and Maurice Strongs!

(Of global climate change! And Oklahoma/Nevada forest fires!)

Of Smithsonians and Brookings and Rockefellers meting out strategic locations! (Laugh!)

Of ("salivating canines"!), 'unconditioned' north-south dialogue(s) and 'conditioned' north-south/ north-north-south/ south-south bilateral/multilateral (or, whatever!) development co-operation (Oh! Such beautiful, deft co-operation (facilitation))!!

Of food on the tables and child malnutrition and hunger in

Darfur...

Of rich, exotic Sedan(s) and poor, enduring Sudan(s)-

Of utter disrespect of other people's faiths and beliefs-

Of 9/11's and the 'global War on Terror' (or, 'whatever', that 'implies' to "most" Westerners); it seems they have no other work to do...

((O! I forget, that the West is an enlightened people(s))-

A chase of WMD'S: Weapons of mass destruction, O! These people are worse than biological weapons (warfare)! I think we ought to send elaborate, confidential letters to them! (Laugh!) (and the Nobel Peace Prize goes to the IAEA, Vienna, Austria, and my heart! Where the "hills are alive with the Sound of Music", said who, the lovely and elegant Julie Andrews)...

Of oil reserves (actually, why do I, we all, keep harping on that one?)-

A nation, pardon me for saying this,

But with policies on

Every other nation on earth-

All this, all another story-

That I might wish to reserve for later-

Forget it! I was not born on the 4th of July-

So, America... is certainly not worth my attention now...

-BUT-

Mr. (Kofi) Annan is:

-Consider this-

He ensured that there was or ought not to be a Third World War. He tried his best on Iraq, and continued to try his best, on Iran, North Korea, as also every other world

nation, until his term expired. He also achieved a 47-member UN Human Rights Council to replace the 53-seat Human Rights Commission (Geneva), overlooking U.S. Opposition, in a bid to reform the world body. (I haven't checked this out though; I really wouldn't know)

I'm afraid I'm getting a bit too personal, though this was never really my intention. Please forgive me, I may have sinned, but then aren't we all entitled to whatever, our respective beliefs, value-systems, thought-processes, reasonings, rationale(s) and emotive patterns?

I am a woman after all!

And someone rather famous said,

'Frailty, thy name is woman!'

I should say I dare disagree- (and I have always loved Shakespeare)

[So, what is all this current global (or, lack of it) disagreement about?]

The World Economic Forum (Davos)

Actually, not even the **"World Economic Forum"**, **Davos** in refrigerated! Switzerland can provide permanent 'solutions' to such hot! Contemporary debates!!

(Especially, with corporate issues being brought 'centrestage', and our globalization 'gurus' relegating other 'apparently less consequential' farmer's and the "developing world's poor's issues to the background?)

And, they all have their issues! From Pensacola to Washington D.C. to NY, from Toronto to Vancouver, from Belfast and Dublin to Liverpool and London, from Prague and Bucharest and Madrid to Berlin and Milan and from Cairns and Canterbury to Sydney, Melbourne and Canberra!

Calling ourselves Afro-Americans and Hispanic-Caribbeans and Aussie-Brits!

"And though we might be differentially (nee white; black and brown) skinned..matters not the diversity: Of race; color of skin; nature of disadvantage or gender..."

It's about giving names to "our" issues and fighting for them (whether these our very issues make sense or not!) – we're all doing it!

To begin with, the Republican Governor of South Dakota (my inherent 'Americanism') it seems though not very recently signed a ban on abortion, challenging the once landmark Roe Vs Wade 1973 US Supreme Court ruling that bans on abortion violated a woman's constitutional right to privacy...

Across the Atlantic, in Britain, Natallie Evans, 34, who had undergone IVF in 2001 with her partner Howard Johnston, ahead of ovarian cancer treatment (that rendered her infertile) found her "pleas (e) may I have a baby from the frozen embryo" going unheard in the European Court of Human Rights as well as in her own country, the British courts of justice!!! Very sad indeed..?

And now it seems Great Britain's compassionate gaze has shifted to Asia... and so the tabloids tell us...

The UK has it seems joined the World Bank and the Asian Development Bank to convene the 'Asia 2015 Conference', London...

How about a 'South Asia 2015' conference or, a 'north-south 2015' conference? How far have we reached? (Our millennium development goals?)

And, how much compassion there is in one's gaze (I mean, the developed world) or ought be that innocent farmers be driven to suicide (everything in INXS, I'm talking of India, my beloved, my bread, my corn, if not my norm) and that innocent children should be sent to God (Lord Jesus, our saviour) by the kind grace of malnutrition..?

"For by grace are ye saved through faith; and that not of yourselves: It is the gift of goa! – Not of works, lest any man should boast!" (Eph.2:8, 9)

Copyright Aug.1984 by Family Services, Zurich, Switzerland.

..And malnutrition hurts...

22

World Hunger Foraging for Food in the Nation's Capitals

PLENTY OF CHILDREN MALNOURISHED

Under nutrition kills about 5.6 million children under five every year in the developing world. 146 million children under five or one out of four – more than half of them (78 million) living in South Asia – are underweight, and at increased risk of an early death. Of the 146 million children under five who are underweight in the developing world, 106 million – 73 per cent – live in just 10 countries. India leads with 57 million, followed by Bangladesh (8 million), Pakistan (8 million), China (7 million), Nigeria (6 million), Ethiopia (6 million), Indonesia (6 million), Democratic Republic of the Congo (3 million), Philippines (3 million), Vietnam (2 million) and finally other developing countries (40 million).

Similar patterns are seen as far as stunted growth goes. It is a result of severe under nutrition. South Asia has the highest levels in the world, with growth of 44 per cent of its children stunted.

Children in rural areas are nearly twice as likely to be underweight as those in urban areas. In Latin America/Caribbean and East Asia/Pacific regions, children living in rural areas are, respectively, 2.6 times and 2.1 times as likely to be underweight as children living in urban areas.

South Asia is the only region in the world where the proportion of underweight girls is higher (47 per cent) than the proportion of underweight boys (44 per cent).

Of the estimated 20 million low-weight births (less than 2.5 kg) each year in the developing world, more than half (11.4 million) occur in South Asia and more than one-third (7.8 million) in India.

Low rates of breastfeeding, iodine, vitamin A and iron deficiency contribute to under nutrition. South Asia has the lowest rate of vitamin A consumption, at 58 per cent, and East Asia/Pacific, the highest, at 73 per cent.

Apart from food, the factors that contribute to malnutrition in children include access to health services, quality of care for the child and pregnant mother, and hygiene.

Vitamin and mineral deficiencies also affect children's survival and growth. Anemia affects 74 per cent of children under the age of three, more than 90 per cent of adolescent girls and 50 per cent of women. Iodine deficiency, which reduces learning capacity by up to 13 per cent, is widespread because less than half of households use iodized salt. Vitamin A deficiency, which causes blindness, increases rate of illness and death among pre-schoolers, is also widespread.

Malnutrition is a problem in industrialized countries as well, but there it is more likely to result from unhealthy diet than from insufficient food.

(Based on information from an international child rights organization)

MALNUTRITION HURTS

-*'Protein Energy Malnutrition'..a nutritional deprivement disease in growing children due to lack of calories / proteins or both...*

-*Large eyes and painfully cache tic...*

-*A life of 'orphan ship'...*

-*Living under a flyover...*

-"Sometimes she holds a baby in her arms. And I wonder if it's hers..she could be a sibling, left with her to tend while

her mother works or begs elsewhere. Or lies in sickness in some hovel. When I see her nuzzling the baby to her breast, I wonder if it is indeed hers, and how she is going to feed it, considering her own fragile frame...

-She is not alone. Across the cities, across the Rich-Poor World! There are many more like her. They have come from God knows where and live under the flyovers and inside the large pipes...

-I look at her and wonder how we can allow anyone to live like that..As today's young woman, she would probably be clear about her future: whether she wanted to pursue a career; what she wanted to do with her life. Instead, here she was, a **beggar**. Definitely not by choice, but because destiny, or chance, decreed it so...

-She is, of course, not alone..There are countless children like her walking the streets by day, sleeping by the roadsides by night, foraging for food or begging for it..This, in a country called INDIA, proud of being on its way to becoming a world leader; in cities that are the nation's capitals and money and commercial capitals..It wouldn't be long before life on the streets reduced these innocent flowers called Children to ill health, and constant childbearing took its toll on their vulnerable bodies, and all that filth and grime added dosages of infection to their lives and those that lived with them...

-Who would care for her then, as she lay sick and helpless? What would happen to the spawn? Would they also be relegated to the streets like she did and grow up into lifetimes and lifestyles of abuse, stealing, fighting and crime?

-Some Men and Women in fine clothes were actually looking at a picture of her on some celebrated gallery wall..Little did they realize how a Life Had Been Wasted..."

(Anonymous)

-Mothered and Suffering, frail, insulted, starved: **No Child Deserved This...**

Malnutrition is characterized by inadequate intake of protein, energy, micronutrients, and by frequent infections or disease. Nutritional status is the result of the complex interaction between the food we eat, our overall state of health, and the environment in which we live. In short, food, health and caring, the three 'pillars of well-being'...

Often an invisible phenomenon, malnutrition casts long shadows..it kills, maims, cripples and blinds..affects especially the poor and vulnerable..Malnutrition is not only medical; it is also a social disorder rooted in poverty and discrimination; and has economic ripple effects that can jeopardize development...

Whose fault is it?

(Says the World Health Organization)..says **WHO...**

23

World Hunger Goes Untreated

(UNTIL THE MEDIA TAKES NOTICE)

For the severely malnourished children in the developing world, providing sufficient food might seem to be the obvious solution. The developed world seems to think that it has fulfilled its obligations after arriving with truckloads of food, that too only in conflict-ridden zones, or after a famine or disaster has been reported from 'some part of the world'. The media suddenly seems to take notice, and any news of a child hunger death gets categorized as a human rights violation, goes into the press and our TV screens, reported to all and sundry! Suddenly everyone begins to take note! It seems it should take a death or a disaster with people being rendered homeless and becoming unfortunate refugees in their own homeland or worse still that people should either die or become incapacitated or swept away by the spate during floods and torrential rains, for that to be enough meat to capture world attention! It's a shame; it's a disgrace that this has happened year after year.

Actually, despite all our efforts, we have failed as educated, enlightened peoples! And on all fronts! The global status of malnourishment has not changed much, nothing has changed! For instance, it has been suggested that cases of malnourishment should be treated in hospitals. But the question of implementing such a strategy in a country like India does not arise, as it lacks the required healthcare infrastructure.

Right now the choice is between 'hospital care' and 'no care' and as a result, the child does not get any care. Severe malnutrition takes months to treat and putting such children in hospital is not possible for the poor. They are forced to make a choice between the child's survival and that of the whole family.

Home-based treatment has been successful in some African countries. Studies in Ethiopia and Sudan show 80 per cent of severely malnourished children treated at home recovered fully. Home-based treatment sometimes encourages parents to understand how to deal with the problem if it recurs.

Sometimes it becomes necessary that we identify suitable food for the affected children. Ready to use therapeutic food (RUTF) has worked well in addressing Africa's malnutrition problem. Such food would need to be developed indigenously, keeping the preferences of the community in mind. The experience in Senegal has shown that both RUTF and the food from the family pot work equally well for home care.

I believe there is a dire need to increase awareness even among parents. Health infrastructure must be geared to provide information about malnutrition to mothers visiting health centers for antenatal checkups or to get their children immunized. Adolescent girls should be educated about the issue as a future investment. Equally important is the need to identify an authority that would be responsible for implementing all such measures in the country in question.

FARMERS GROW OUR FOOD, BUT ARE FORCED TO EAT RATS!

Farmers need plenty of patience and faith. They can't expect the world to change overnight, but must very patiently wait for the plants to grow and the animals to produce..God helps in a mammoth way: He sends the sun and the rain and ensures that the crops grow..and that the animals produce. About all the farmer can do is trust the Lord and not worry about it...

We ought to take a lesson from the Farmer! Besides, many of these farmers who actually grow our food are either forced to survive on the fringes of civilization or worse still, commit suicide in sheer poverty and desperation as it is agriculture in India is so dependent on the vagaries of the monsoons! Farmers ought to be insured! I mean a "social safety net" for our farmers!!! Farmers ought to be heard!

24

Dehumanizing Poverty- It seems we all want an Unequal World

SOME REGIONS OF THE WORLD ARE DESPERATELY POOR

Some regions of the world are desperately poor. Too poor to buy essentials, I mean! Too poor to fulfill the average man's basic needs! Where little children die of preventable causes! Where mothers die in labor or out of complications arising out of birth! Where a man is not able to read a letter or write his name! Where people either die in large numbers or become permanently disabled so as to say (the corporate sector refers to them as 'differently abled' without actually doing much!) Where people are forced to live on the fringes of civilization, in refugee camps (and under desperate conditions!) for instance! Where many people are being forced out of their habitat (a process called 'displacement') in the name of development. Many are forced to live on less than $1 a day, just unable to put enough on the table at the end of the day! Our policy-makers call this process 'Poverty' and such people 'poor' without actually doing much about the whole thing! The process referred to as 'Globalization' has brought in its wake a phenomenon one might call 'Mindless Consumerism', an extravagant form of material consumption marked by a lavish display of wealth on the one side and very little/nothing on the other, dividing global society into the so-called 'haves' and the 'have-nots', an enormously skewed world economic order, and in the final instance, what I would call ***'inequality'***, both within and between nations.

The social implications, as would be the political ones, are simply enormous! A major percentage of world spending goes on meeting the costs of War(s) and threat of War(s)! Some regions of the world are still in 'Conflict', with some of these marked by 'child conscription' and draining heavily on the exchequer. It is a shame, this very employment of children as soldiers; they should be in school instead! This is indeed a murder of 'human dignity' in the first instance, but we, the so-called educated, enlightened and "civilized" nations and peoples of the world cannot blame our innocent brethren, considering especially the fact that while on the one hand, disease can be erased by greater progress in medical science, it would be somewhat difficult if not impossible to erase ignorance, money can make for a healthier population, but can money erase years of official neglect, a general apathy towards the poor and the evil of ignorance!

My mind travels to Darfur (the Sudan)! This region of the world has become infamous recently and there has been a global outcry about the ongoing conflict! What most audiences (including the West) fail to realize is that Africa (rather, development in Africa) needs a new direction! Nothing much should come out of all these global online campaigning and other similar efforts towards solidarity unless we start a program of social and economic reform.

Both social and economic reform is needed. Mindsets have to be changed before bridges are built! And all bridges must be built on a firm foundation, to address first the prevalent social issues-illiteracy, ignorance; disease and neglect that still ail the Third World before we can press for economic reform. A more pronounced social reform is needed; I mean to say, in the Third World!

DEHUMANIZING POVERTY

Poverty cannot be solved unless we actually go to the poor. You feel guilty, really bad, when an enormous

amount of money meant for the poor does **not** go to the starving? At one end, are those releasing the money, and at the other, are those reeling under starvation and debt, and who would probably never be receiving what is actually meant for them. These are the "**outcasts of the global village**", those far away from the realm of social and economic-decision-making...

> The 1st world has its own agenda-the world AIDS pandemic, (a sudden feeling of vulnerability) on terrorism, civil and political rights, etc. And there is also, I admit, **concern** over and talk of the "**heavily-indebted poor country initiatives**" (let us forgive the poor countries for their debt) and "charity commissioners"..we **must,** as a matter of urgency, renew our efforts to fight **HIV/AIDS**. We must, also, deal with the fact that an enormous sum of money is being paid per week by Sub-Saharan Africa on, putting it mildly, debt ..let us address all these issues with firm commitment...
> Now, this question should arise in your minds, namely, what would be the root causes of hunger**?** Firstly, we have poverty: Poor people do not have the resources-whether land, tools or money-needed to grow or buy food on a consistent basis. Secondly, we have armed conflict: War disrupts agricultural production and governments often spend more on arms than on social programs. Thirdly, there is the factor of environmental overload: Over-consumption by wealthy nations and rapid population growth in poor nations strain natural resources and make it harder for poor people to feed themselves. However, we must remember that although rapid population growth and topsoil loss may lead to temporary shortages, on the whole, global food supplies still outpace rising demand. Another important factor happens to be discrimination: Lack of access to education, credit and employment-a recipe for hunger-is often the result of racial, gender or ethnic discrimination. One way to deal with the problem would be combining credit with education..finally, we have lack

of clout: In the final analysis, hunger is caused by powerlessness. People who do not have the power to protect their own interests are hungry. The burden of this condition falls most acutely on children, women and the elderly.

(Bread for the World Institute, "The Causes of Hunger", 1994)

There are many paradoxes to the present crisis:

- Firstly, the world economic situation was never considered a crisis as long as phenomena such as high rate of unemployment, poor resources, high incidence of **poverty**, etc. were confined to the developing countries even though they accounted for 2/3 rd of the world population. The situation became a crisis as soon as the same phenomena started engulfing the developed countries those have near total command over the reins of the world economic system;
- Secondly, surprisingly, the problems which the South presents to the North – such as **poverty**, resource constraints etc. are being experienced by the North itself. It is to be noted that developed countries are not so much concerned about the South which are restructuring the world trading system, as they are for themselves;
- Again, paradoxically, at a time when the South was trying to realize better and fairer returns to the producers of primary products, it was being punished by significant falls in commodity prices;
- Fourthly, countries claiming to be intellectually rigorous are "disastrously" adopting restrictionist policies to meet their internal crisis. Further, those countries professing liberalism and a free environment for production and trade have themselves adopted highly protectionistic policies...

Even as way back as 1977, many thoughtful men had pleaded before the Joint Economic Committee of the U.S. Congress, that the government need not take drastic measures in response to the trade deficits of 1976, 1977. Professor Cohen argued: '...I do not view the present U.S. Trade deficit with alarm, nor do I feel that radical revision of current U.S. Economic policies is warranted...the present trade deficit signifies neither a serious deterioration of our competitiveness in international markets nor a significant loss of a capacity of world economic leadership, although the fact of a deficit remains...'

It is clear that the main question is, how should the South pursue its objectives, particularly, the combating of **poverty** and fusion of internal **peace** and security with development? The "poor" South has long lived under the illusion that the North is extremely generous in its attitude...

Partial delinking with the North and more effective "South – South" cooperation is necessary. More attention should be diverted towards bodies such as OPEC, ASEAN, SAARC, NAM and the Colombo Plan. A separate Third World secretariat located at a Third World Country (particularly, one ranked low on the Human Development Index), holding of independent Third World Summit meetings and encouragement of preferential arrangement for intra-south flows of goods, manpower resources, etc, are the needs of the hour. A center for science and technology for developing countries, a "bank" (particularly, micro-credit) for developing countries, a "research and information system", a "solidarity fund" for economic and social development, are now just for remaining on "official machinery papers". Concrete action programs should back them. We can also have a "consortium" or "group" of debtors...

There is need for a new strategy for development. It is high time developing countries built up more efficiency in agriculture, agro-based industries and optimum land utilization. W.W. Rostow in his suave analyses of the world

economy has also argued for a shift in "thinking" from "lame" industrialization to agriculture.

Finally, the World Economic Crisis should be viewed in its wider perspectives through less of debates and more of concerted action following **"dialogues" between the North and the South.**

The critical role for official development assistance: (Developing countries) **(source: BIS Review):**

Developing countries have to be managed well to achieve internal stability and implement development policies. Aid is a very critical resource in that it helps countries improve their policies by providing technology, training people and strengthening institution building.

The question is, how much has actually been accomplished in terms of aid?

Much of the world has changed. We can now communicate across the globe instantaneously. Countries are now more interdependent. Firms are producing globally and bankers moving money quickly from one part of the world to another. The capacity to develop has been improved by advances in science and technology. Yet, **Poverty** is far from being solved, and gaps between the world's rich and the world's poor have widened. And, there are now serious problems not earlier perceived, like the depletion of the ozone layer and earth warming, or the "Greenhouse Effect".

The aid community now knows that problems are more complex and more diverse, and human and institutional factors are now more important to change, as never before. Extraordinary progress has now been made, life expectancy at birth has gone up, and now there are medicines and cures for virtually every ailment...

Aid is only one influence in a complicated process, which involves factors such as open trade policies, trends in commodity prices, the weather and **accumulated debt...**

Yet, aid is still not unimportant apart from the uses

outlined above, it also communicates ideas and encourages initiative. It helps build much needed infrastructure and finances goods needed for production. Aid is important in disaster management, and has a humanitarian role to play.

It is important as to how funds will be used and what will be achieved. It is heartening to note that countries are moving forward through bold policy reforms and more commitment.

In a number of low-income countries, especially in Asia, additional aid could translate into accelerated growth, creation of jobs, rural infrastructure, and investment in human resources. **A former World Bank Vice-President for Asia described two Asias: first, the high growth, industrializing economies, and second, an Asia with massive problems of development and containing more than half of the world's poor, but which have been able to avoid payments crisis through prudent management.**

What are some of the key areas where aid can play an important role in the years ahead?

Our ozone layer is depleting, we now (as never before) need to find solutions to earth warming, air and water pollution, loss of soil, deforestation, and desertification. Some **environmental issues** can be mitigated by direct investment, while others require a change in values and life styles or simply development.

Every year, large numbers of people enter developing country job markets, where there is a need for power, **water,** communications, transport, and ports, and improved financial institutions. Aid can help in these, as well as in facilitating **foreign private investment.**

In only a few decades, a majority of people in the developing world will live in cities, therefore, more aid agencies are focusing on **urban issues** these days.

Poverty forces millions of children under five to die every year. Aid can complement political commitment and

management of developing countries in providing low cost inoculations and oral rehydration and education for children (in developing countries).

World population is increasing rapidly every year. If, country by country, societies could speed up the "demographic transition" i.e. reach the years of lower population growth sooner, this would reduce death rates, make higher quality and universal primary education and training more feasible and make sustainable development more manageable. Aid has a critical role to play.

At least another five billion people are expected to be added to the total world population over the 21st century; leading in turn to greater demand for food. For most developing countries, overall economic growth will be led by high – technology agriculture. There is now an increasing need to give priority to agriculture.

Aid has to assume a new role. No development program can be successfully implemented without political commitment, good policies, and improved management in developing countries. In addition to sound macroeconomic policies, sector and sub-sector plans need to be thought through. There arises a need for much better aid management. Donors need to respond to areas of need. Common vision of needs and high-quality national planning and management have to be combined. Global problems need to be solved locally, country by country.

In this complex world, there is no right level for official development assistance. **Yet, there is no doubt that faster growth could be made in the world if donors could increase their aid levels significantly.**

And aid (which provides important resources) has to assume a new role, the role of a "Catalyst" in development...

– As new demands of human security arise, a new and more positive relationship between North and South – a new era of "Development Co-operation" becomes the need of the hour. Developing countries argue that most of their economic problems arise from an inequitable international order. But, now they have come to recognize that "no amount of external assistance can ever substitute for the fundamental reforms needed in their domestic economies".

India: The Indian social system is in a flux. We have become one of the most corrupt societies anywhere in the world. There are still areas that are extremely poor, there is grinding **Poverty** in many areas. Another very major economic factor has been **our total inability to check the population explosion.** This has been one of the great disasters and tragedies of free India. Our population is growing at the rate of over a million people a month, a crore and a half of people every year.

That is, we are adding one Australia every year to our population. How are we going to abolish POVERTY? What meaning does all this talk of POVERTY abolition have when millions of people are coming into the job market every year, and you are unable to provide for them? We still have over 50,000 villages with no drinking water. Many children still don't go to school.

Why is our social revolution unfinished? Why is it that there are temples where "Harijans" (Mahatma Gandhi "Children of God") are not allowed to go? It is a shame and a disgrace.

We also find a sharp and growing confrontation on the basis of religion. We have to use religion in a creative manner. The message of religion is love, compassion, harmony and helpfulness, not conflict.

We need a "Revolution"- the kind of the Indian Renaissance, the sort of revolution that took place in Bengal in the middle of the 19th century – with Raja Rammohan

Roy, Keshab Chandra Sen and Ishwar Chandra Vidyasagar, with Bhandarkar and Ranade and other great reformers, with Tilak and Sri Aurobindo, the great seers and visionaries, with Vivekananda and Shri Shri Ramakrishna. This is the sort of renaissance that we require if we are going to build a truly great country.

Because India has a lot to offer to the world. Her sheer size, her cultural continuity, her extraordinary vivacity, and her "Spiritualism" make it important for India to play an important role.

May God Bless Our Country.

Oh India! - It is true that in 1995, the country's granaries were overflowing with unsold grain. At the same time, more than 300 million people were living below the **Poverty** line.

Our countrymen are too poor to purchase the food produced in their home country. **Kalahandi district in Orissa is best known for its starvation deaths.** In 1996, the district suffered from drought and people died of starvation. Yet the same year, rice production in Kalahandi was higher than the national average. What often happens is that rice is exported to the center, while some grain is diverted to the black market (Some people get away with fake ration cards!)?

Stark, isn't it?

India is trying to build more sophisticated weapons, but has it been able to provide a decent education to its **Children**? What do you have to say about the fact that poor, rural women have to walk miles and miles in parched heat to fetch drinking water? Or, get to the nearest clinic? What about those who are forced to live, eat and wash on the roadsides? About traditional practices such as Sati, Lausa, Dowry and Female infanticide? About the highly unfavorable sex ratio? What about the fact that owing to lack of sanitary latrines, unfortunate slum dwellers have to

defecate on the streets, river banks, parks; etc. under conditions detrimental to health and the environment? Also, the fact that endemic dysentery and diarrhea carry away millions of **Children** every year? What about the high value placed on entertainment, especially films? And sex, violence and obscenity? Rampant consumerism? Corruption? Debt? What about the damage being caused to our fragile ecosystems?

May God Bless India,

May God Bless Every Country.

Food and Famine: Starvation amidst plenty – the Bengal famine of 1943: (Source: Human Development Report, date could not be recalled)

Nature often avenges herself on hapless humanity in one very dangerous manner – local food shortages, which turn to famine in the hands of man. People go hungry not because food is not available – but because they cannot afford it. This is what happened in the Bengal famine of 1943. Between 2 and 3 million lives were lost, even though there was no overall shortage of food.

The famine was partly caused by an economic boom. War-related activities suddenly increased, exerting powerful inflationary pressures on the economy and causing food prices to rise. In the urban areas, those with work could pay these prices. But in the rural areas, agricultural laborers and other workers found that they could no longer afford to eat, and many people headed for the cities, particularly Calcutta, hoping to survive. Prices were then driven even higher by speculation and panic buying.

Timely government action could probably have averted the famine. But the colonial government did nothing to stop hoarding by producers, traders and consumers. They only "waited and saw". Relief work was totally inadequate, and the distribution of foodgrains in the rural districts was inefficient. Even in October 1943, with 1,00,000 sick and

destitute people on Calcutta's streets, the government still went on denying the existence of a famine.

What resulted was one of the largest man-made catastrophes of our time.

And this has a direct impact on **Poverty**.

What then, does "Food Security" Mean?

It means that all people at all times have both physical and economic access to basic food, which requires not just enough food to go round. People should have ready access to food – that they have an "Entitlement" to food, by growing it for themselves, by buying it or by taking advantage of a public food distribution system. Therefore, that food is available, is not a sufficient condition of security, and people can starve even when enough food is available – as has actually happened during many famines.

Food is available in the world. And there is enough food to offer everyone in the world around 2,500 calories a day – 200 calories more than the basic minimum.

But not everyone gets enough to eat. The problem is the poor distribution of food and a lack of purchasing power, among other factors. **Some 800 million people around the world go hungry. In Sub-Saharan Africa, food availability has considerably increased in recent years, and yet about 240 million are undernourished and in South Asia, 30 percent of babies are born underweight, a sad indication of the fact that people, particularly women (who often eat after the entire household) have inadequate access to food. Access to food comes from access to assets, work and an assured income; therefore, these are the problems that the state has to tackle at the earliest.**

The World as It is

'..A Sequel to what lies ahead...'

"Let us be clear as to what is our ultimate aim. It is not

just the negation of war, but the creation of a world of security and freedom, of a world which is governed by justice and the moral law. We desire to assert the pre-eminence of right over might and the general good against selfish and sectional aims."

- Clement Attlee, British PM, in 1946

...There are the prosperous nations such as those of Western Europe and North America, and the poorer developing countries that cannot afford to provide adequate food, water, health care, and education for their people...

- Vastly improved communications and the growth of international trade have made the world "a smaller place" with nations increasingly dependent upon each other.

And yet, today, we are becoming increasingly envious of one another, and prepared to take up arms. Conflict within countries is now more rampant than ever before...

There is much human suffering and people are on the brink of starvation in many countries of the Third World...and then there are war casualties and severe shortages of food and other essentials like fuel, housing, work, clothing and education...disease is rife...and then, there are the world's "Refugees" (remember Sarajevo?).

Children are suffering from hunger, disease and illiteracy. Clean water has to be provided, schools have to be repaired and **Children** have to be taken care of. Relief has to be brought to **Children** caught up in civil strife, epidemics of disease or natural disasters.

We have witnessed a gross violation of **Human Rights** across the globe...the fact that the nearest antenatal care clinic for pregnant mothers in rural areas is often miles away...is so disheartening...and that development projects often displace thousands of people...

Poverty is the worst disease known to mankind. "**Poverty**" does not mean merely not having enough money to buy everything the developing countries want. It means not having enough to provide people with essentials such

as sufficient food, shelter, health care, work and education. In the cities, people have to "fight for survival" in any way they can. Survival was beyond the victims of the drought in the Sahel region of Africa hit by decades of crop failure. Millions suffer from extreme malnutrition.

One of the ways of measuring **poverty** is to look at "life" in different countries (for example, life expectancy). We can also count the number of babies who die in the first year of life (in Afghanistan, one out of five babies does not survive until its first birthday). As for food, an intake of about 2300 calories a day is regarded by nutrition experts as the average daily nutritional requirement for most people (in Bangladesh, the average calorie intake is less than two-thirds of what is needed for good health). Another indicator of **poverty** is the availability of clean water. Germs carried in impure water spread many fatal diseases (e.g. Cholera and dysentery). According to estimates, over a quarter of the world's population cannot obtain safe water for their everyday needs. In health care, also, there is a huge difference between developed and developing countries.

In many poor countries, shortage of energy supplies holds back economic progress. There is a need to explore new energy technologies, for example, power using geothermal heat from deep inside the Earth's crust.

"Development" goes beyond providing seeds and equipment. It also involves developing a country's farming skills and much-needed knowledge and expertise (on training) which will finally guide a developing country to food-sufficiency.

For some developing countries, it will be difficult for farming to bring prosperity. Nepal, which is one of the world's poorest countries, is dependent almost entirely on farming. However, only about one-fifth of its land is suitable for farming. Most of Nepal's population lives in the hills, where the terrain is sloping, the soil is of poor quality and the climate unpredictable and often violent.

Countries like Nepal are the most challenging to development planners. Very often, floods and landslides can ruin work by carrying away irrigation channels, together with the growing crops. Also, forests get depleted, loosening soil for agriculture. Yet, "Hill farmers" have no other source of fuel for cooking and heating.

The size of the "Gap" between rich and poor countries is mammoth. This calls for enormous investment.

"... It is not true that there is insufficient food to go round...", so said John Ferguson, in "Not Them But Us", ... "The grain produced, if properly distributed, would give every human being ample protein and more than 3000 calories a day. But a third of the grain produced is fed to animals. There are terrifying anomalies. In 1971 during acute drought the countries of the Sahel actually exported 15 million kilos of vegetables, mainly to Europe. In 1974, after the floods in Bangladesh, people could not afford the rice which was actually available."

And, then, there is the darker side of development. A great deal of aid is in the form of loans that the countries must pay back with interest. This burden of "Debt" adds to the problems of the poorest countries.

"If the governments cannot agree to feed the world, they cannot agree about anything", said Boyd Orr.

The Sahel is a strip of land along the southern edge of the Sahara Desert in Africa. Drought and overgrazing of the sparse vegetation in the past led to expansion of the desert, resulting in starvation and death for herdsmen, their families and their animals. Ethiopia and Somalia were the worst sufferers. The crisis worsened with civil war and a rapidly growing population...resulting in one of the greatest human disasters in history. In 1985 and 1986, humanitarian aid poured in from all directions, but over one million people perished of starvation. This vicious attack stunned audiences all over the world. As for Uganda, even in normal times, Ugandans eat, on an average, much less food than they need, which leaves them disease-prone, and in cases of crop failure, to famine.

I feel sorry for the poor. We go on...

The "Green Revolution" aimed at improving the productivity of farmers in the developing countries and enabling them feed themselves. Between 1950 and 1985 the total land area of the world made fertile by irrigation doubled. New strains of cereal seeds were introduced; alongwith the use of artificial fertilizers and pesticides. World cereal production went up. Countries like China and India greatly benefited. And yet, poor (small) farmers using hand tools, failed to afford the new seeds or the fertilizers, and the small size of their farms made it difficult to employ agricultural machinery. The revolution definitely led to better crops and less hunger. But it produced adverse social and economic effects. In recent years, more emphasis is being placed on agricultural development projects targeted at small farmers.

"Development aid" is a very complex issue. The money is not always well spent. Some of it goes on government palaces and such luxuries as artificial sport(s) turfs and conference halls. The money does not always reach the target groups, but percolates down into the pockets of politicians and officials, or is used to pay the defense forces. The "Gap" remains...

World War III? By the mid-50s, many renowned world figures – like the British philosopher and mathematician Bertrand Russell and the American scientist Linus Pauling – doubted whether the world would survive to the year 2000 without blowing itself to pieces.

There has been no world war during the life of the United Nations. Since 1945, no nation has dropped a nuclear bomb on another nation. There has been no nuclear war. Space, which could have been a kind of storehouse for nuclear weapons, has been kept free of arms. (How long will this continue???)

The message is love; we all live in the same world and must learn to share it-or perish.

We have survived, and yet there are many more miles to go...

25

War, Famine, Crime, Disasters and Starvation

(THE EVOLUTION OF NATIONS - A WORLD IN TRANSITION)

And, we're all "Peace Loving Nations.." we only profess to love peace, no wonder the UN has not so far been able to 'come close to fulfilling the hopes and dreams of its founders..'.

The consequence:

"Wars and rumours of wars.." at the 21st session of the International Red Cross in 1969, it was reported that more than 90 million people have been killed in wars since the 20th century began, over 2 trillion dollars have been spent on arms and over 130 conflicts on five continents have been waged!

"Famines and pestilences..": The WHO estimates that about one-third of the world is well-fed, one-third is underfed and one-third is starving! Four million people die each year of starvation, 70% of the world's children under six years old are undernourished, and 30 persons die of starvation every minute!

"Earthquakes in divers places.." : The world almanac tells us that there were only six earthquakes of major strength between 1800-1896..the dramatic increase of quakes..led many scientists to predict that we are entering a new period of great seismic disturbances.

"The modern means of communication and

transportation..": In this very short period of time, mankind has advanced from a state little different from Adam's to one in which man not only drives at enormous speeds, but flies and even goes to the moon!

People travel more today than they ever travelled before! International tourism is a huge multibillion dollar business involving over 200 million people traveling outside their own countries every year throughout the world!

When you realise that there are people alive today..a jet can fly around the world in 24 hours, a spacecraft can cover the world in 80 minutes, and in less than one second a radio message can reach the ends of the earth!

Now imagine the ancient prophet seeing a vision of future highways, today's super highways, with hundreds of cars speeding along with their headlights on at nighttime! —..And they certainly jostle one another in the broadways! – Thousands of people are killed every year from this jostling!

"And knowledge shall be increased..": Knowledge has been increased..almost beyond imagination! – To where computers are now even taking over the thinking of man and are able to do feats of calculation and memory and computation and even thinking, far beyond the limits of man's own mind!

A few years ago it was estimated that the sum total of man's knowledge was doubling every ten years! It is a known fact that more than 80% of all the scientists who have ever lived are alive today!...Dr. Malcolm Todd, one-time President of the American Medical Association, said that about half of medical knowledge is outdated every 10 years..it is estimated that..throughout the world, more than 1,000 new books are published every day!—knowledge certainly has been increased!

But although modern man has all this knowledge and has made so many amazing scientific discoveries and technological breakthroughs, what good has it really done

him?—while much of the world tolls to try to scrape together enough to eat for its massive populations and to try to solve the pressing problems of world peace and pollution, extravagant misguided western scientific genius is largely devoted to silly scientific toys, looney luxuries, idiotic idols and horrifying, wasteful weapons of war! And although they have the most "advanced" and expensive educational systems the world has ever known, they're turning out the most ignorant and violent children they've ever produced!

Yes, "knowledge" has "increased"!—but without god and without his word, things are so confusing, so complicated and so complex that by the time they complete their modern education, most people are more mixed-up than when they began!...what a picture of today's universities and hallowed halls of so-called "higher learning"!

Do you know which age group has had the biggest increase in crime involvement today? Fifteen is now the age of the largest increase of arrests for all kinds of crimes, including major crimes... according to FBI and Department of Justice reports. When I was a young man, the age group of criminal involvement was in the 20's, 24 as I recall...

Is the world full of violence today?—in the U.S., violent crime has risen by 1,600%...the surgeon general reports that "violence in all its forms, from murder to child beating, is now the nation's number 1 public health problem!"

Experts have calculated that by the time the average American child is 15 years old, he will have personally witnessed the violent destruction of more than 13,000 human beings on television!—and yet they wonder, "where did we go wrong?", In one week, the following acts were observed on television during children's viewing time: On the 185 programs viewed, there were 281 assaults, 117 killings, 19 robberies, 16 kidnappings, 10 murder conspiracies, 3 arsons, 3 extortions, 3 jail breaks, 1 lynching, 1 bombing and 1 suicide! On the average station there are 800 acts of violence per week!—it's hard to imagine that even "the days of Noah"

were as violence-filled as those in which we are now living!

"And there shall be upon the earth distress of nations, with perplexity; the sea and the waves roaring." (Lk.21:25.) the peoples of the earth are often likened unto the sea and the waves in the bible. So here he's actually speaking symbolically of the peoples and nations of the world—their wars and rebellions and riots and terrorism—the waves of their various wars and conflicts and uprisings. Every time you turn the news on the television, it roars! Every time you turn on the radio, you can hear the waves of a new war roaring, a new riot, a new rebellion, a new revolution, more terrorism, more strikes, more problems, chaos!

I can remember when I was young, people were not living in constant fear and terror as they are today! – They might have been living poverty and destitution, but they didn't live in constant fear of getting murdered on the street or being annihilated by an atom bomb in a nuclear war! But ever since World War II and the U.S.' nuclear annihilation of over 100,000 innocent people in Hiroshima and Nagasaki, Japan, it seems like almost everybody abandoned their faith in God, lost their faith in peace and got scared stiff of blowing themselves to hell, and still are!

..The tremendous and unprecedented upsurge and interest in the occult, psychic phenomena, spiritism, demonology and witchcraft which the world is experiencing today..many young people have, in their pursuit of genuine spirituality and real religion and the actual supernatural and miraculous, gone into ancient mysticism, drugs and the spirit world..and now the youth from so-called Christian backgrounds are following many modern-day false prophets by the millions!—"for many false prophets shall rise, and shall deceive many!" (Mt.24: 11.)

Besides these commonly recognised demonic mediums, the devil in recent years has raised his ugly head and literally roared his message loud and clear through another medium: Popular music!—"hard rock", "acid rock", "punk

rock", etc. Have deceived youth particularly and misled them into the horrors of drugs and hell! Much of the music is literally demonic, invoking demons and seducing people to yield to their influence! It puts many people in tune with Satan to where they get his messages and carry out his will, his diabolical design! Much of its jungle rhythms and screaming savages are the sounds of horror, the sounds of hell, tortured souls with tortured minds producing tortured music that's literally driving this generation **insane**!

Copyright Aug. 1984 by Family Services, Zurich, Switzerland.

(In search of help... *Geneva..no good...*

In search of justice... *The International Court of Justice...no good..it always sits in "permanent session"at the Hague...!*)

Come to my beautiful country, my friends! Incredible India is well-versed in all kinds of therapy: *Temporary and permanent,* traditional western, Indian and Continental, alternative, physical, spiritual, metaphysical and transactional!

India will sure heal your tortured minds and arrest your cardiac whatever and hypertension and skin disorders and migraines and asthma and dichotomies of Trichotomy and Trichology with her soothing balms of loving care and compassion! Mark my words, India is really good! And highly adept at it!)

Don't we all need some therapy
For freedom, liberty, equality and fraternity?

26

Born for Freedom, Liberty, Equality and Fraternity

We Live for our Nations

“Born free...”From human beings (us ordinary mortals) to a lovely little tiger cub...to a bird (that flies from the lake to the tree!)..to a shy orchid...to a mammoth redwood giant..rich and poor/as also every other anomaly in life’s equation...

We are all God’s children..right?

We are simply all ‘born free’...(That’s what we are)...

(It is just that life has been harsh on some of us and less harsh on the rest..)

(And, the real antagonism, my dear friends, all these wars/ethnic conflict/gore/malnourishment/abuse arises when we actually stop being able to relate to the very ethos of the word ‘freedom’, stop respecting what the creator had in mind for us, and start practicing our very own ‘whims’ and ‘fancies’, when ‘material’ takes over the ‘spiritual’/ethereal , causing untold harm and misery not just to ourselves, but our common ‘fellowship’ as well..)

Forget it, who cares, this is, after all, another one of those stories..unheard..unlistened..unappreciated...

Maybe its all about a ‘Maverick’, a complete ‘non-conformist’, unfettered, unleashed..sorry! Unappreciated...

Maybe, without blaming my friends..I should just talk about ‘freedom’..as I have perceived it...within this tiny tot

age of 30+..gosh! I only wish you would appreciate my self-testimonial...

"Shoot..they said...this could be your only opportunity..what..does 'freedom' mean to you, little girl..not yet a woman...(Very Britney Spears! all I need is time..a moment that is mine..!) And, I add..to explain myself..!

Here I come, take me..or, leave me..I have very restricted 'choice' anyway...

Okay, please enable me concentrate..this is taking me oceans of courage..coz' confessing the truth can be actually harder than you might ever think..So! How..and from where..do I begin..period..well! It is all about an abnormally high level of prolactin in the blood..actually...

Actually...

"People (nee society) have almost always asked me what my real perspective on life is..what 'freedom' means to me, and I believe that as a strongly principled person (please, may I, and I am asking you, dearest society, my respected elders and beloved friends, can we use that word for me?), I should be honest with you to the point of actually learning to relate to this beautiful word called 'freedom'/ or, just 'life'...

Because we are all God's children..we are all 'born free'... (There was this very beautiful movie about a human being and a tiger cub!)

Who are we to decide? The constitution, law, the police? The courts? Its like saying that : because you're rich, you would escape the law even if you were, say, all foreign liquor, women (nee men) and vice, but not vice-versa, say, something like you're poor, so, you would be inevitably punished if you were caught indulging, in say, illicit liquor, hooch/haria (well, when you really cannot put sufficient on the table, what would you, or, for that matter, anybody else in your position..do, for Christ's sake..and I'd much rather stay away from religion..the papacy, the abortion, the contraception, the gender-gap, all those scandals..being

thrown out of hospital in labor when she couldn't write her husband's last name..)...

I only wish that as a nation with a name to reckon with, we were more tolerant..and democratic..or, understanding (global/national (with a 'rationale'..regional, and yes, local!)..and, off course, truly educated (not, degrees, we get some fake ones in the market, too!), but, like, enlightened...

Maybe, the West, maybe, progress, maybe, just some careful, in-depth..independent thinking...just 'free (dom) thinking'...

We're coming to my conscience, my heart, just issues!

In fact, "freedom", "progress" and "liberation" are just terms we often confuse..thanks to some very restricted outlook..Freedom is really not about short dresses, or beauty pageants or the make of car and the proud ownership of either/each/all, it is about "space" (nee privacy), about "choice", it is about "mutually respect(ing)" those in your immediate environment as also distant, as they say, "to each his/her own"..one should always be "free" to "choose"..from profession/career..to partner...

"Freedom"..should also be..the "power" of "decision-making".

But "freedom"/power/pelf should never be misused..not for all the wealth in the world (including King Midas!) would/ought I do something like that..we all make mistakes, but mistakes should be forgiven (if not forgotten!) and I may have gone wrong somewhere, somehow..well, in Buddhism, we call them our 'Karma'...

"..I remember the time I first learnt of these terms (during a brief visit to a government department when in college in Delhi, India). I was a bit curious, considering the immense importance I was attaching to them (the terms). I was wondering whether these terms had something (in fact, anything!) to do with *global instability*, about which I had nurtured strong feelings ever since I was in school. I was

pleased to know that they did indeed, looking at them my way. A visiting counselor had advised us to follow a "vocation of the heart", or, in other words, choose a profession that would be based on what one heard from one's conscience. It would be conceptually, as it was said, "work with feeling"...

With time, there were questions (related to contemporary issues, largely war/conflict in developing economies) that were to start haunting me, more so as I happened to be a developing country national. Some of these would have been like the following: how best could reduced world military spending be channeled into social development? Why would innocent children, such "innocent flowers" be forced into conflict? Could law intervene to bring about progressive social change? Would social change be an effect or a cause???? And, why would people commit "crimes against humanity", as during war and/or ethnic conflict? The issues that haunted the then "young mind" were endless. I was in a state of utter confusion.

It was following my undergraduate studies that I started looking at these issues from the grass root level(s). The question was: how could one alleviate them?

I started working for these "hapless" people. I started moving about with them. I started breathing the very air that they breathed. I started assimilating their problems as if these were mine. I could feel the change in me. The person, who wore the shoe, knew exactly where it pinched! I started feeling (emotions) for them. I started hoping for them. I started getting, well, involved with small human rights, peace and social development issues and initiatives. However, I would still be hoping...

But hopes would not be castles in the air. These would need to be developed on a logical foundation so that they could be transformed into reality. They would need nurturing and caring... say, for instance, higher education ..could open up the door(s) to the mind. They could be a gateway for understanding the cause effect relationship...they could give

an insight for questioning our basic norms, our accepted principles, at the same time, laying the foundation for an approach towards challenging age old social traditions/taboos/concepts and/or idiosyncrasies ...

I could then, for instance, study fresh political, philosophical, social and scientific perspectives primarily on the "parent issue", which I later learnt, was called "peace and conflict/human rights/justice"; their causes, as indeed control of gross violations; how to practice such work in intergovernmental and international organizations as well as in current issues and controversies, with a much-anticipated exposure to the global human rights and stability situation. Another closely-related area would be conflict resolution. Its nature would make it not just an object of study, but a matter of policy, intervention and practice as well. We would be motivated to think about and do something about these very issues.

It was only now (much to my satisfaction), that I could gather more specialized knowledge in the field, particularly, one that each of us hoped to choose for our respective objectives. There would, presumably, be scope for exposure to key international debates over a "culture of peace" (something I could associate, only now, given my somewhat increased 'peace vocabulary', with an agency like UNESCO) and "peaceful transformation" (with scope for analyses of concepts such as gender, race and class in a larger perspective of 'peace'). Moreover, some of us, coming from nations of the world (and, as in my case, India), where those like Gandhi, have walked across the land, would really have much to gain, from, as I noticed, a study/practice of the concept of 'non-violence'...

In fact, I am myself preoccupied with and strongly wishing to work to unearth the causes underlying the absence of peace, beginning on the firm conviction that there would be hardly any, if at all, instability, if "we" were to guarantee a better (in terms of food, drinking water,

medical care, education, and yes, much-needed love and affection!) world to our children, our future..in other words, were "we" to concentrate on the marginalized and poverty-stricken, I guess there wouldn't be much need for conflict and post-conflict reconstruction...

Because I have been "disturbed" by what I have seen, namely, images of undernourished, thin or lean, wasted and emaciated children in places as diverse as Sub-Saharan Africa, and, off course, South Asia, including my home country, India, off course, within the boundaries of my (own) human limitations!

I strongly believe in "solidarity between nations", and I have no doubt, whatsoever, that with much-cherished support, I could be what I wanted to be some day!

I would like to make certain general comments about conflict(s)/human rights, as I would see them. A study of them would involve the world we lived in, and why it were the way it actually were. Facts as quoted after studies would be mind-boggling: "ten million more people will stay poor..due to the events of September 11th". The goal of the new millennium should be the "development goal" of 'eliminating' world conflict. When we read the papers, watched TV or listened to the news, we would be bombarded with images of the poor, of wealth, fame and power, and, obscene conflict. These would be issues that needed to be looked at not only by human rights and/or peace/conflict practitioners but us ourselves as well. This would be the greatest challenge for the coming generation... this would be the question for which we would need an answer for the new world that is emerging, like work with refugees, for instance...

These would be my thoughts and comments. I do realize that there are certain issues that merit immediate attention, and these would include poverty, ecological damage, war and conflict, gender inequality, and that, the fact that these issues existed, made for the immense importance of this

discipline(s) (of "conflict"/human rights) to contemporary society...

I guess we would then, together, be able to contribute to the attainment of peace and harmony and the complete realization of the dreams of those who formulated the "Universal Declaration of Human Rights".

They say, "Tiny drops of water make up the ocean". I strongly believe in the "ripple effect". Let each one of us contribute his/her bit! Only then can we make the world a more peaceful place to live in..!!!

Born for freedom, liberty, equality & fraternity, I finally realize that's what we are in the first place...(Dreaming!)

"Those who are equal before God shall now also be equal in the polling booths, in the classrooms, in the factories, and in hotels, restaurants, movie theaters, and other places that provide service to the public..." (President Johnson, after signing the Civil Rights Act, July 2, 1964)

"..Free at last, Free at last. Thank God Almighty I'm Free at last..." (From R.J. Owen: "Free At Last" & Flip Schulke: Martin Luther King, Jr)

In Dec 1955, an African-American woman named Rosa Parks was arrested in Montgomery [the capital of the southern state of Alabama] an incident that led to the famous Montgomery bus boycott..The leader of this movement was Martin Luther King Jr., who was to wage a tenacious struggle against discrimination through an unwavering commitment to non-violence..The Civil Rights Movement had spread to every nook & corner of the United States..shortly thereafter, the US government passed the Civil Rights Act of 1957, which promised to facilitate equal voting rights for Afro-Americans...

"..Attitudes changed as they saw Negroes being watered down with fire hoses..innocent children being bombed in churches, there was a reaction to this type of thing..." (William Nix, Morehouse College)

"..One of Eleanor's (Roosevelt) closest friends was the great Education and Civil Rights leader, Mary McLeod Bethune..white racists called her (Eleanor) a "nigger-lover"..in May 1936, she organized a garden party in the grounds of the White House for the mainly black inmates of a training school for delinquent girls where disease was rife and conditions miserable..she was said to have entertained "a bunch of nigger whores at the White House"..when she uncovered similarly dreadful conditions at an old people's home for black people..she said: "we should be ashamed. I was sickened. If that is the way we care for people who are not able to care for themselves, we are at pretty low ebb of civilization..". (David Winner)

Fifteen years had passed since the end of World War II, yet humanity's hopes for peace still remained in vain. The East and West had become mired in a Cold War with no end in sight. At the same time, there was a dramatic escalation in the nuclear arms race among the major nations of the two Blocs, led, respectively, by the Soviet Union and the United States..Conflict in Africa involved struggles for independence against colonial rule erupting in each area, while racial and ethnic strife flared in various parts of the globe...

Everywhere people were quailing under the threat of **nuclear holocaust,** continuing to live in fear amid **civil strife** or suffering from discrimination, cruelty, poverty and disease. Yet, all surely cherished the hope of witnessing a dawn of peace and happiness!

Happiness is life's goal. Peace is what people of the world desire. The course of human history must move towards peace and happiness. The race should search for a firm guiding principle that will lead in this direction...

I remember what a friend of time once asked me in all earnest: 'Every day we read in the newspaper or hear about the "War on Terror(ism)". Who are these terrorists? Wherein their origin(s)? This question really shocked me! I was myself

in search of an appropriate answer! They are our own people, whom we sometimes create through political and economic isolation, or they could be fanatics, sometimes sponsored by hostile nations, trying to disrupt normal life through terrorism. In the Ramayana, the battle is between the divine hero Rama and the demon king Ravana. It is a long-drawn battle that finally Rama wins. In the Mahabharata, the battle at Kurukshetra is a battle between good and evil, and Dharma wins. The battles are many but finally **peace triumphs**.

In our times too we see good battling evil- for instance, the Second World War. It seems to me both good and evil will survive side by side. The Almighty does help both to varied degrees! How to minimize the evil through our spiritual growth is a question that has persisted throughout human history...

I can recall the words of Stephen Jay Gould, writing in The New York Times following 9/11: "Good and kind people outnumber all others by thousands to one. The tragedy of human history lies in the enormous potential for destruction in rare acts of evil, not in the high frequency of evil people. Complex systems can only be built step by step, whereas destruction requires but an instant. Thus, in what I like to call the Great Asymmetry, every spectacular incident of evil will be balanced by 10,000 acts of kindness, too often unnoted and invisible as the 'ordinary' efforts of a vast majority."

Great symbols of kindness lived at different times...

Alexander the Great *born in 356 B.C. in Macedonia, pupil to Aristotle, acceded to the throne in 336 B.C. at the age of 20, and two years later went to war with Persia in the east..After defeating the Persians in a preliminary engagement; Alexander liberated Egypt, which had been under Persian rule..In the final phase of his long expedition, Alexander crossed the River Indus, entering the unknown land of India. At this point, he turned back why? Because*

he never gave in to petty ambitions or the lust for power, but rode on at the head of his great expedition. All because he wanted to realise a dream – the dream of linking East and West and uniting all humanity..! While in Egypt, he had a revelation that all humankind was one. Henceforth, he was to make that ideal his life's goal! Though he used military force to make his conquests, he never looked down on the Eastern peoples, treated them well, and although none of Alexander's soldiers could understand his grand ideal of uniting the world, he made positive efforts leading to the emergence of a cross-pollinated culture in Gandhara in northern India in later centuries!

Beethoven was differently-abled, and impaired of the senses, and yet "each musical composition has a unique rhythm. Beethoven's works reflect his inner rhythm, which transcends the barriers of nationality, language, culture and religion and affects all who hear it. .."

"..Josei Toda often said a common understanding would be quickly achieved if the original teachers of the major religions – Nichiren Daishonin, Shakyamuni and Jesus **Christ** – could all get together in one room and hold a conference..". These leaders of the world religions lived at different times and in different historical circumstances, but all fought for the happiness of mankind amid persecution and fierce opposition..these revolutionaries have been there with us for as long as mankind has existed or will continue to exist..for as long as deep-rooted tensions exist between nations...

Following the deep-rooted tensions of the Cold War, the year 1960 opened with hopes of a thaw in East-West relations. The leaders of both nations had begun to understand the dangers inherent in a cold war where both sides were engaged in heated competition to develop and stockpile nuclear weapons. At the UN General Assembly, Soviet Premier Nikita Khrushchev outlined a plan towards peaceful coexistence wherein each nation of the world would

do away with its armaments in four years, and President **Dwight Eisenhower** also pledged that henceforth not military force but peaceful dialogue would be employed to settle international problems..a tremendous landmark in the history of man!

Or, Woman!

She (**Helen Keller**) will live on..the woman who showed the world there are no boundaries to courage and faith..Her eyes were taken away, but she remembered Milton's Paradise; her ears but Beethoven came and wiped away her tears; her tongue but she had talked with God when she was young who would not let them take away her soul possessing which she still possessed the whole...

Kemal Mustafa Ataturk (1881-1938), 'Father of the Turks' and the first President of the republic, was born in what is today the Greek city of Salonika..When the Ottoman Empire allied itself with the other Central Powers in World War I, defeat seemed almost certain. The people were fatigued from the long succession of wars that had confronted them. But Ataturk would not give up! Executing brilliant diplomacy, he negotiated the Allies' territorial demands and thereby achieved **Peace!** After becoming President, Kemal Ataturk set himself to giving women the right to vote and initiated numerous other progressive measures..To implement a new romanised Turkish alphabet, he traveled around the country, personally teaching it to people. He would set up a blackboard in the village square and demonstrate the new alphabet! ('I can write my name..'!) This excitement spread throughout the land, until all of Turkey was transformed for a time into a giant classroom, leading the British historian Arnold J. Toynbee to comment thus ('**The World and the West**'): "In the 1920s [Kemal] put through in Turkey what was perhaps as revolutionary a programme as has ever been carried out in any country deliberately and systematically in so short a span of time. It was as if, in our Western world, the Renaissance, the

Reformation, the secularist scientific mental revolution at the end of the 17th century, the French Revolution, and the Industrial Revolution had all been telescoped into a single lifetime and had been made compulsory by law..."

It was time for **Louis Braille's** genius to be recognized..He built a large, firm stairway for millions of sense-crippled human beings to climb..On the highways it was common to find groups of sightless people..These people were regarded as incomplete beings, ignorant and simple..Homeless blind people of all ages roamed the streets of most large towns, and even well-educated men and women seemed to find it amusing to watch them groping their way and bumping into buildings. They would throw things at them or trip them up, and then burst into laughter..At the Fair at St. Ovid, in 1771, **Valentine Hauy** saw blind people clowning to the shouts and jeers of the audience. The sight of human beings so degraded and so helpless before the cruel laughter of others shocked him profoundly. It set his feet on the path which led to the foundation of the world's first school for the blind (visually handicapped) where Francois Lesueur was Hauy's first pupil...

Socrates' disciple Plato was 28 at the time of Socrates' trial. The pupil spent a greater part of his youth alongside his teacher. His beloved teacher's execution was a tremendous shock to Plato, but he wiped away his tears of rage and powerfully resolved to devote his life to letting the world know that his teacher had been right, and to making his nation just and principled, as had been his mentor's dearest wish..For about 50 years, until his death at 80, Plato composed enormously..he also founded the Academy, devoting himself to educating youth and nurturing talent. The theme to which Plato dedicated his life was the basic problem of **how to achieve a just world..!**

..And a just world would consist of nations...with sincere effort, nations of the world can accomplish all it could ever

want: Alternatives to violence; peaceful conflict resolution and post-conflict reconstruction; and alternatives to war; build up pre-disaster warning systems; renewable energy; and achieve the application of a positive Scientific Temper to the common problems of Man – poverty, hunger, disease, bloodshed and civil strife that take away so many people each year..!

..and Life is Precious; all of Life..!

Ask a heart patient who carries KR coronary stent in his artery and a physically challenged child who has just been fitted with the lightweight Floor Reaction Orthosis (FRO) calipers and who find their life difficulties eased somewhat!

Both of these surely come as spin-offs from missile technologies!

Nations of the World will not be nations of cities! But networks of peaceful, prosperous communities empowered by telemedicine, tele-education and e-commerce! By biotechnology, biosciences and agricultural and industrial sciences and renewable energy! We will try and minimize the rural-urban divide and once and for all, the problems of urbanization, so prevalent in the modern era!

But every change comes at a price!

"..A man is said to pass through different stages in his lifetime..Dr Wayne W. Dyer, in his book 'Manifest Your Destiny', **makes an interesting categorization of them as athlete stage, warrior stage, statesperson stage and spirit stage...**

Nations too make a similar transition although the stages do not follow in sequence necessarily; they can be coexistent, with one aspect dominant...

A Rocket man works with stages. Each stage is jettisoned after taking the rocket further along its intended trajectory..As space research intensifies and we orbit, we

learn control, guidance, propulsion and aerodynamics, besides the ability to design various rocket systems..but technology can and ought be denied through the instruments of The MCTR (THE MISSILE TECHNOLOGY CONTROL REGIME) and the **"NPT" (THE NUCLEAR NON-PROLIFERATION TREATY)...**

At this moment, an "ICBM" (Intercontinental Ballistic Missile) has been fired!

As Nations of the world become Underdeveloped, Developing and Developed respectively, each one will probably experience a Period and Process of Transition..Sometimes, these transitions can be painful, history is witness to several such painful transitions, in which an entire species of peoples had to undergo the 'Horrors' of War- killing, loot, plunder, mayhem and being forced into Refugee Camps..The French Revolution of 1789 is a case in point!

Every nation has struggled to achieve the goals of Humanity! Generations have given their best to make life better for their offspring! There is absolutely nothing mysterious or hidden about this, no alternative to effort..And yet we fail to follow the Right Path! More than the problems outside-globalization, recession, inflation, insurgency, and instability and so on- we ought be concerned about the inertia that has gripped an entire species of peoples, the human race, and the mindset of defeat!

But War is Never! The Answer!

What are in fact the forces which lead to the rise or fall of nations? For a people and nations in general to rise to the highest, they must have a common memory of great heroes and exploits, of great adventures and triumphs in the past. Britain rose to great heights for men like Lord Nelson, the Duke of Wellington and Churchill. Japan rose out of the ashes of Hiroshima and Nagasaki to become a major economic superpower!

All nations which have risen to greatness have been characterized by a sense of mission. In the course of three decades, Germany was twice all but destroyed. And yet, its people changed its destiny. From the trenches and incinerators of the Great War, it has emerged as an economically powerful and politically assertive nation!

War is suffering! Immense Pain! Ask the Victims of War Crimes, Genocide (the mass graves) and Crimes against Humanity!

...Ask the Victims of Vietnam..all those trenches and Sirens, all the gore..the survivors of Hiroshima and Nagasaki as Akio Morita built a new Japan out of the Ashes, ask them how the intense Radiation must have felt on their charred bodies, some are yet to recover from the aftereffects of the trauma; ask the survivors-of the Rwandan Massacre; ask the Jews about those loathsome Concentration Camps; ask Anne Frank how she survived..ask the survivors of Slobodan Milosevic's Exploits; Idi Amin's Uganda; ask how a contingent of innocent Athletes were gunned down in 1972 in Munich...

Ask the Prisoners of War in Afghanistan, the Ghosts of Abu Ghraib; the detainees at Guantanamo; ask the survivors of Landmine Attacks in Cambodia...

And listen to the Voices of the Victims of that one most suffering region of the 21st Century – DARFUR..!

Ask also the Child Soldiers of Angola as they get CONSCRIPTED!

Without Peace, there can be no Progress!

I often wonder why the human race, the best of all of God's creations, has been so deeply divided by violence! I see myself in a desert with miles of sand all around! The moon is only partially visible but the stars shine bright!

I can recall the 'Battle of Kalinga' which claimed the lives of at least 300,000 people with an equal number being wounded. Victory had been obtained at heavy cost..And

Emperor Asoka looked down at the horror he had created, a horror of bloodshed and more gore..At that moment that was to go down in the annals of history, **Ahimsa Dharma was born..**The remorseful King embraced God's command to propagate love for human beings through this doctrine!

The Mahatma thus spoke: 'Friends, the divine message we are hearing is the message of creation. Since we all belong to Planet Earth, we may give a message to mankind, how people of different races, religions and languages can live peacefully and prosperously together..."

Asoka said, 'Friends, there is one thing I have realized, there is no victory in causing suffering. Triumph is a peaceful kingdom..'.

The Great Albert Einstein once famously remarked, 'You know, in the West we have built a large, beautiful ship. It has all the comforts in it, but one thing is missing: it has no compass and does not know where to go. Men like Tagore and Gandhi and their spiritual forebears found the compass. Why can this compass not be put in the human ship so that both can realize their purpose?'

Abe Lincoln once remarked: '..Perhaps there is so much conflict between peoples and nations because in our pursuit of prosperity and power we have lost sight of ethical values. We must ask ourselves, what is the role of human consciousness? Does it have a part in political thinking, scientific thinking and theological thinking? Is spirituality acceptable in the business of life?

Sage Ashtavakra had once propounded that the business of life ought be peace and prosperity, and not exploitation and conflict...

Just like Nature! Nature gives without reservation, like the mango tree- people throw stones at it, break off its branches, but it still offers its shade to the weary traveler, and its fruits to the hungry!

Then wherein we..?

The history of the world shows the forces of good struggling hard to make life better for mankind while we human beings show a terrible capacity for destruction...Thus we have Gandhi on the one hand, striving relentlessly towards Non-Violence, while on the other hand, millions die in the Second World War and Pearl Harbor and the atomic bombing of entire cities. Several thousands perish in Bosnia-Herzegovina..a war rages in the Gaza Strip between Israel and Palestine...

And on 11 September 2001, the Twin Towers of the World Trade Center in New York City fall and innocent lives are lost..In India, in the Bhopal gas tragedy, 30,000 people die as the result of the carelessness of a multinational company, and Chernobyl and the daily Violence in the Kashmir Valley...

Where are we going? Are we doomed to destroy ourselves?

No, we have to find an everlasting solution...

In the modern era, there are few such examples, of those who embody the qualities that come from realizing the nature of the mind 'Atmabodha'. We are too much preoccupied with ostentatious displays of wealth and personal freedom!

Actually, how humane or civilized or compassionate or tolerant are we? There is still a long way to go...

Glaring inequalities in society exist along with obscene hunger..Those wallowing in luxury and privileges beware. Unrestrained open displays of wealth and privileges and indifference to the poor might one day arouse such rage as to cause a bloody revolution as happened in France!

Wherein We..?

Actually, there is nothing mysterious about the abundance in developed nations! Historically, the people of these nations- the **G8** as they are called- believed over many generations that they must live a good life in a strong and

prosperous nation. This reality became aligned with their aspirations...

But abundance and spirituality are not mutually exclusive nor is it wrong to desire material things..Nature too adopts full measures; you would observe that if you looked around you! Inside a garden, there is a profusion of flowers. Even better still, if you looked up, you would see the vast Universe stretching into infinitude, unbelievable really!

All that we see in the world is an embodiment of energy, as Sri Aurobindo says. Therefore it becomes wise to appreciate that spirit and matter are both part of existence, are in harmony with each other, after all, it is the realization that it is wrong to feel that it is shameful or non-spiritual to desire material things that matters...

But one ought not be led to rely entirely on this premise. Mahatma Gandhi led a life of asceticism, making do with the minimum, but in his case as in ours it has to be a matter of choice. Follow a lifestyle that suits you, but make sure you do not interfere with the basic Rights of others!

Whatever you do must come from the heart, express your spirit, and thereby you would also spread love and joy around you!

'But how do you love when you don't love?'

In the great literature of all progressive societies, love is a verb...Love is something you do: the sacrifices you make, the giving of self, like a mother bringing a newborn into the world. If you want to study love, study those who sacrifice for others, even for **people who offend or do not Love in return...**

We Must Love and Dedicate and Re-Dedicate Ourselves...to..well, I understand I am writing for elite, enlightened readership!

..Look at **Gandhi**. During the time that his accusers

were in the legislative chambers criticizing him for having refused to join them in their condemnation of the British Empire, Gandhi was out in the paddy fields slowly and steadily expanding his base among the laborers... thus being able to build up a swell of support in the countryside...Gandhi had no office or position to fall back upon... most certainly an exemplary in compassion, courage, fasting and moral integrity...

Non-violence is a powerful expression in **silence!** A powerful way to heal, transform and empower our lives and our communities! Inspired by the thoughts and vision of Mahatma Gandhi and Dr. Martin Luther King Jr., for an empowered, non-violent world!

We seek to honor those who are using non-violence to build a community that honors the dignity and worth of every human being!

We seek to prove to ourselves and to the world that non-violence is the weapon through which every individual can move the world in the direction of peace as a matter of choice in daily living...! A powerful way to heal, transform, and empower our lives and an educational and community action campaign, we are honoring those who are using nonviolence...

The "**SYMPHONY OF NATIONS after all is – LIFE... WE LIVE FOR OUR NATIONS, WE LIVE FOR LIFE...**"

27

9/11 and the War on Terror-Hate, the Politics of

MAMA! DO TERRORISTS REALLY EXIST, A CHILD ASKS

(From Afghanistan to Abu Ghraib, via Guantanamo - slavery, torture and the horrors of abuse, no one questions 'America's Human Rights record)

"When I look upon the tombs of the great, every emotion of envy dies in me; when I read the epitaphs of the beautiful, every inordinate desire goes out; when I meet with the grief of parents upon a tombstone, my heart melts with compassion..when I see kings lying by those who deposed them..or the holy men that divided the world with their contests and disputes, I reflect with sorrow and astonishment on the little competitions, factions, and debates of mankind... I consider that great day when we shall all of us be contemporaries, and make our appearance together..." (Joseph Addison)

11 September 2001 – four US commercial airliners are hijacked. Two are crashed into the World Trade Center in New York, one into the Pentagon and one into a field in Pennsylvania. Almost 3,000 people are killed in this serious crime against humanity.

7 October 2001 – the USA leads military action against the Taliban government and members of the *al-Qa'ida* network in Afghanistan.

10/11 January 2002 – the first detainees are transferred from Afghanistan to the US Naval Base in

Guantánamo Bay, Cuba, in conditions that amount to cruel, inhuman or degrading treatment.

7 February 2002 – the White House announces its decision that the Geneva Conventions do not apply to *al-Qa'ida* suspects captured in Afghanistan, and that neither they nor Taleban members would be eligible for prisoner of war status.

June 2002 – Hamid Karzai appointed as President of interim Afghanistan administration. US forces continue to carry out military operations and detentions in Afghanistan to this day.

20 March 2003 – US-led Coalition forces attack Iraq. On 1 May 2003, President Bush announces that the main combat operations in Iraq are over. A major insurgency against the occupation develops.

28 April 2004 – photographs of torture and ill-treatment of Iraqi detainees by US soldiers in Abu Ghraib prison outside Baghdad are broadcast by CBS News and subsequently around the world.

22 June 2004 – the US administration releases several previously secret memorandums discussing "war on terror" detention and interrogation options "to set the record straight" following leaks.

28 June 2004 – the US Supreme Court rules that the US courts have jurisdiction over the Guantánamo detainees, hundreds of whom have already been held for more than two years without any judicial review, charge, trial or access to legal counsel or relatives.

2001-2004 – The US military has taken more than 50,000 people into custody during its military operations in Afghanistan and Iraq. In Afghanistan, the US has operated some 25 detention facilities, and in Iraq another 17. More than 750 people have been held in Guantánamo. The Pentagon states that 202 have been released or transferred, leaving "approximately 549" in the base by 22 September

2004. An unknown number of detainees have been held in undisclosed locations by the USA or transferred to the custody of other countries.

A familiar path to torture

Apologists for torture generally concentrate on the classical argument of expediency: the authorities are obliged to defeat terrorists or insurgents who have put innocent lives at risk and who endanger both civil society and the state itself...The accumulated evidence also gives a clear picture of the 'preconditions' for torture..Incommunicado detention, secret detention and 'disappearance' increase the latitude of security agents over the lives and well-being of people in custody. Amnesty International, Torture in the Eighties, 1984.

The image of New York's Twin Towers struck by hijacked airliners on 11 September 2001 has become an icon of a crime against humanity. It is tragic that the response to the atrocities of that day has resulted in its own iconography of torture, cruelty and degradation. A photograph of a naked young man captured in **Afghanistan**, blindfolded, handcuffed and shackled, and bound with duct tape to a stretcher. Pictures of hooded detainees strapped to the floor of military aircraft for transfer from Afghanistan to the other side of the world. Photographs of caged detainees in the United States (US) Naval Base in **Cuba**, kneeling before soldiers, shackled, handcuffed, masked and blindfolded. Television images of orange-clad shackled detainees shuffling to interrogations, or being wheeled there on mobile stretchers. A hooded detainee in **Iraq** sitting on the sand, surrounded by barbed wire, clutching his four-year-old son. And the photos from **Abu Ghraib** – a detainee, hooded, balanced on a box, arms outstretched, wires dangling from his hands with electric torture threatened; a naked man cowering in terror against the bars of a cell as soldiers threaten him with snarling dogs; and soldiers smiling, apparently confident of their impunity,

over detainees forced into sexually humiliating poses. The United States of America (USA), and the world, will be haunted by these and other images for years to come, icons of a government's failure to put human rights at its heart.

The struggle against torture and ill-treatment by agents of the state requires absolute commitment and constant vigilance. It requires stringent adherence to safeguards. It demands a policy of **zero tolerance**. The US government has manifestly failed in this regard. At best, it set the conditions for **torture and cruel, inhuman or degrading treatment** by lowering safeguards and failing to respond adequately to allegations of abuse raised by Amnesty International and others from early in the "**war on terror**". At worst, it has authorized interrogation techniques which flouted the country's international obligation to reject torture and ill-treatment under any circumstances and at all times.

The US administration has said that it is "strongly committed" to working with non-governmental organizations "to improve compliance with international human rights standards." President George W. Bush has recently said that the USA "support[s] the work of non-governmental organizations to end torture and assist the victims". With this in mind, Amnesty International seeks to provide a framework in this report by which there can be a full accounting for any torture or cruel, inhuman or degrading treatment by US agents, and to **prevent future violations** of international law and standards.

Throughout history, torture has often occurred against those considered as "the other", those in custody being removed from Afghanistan to Abu Ghraib. The unequivocal and non-derogable international legal prohibition on torture and cruel, inhuman and degrading treatment has been flouted. Respect for **human rights** is the route to **security**, as the US government itself claims, not the obstacle to security, as appears to be the administration's true belief if its detention and interrogation policies are the yardstick.

Amnesty International has come up with a *12-point Program for the Prevention of Torture by Agents of the State.* The organization has been working against torture for more than three decades. In addition to its daily efforts against this most tenacious and pervasive of human rights violations, it has conducted three worldwide campaigns for the **abolition of torture**, launched in 1972, 1984 and 2000. The 12-Point Program that forms the basis of this report was adopted for the most recent of these campaigns and reflects Amnesty International's key findings on how best to prevent torture.

Point 1 of the 12-Point Program is **"Condemn Torture"**. In other words, the highest authorities of every country should demonstrate their total opposition to torture and other cruel, inhuman or degrading treatment or punishment. They should condemn torture and ill-treatment unreservedly whenever they occur. They should make clear to all members of the police, military and other security forces that torture and ill-treatment will never be tolerated.

In June 2004, in one of several statements by senior United Nations (UN) officials responding to the US "torture memos", **Secretary General Kofi Annan** emphasized the absolute prohibition on torture and other cruel, inhuman or degrading treatment. He stressed that the prohibition is binding on all states, "in all territories under their jurisdiction or control", and in times of war as well as peace. He added: "Nor is torture permissible when it is called something else. Euphemisms cannot be used to bypass legal obligations."

There is a tendency, to euphemize aspects of war and violence. Killed and maimed civilians become "collateral damage"; torture and cruel, inhuman or degrading treatment become "stress and duress" techniques; and **"disappeared" prisoners** become "ghost detainees". Euphemizing human rights violations threatens to promote tolerance of them.

Impunity allows torture and ill-treatment to thrive. All

allegations must be thoroughly investigated, including all deaths in custody. (Point 6) **Perpetrators** of such human rights **violations** must be brought to **justice**, preferably in ordinary civilian courts rather than military tribunals as an emerging **international consensus** now recognizes (Point 7). At the same time, the necessary **safeguards** must be put and kept in place to prevent any recurrence of torture and ill-treatment. Secret detention must end immediately (Point 3). So too must the use of incommunicado detention, with lawyers, doctors, relatives, and independent monitors granted immediate and continuing access to and information about detainees, and with detainees brought before a judicial authority as soon as possible after arrest (Point 2). There must be a clear delineation between powers of interrogation and detention, with detention conditions fully meeting international standards. **Vulnerable detainees, including children and women**, should receive particular protections demanded by international law (Point 4). Coerced statements must not be admitted in any trials. Military commissions set up to try "war on terror" detainees, with the power to admit such statements, must be abandoned (Point 8).

Any victims of torture or ill-treatment are entitled to reparations, including compensation for the families of anyone who died as a result of such treatment in custody (Point 10). Training of anyone who comes into contact with detainees is essential, and must include relevant **cultural awareness education** as well as training in the international prohibition of torture and ill-treatment (Point 9). In accordance with international human rights law, international security cooperation must rule out the transfer of detainees in conditions or to places where they are at risk of torture or other cruel, inhuman or degrading treatment or punishment (Point 12).

On **11 September 2001**, President Bush said that "America was targeted for attack because we're the brightest beacon for freedom and opportunity in the world. And no

one will keep that light from shining."(6) Three years later, the catalogue of human rights violations alleged or known to have been committed by US agents in the "war on terror" tells a different story...

And because each story is different, no story is meant to be repeated..!

Why War is Not the Answer to Despots

"The ultimate weakness of violence is that it is a descending spiral, begetting the very thing it seeks to destroy. Instead of diminishing evil, it multiplies it. Through violence you may murder the liar, but you cannot murder the lie, nor establish the truth. Through violence you murder the hater, but you do not murder hate. In fact, violence merely increases hate.... Returning violence for violence multiples violence, adding deeper darkness to a night already devoid of stars. Darkness cannot drive out darkness; only light can do that. Hate cannot drive out hate; only love can do that."

28

Human Dignity Denied: Torture or Ill-Treatment of the 'other'

A basic human dignity of the poor and the wretched of the earth

Make no mistake: Every regime that tortures does so in the name of salvation, some superior goal, some promise of paradise. Call it communism, call it the free market, call it the free world, call it the national interest, call it fascism, call it the leader, call it civilisation, call it the service of god, call it the need for information; call it what you will, the cost of paradise, the promise of some sort of paradise...will always be hell for at least one person somewhere, sometime.

Ariel Dorfman, Chilean writer, May 2004 (73)

I Can Recall Hubert Humphrey

"There is no such thing as an acceptable level of unemployment, because hunger is not acceptable, poverty is not acceptable, poor health is not acceptable, and a ruined life is not acceptable..In the minds and hearts of the American people, there is a great hunger for peace based on a universal recognition of the values of freedom and human dignity."

Principle of Human Dignity

The intrinsic worth that inheres in every human being. From the Catholic perspective (among other Christian perspectives), the source of human dignity is rooted in the concept of *Imago Dei*, in Christ's redemption and in our ultimate destiny of union with God. Human dignity therefore transcends any social order as the basis for rights and is neither granted by society nor can it be legitimately violated

by society. In this way, human dignity is the conceptual basis for human rights. While providing the foundation for many normative claims, one direct normative implication of human dignity is that every human being should be acknowledged as an inherently valuable member of the human community and as a unique expression of life, with an integrated bodily and spiritual nature. In Catholic moral thought, because there is a social or communal dimension to human dignity itself, persons must be conceived of, not in overly-individualistic terms, but as being inherently connected to the rest of society. Because the tradition emphasizes the integral nature of our body and spirit, the human body takes on greater significance and value than in the prevailing dualistic conception of the person (principle of respect for persons).

The normative implications of this conception of human dignity impacts much of Catholic moral thought as it pertains to a range of human life issues, including health care ethics. For example, the principle is foundational for the tradition's understanding of distributive justice, the common good, the right to life and the right to health care. Other perspectives, both religious and secular, may conceive of human dignity in similar terms with a similar sense of its inherent worth or value and other implications, but may posit different sources for that dignity.

We are often forced to ask ourselves: What happens when rights and dignity are violated? What are the long-term effects? What is, for example, the long-term effect on people who are born, live and die as refugees, in refugee camps? What are the inter-generational effects? How are second and third generation refugees affected? This is surely living a degraded existence!

((Source: Research conducted in conjunction with United Nations University, HumiliationStudies.org))

World Conference on Bioethics (Gijón, Spain, 2002)

Observing

- That full dignity is an attribute of humankind, and that its recognition is a fundamental right of each and every individual which must be respected and protected.
- That, in spite of this fact, in far too many places in the world, such norms or principles are still restricted or even deliberately violated because neither the dignity of the human being nor the rights that follow from it are recognised in their full scope.
- That millions of people are suffering from hunger, lack of clean and drinking water and proper housing facilities, from diseases (AIDS being the most dramatic example), from indigence due to poverty and scarcity of essential goods or services - all of them evils that could be easily and readily overcome, conditions that are turning individuals into completely dependent beings, or are leading them to extermination and death, while the affluent society - the smallest part of the world's population - are enjoying wealth and abundance and are even squandering global resources.
- The nature, biodiversity and environment are undergoing an increasingly alarming decline with the progressive reduction of green areas, the extermination of animal species, the accumulation of waste and garbage in continental and maritime areas, the degradation of soil and waters because of global pollution levels, regardless of the fact that these are the habitats, resources and spiritual resorts which are essential to the human beings.
- That intolerance and violence be it physical, psychological, moral, technical or social, is irrational behaviour which is anti-cultural and contrary to the dignity of human beings.

- That abuse of power, wars and armed conflicts, terrorism, political or religious persecution, forced emigration, attacks on cultural diversity and most particularly on that of indigenous peoples, racism, xenophobia, social exclusion, exploitation and abuse of women and children, the abandonment of the elderly, the promotion of selfish economic interests and the abuse of scientific and technological superiority, make evident the many violent and daily acts that affect all layers and domains of humanity, acts that are increasing in number and intensity and often carried out with total impunity.

The world talks about Human Rights and Equal Dignity. Article 1 of the Universal Declaration of Human Rights of 1948 states that "all human beings are born free and equal in dignity and rights." They talk about achieving the Millennium Goals and a Free and Fair Trade to achieve Equal Dignity. I am concerned that ten million children under the age of five die each year, the majority from preventable diseases and malnutrition. An estimated 1.2 billion people worldwide survive on less than $1 per day.

To me, it is obscene that some people should be regarded and treated as inherently *higher* beings and others as inherently lower or shall I say lesser beings. Our world believes in the human rights ideals of equal dignity and yet 'ranks' people by wealth and status.

I would thus not attend to world poverty and treat the poor as human beings with equal dignity. But what about manual scavengers for instance, wouldn't they carry more than the litter of the streets on their backs?

What do we mean when we say let us "treat the poor as human beings with equal dignity"? Are we not exploiting them, the poor and the wretched of the earth? That instead of giving them an equal chance, or an enabling environment, we should stand by as mute spectators cheering on the predators as they stand ready to devour those innocent slaves?

What do we Mean by A Decent Global Society?

Avishai Margalit wrote the book *The Decent Society* (1996), in which he calls for institutions that do not anymore humiliate citizens. He states that it is not sufficient to merely aspire to building *just* societies, *decent* societies should be implemented that do not entail humiliation. Humiliating living conditions are not only unjust; they are also *obscene*. *Decency* reigns when dignity for all is made possible. *Decency* calls for a joint effort to attain the goals of the *United Nations Millennium Declaration* of September 2000.

Traveling from Social Exclusion to Equal Dignity

Ruth Lister writes (2004): "People living in poverty and their organisations should be empowered by involving them fully in the setting of targets, and in the design, implementation, monitoring and assessment of national strategies and programmes for poverty eradication and community-based development, and ensuring that such programmes reflect their priorities."

There is a need to make World Leadership more transparent and accountable. We have to promote a World Dialogue of sorts.

In order to promote our vision of a world of equal dignity for all, away from practices of humiliation; we have to work for dialogue, locally and globally.

(Human Dignity and Humiliation Studies.org)

"***Human Security***" binds together all people and all nations, and it can be addressed only through "sustainable human development" strategies, not through the acquisition of ever-more-powerful weapons. This security consists of the security of people in their homes, in their jobs, in their communities, in their environment. There is always a need for preventive diplomacy on the part of the international community...Also, any decline in global military spending can be (translated into improved human development) and used to finance the world's social agenda.

What we need now is a pressurizing for reduced global military spending and to make an explicit link between reduced military spending and increased social spending...

The industrial nations should be persuaded to close their military bases, phase out their military assistance and eliminate their subsidies to exporters of arms...

A major concern of many countries in the future must be to avoid violent social dislocations-especially-ethnic conflicts. To achieve "social integration", measures to promote more equal opportunities for all include:

- Equality before the law – to bring about an integrated society, we must ensure basic legal rights for all;
- Rights of the minority – countries must ensure minority rights, including those related to minority culture;
- Antidiscrimination policies – Measures to counter discrimination (and application of penalties for violation) should be taken by governments;
- Education – Governments must ensure that all sections of society have access to basic education respecting local cultures and traditions;
- Employment – The state should make employment opportunities available to disadvantaged and marginalized sections like women; and
- Governance – should be brought closer to the people, through decentralization and accountability, by promotion of grass-roots organizations and by creation of avenues for people's direct participation.

- (Source: Human Development Report, UNDP,' 94).

"They shall beat their swords into ploughshares, and their spears into pruning hooks. Nation shall not lift up sword against nation. Neither shall they learn war any more."

This prophecy did not come true with the end of the Cold War. At any one time, many military conflicts are going on in "trouble areas" globally.

These conflicts are increasingly threatening the lives of military as well as civilian populace. At the beginning of the 20th century, around 90% of war casualties were military. As of now, about 90%, disastrously, are civilian!

One of the greatest worries of the 20th century was the extent to which whole societies were militarizing themselves. This fear is pervading the 21st century as well...

In weak democracies, armed forces have been positioned strong enough to direct the political process and subvert democracy.

– War Crimes Court: The world's first permanent 'War Crimes Court' will try war crimes, genocide and crime(s) against humanity.

Former U.S. President Bill Clinton is said to have remarked: "In taking this action.. We reaffirm strong support for international accountability and bringing to justice perpetrators of genocide, war crimes and crimes against humanity."

- 25 years after the Vietnam War, the people of Vietnam gave a red carpet welcome to U.S. President, Bill Clinton, when he visited their country...even when they are still suffering from the war's after-effects – the Vietnam landscape still hiding hundreds upon thousands of mines that still kill and maim many unaware innocent citizens..A dear price for the scourge and cruelty of war...

Armed Conflicts within states increasing: Of the 82 armed conflicts between 1989 and 1992, only 3 were inter-state. Most conflicts are in developing countries. But, practically, all regions have experienced conflicts-Bosnia-Herzegovina in Europe; Iraq, Israel and Lebanon in the Middle East; Colombia and Guatemala in Latin America; India, Myanmar and Tajikistan in Asia; and Angola,

Somalia, Sudan and Rwanda in Africa. More than half of conflicts in 1993 took the lives of 4 to 6 million people. These conflicts have caused millions to flee their countries to avoid repression and death, creating a trend in "War-induced international migration".

Since 1945, millions of people have perished in wars and other conflicts and the numbers are simply not abating. Kashmir, a center of strife within the Indian sub-continent has seen thousands of casualties in the past years. Unless national and international communities take concrete action, deaths will continue unabated.

Despite all the brouhaha over the global agenda of human insecurity, world military spending still equals the income of nearly half the world's people (as of 1992).

The Continuing Nuclear Threat: The threat of nuclear war has definitely dwindled, but it has by no means disappeared. A major concern is nuclear proliferation. In addition to the five nuclear powers (China, France, Russia, the United Kingdom and the United States), there are states like India, Israel and Pakistan which have the capacity to deploy nuclear weapons on short notice. On the positive side, 3 other states (Argentina, Brazil and South Africa) had halted nuclear weapons development as of 1992. It was further proposed to extend the 1967 Non-proliferation Treaty after 1995. However, some countries complain of "Nuclear Apartheid", and some developing countries feel that nuclear technology can have "Non-nuclear" uses. Some countries feel threatened by their neighbors and value the possession of nuclear weapons. What is most important is removal of the causes of conflict.

The human cost of military spending in developing countries is enormous. As of 1992-94, 12% of military spending could be diverted to health (preventable, infectious disease, malnourishment, access to safe water, primary health care including immunization), 4% to education (primary education, adult literacy, female literacy) and 8%

to population control (basic family planning services and family welfare)...In developing countries, people are 33 times more likely to die from social neglect (malnutrition and preventable diseases) than from war. Yet, there are 20 military personnel for 1 doctor...

Arms spending eat up precious resources than could otherwise be spent on human development. Some of the world's poorest countries – Angola, Ethiopia, Somalia, Mozambique and Pakistan spend more on their armed forces than on public education and health.

High Military Spending Among Poor Countries

Country	*GNP p. capita ($US) 1991*	*Military Expenditure p.c. ($ US) 1990/91*
Sudan	400	23.3
Ethiopia	120	14.9
Chad	210	10.7
Burkina Faso	290	10.5
Mozambique	80	9.5
Mali	270	6.8

Promoting human security globally will be a tedious process. The future of world disarmament demands higher goodwill between the 'North' and the 'South'- the creation of new fora for PEACE discussions, regulation of trade in arms and a novel role for the United Nations. The Third World urgently needs disarmament. The job is only half done. Let us :

(i) Establish fora for disarmament: First of all, let us start with existing fora such as the Organization of African Unity (OAU); the Organization of American States (OAS); the South Asian Association for Regional Co-operation (SAARC); the Association of Southeast Asian

Nations (ASEAN); the Non-Aligned Movement; etc. Some neighboring countries can apply some pressure towards PEACE. The Tegucigalpa Commitment (Dec. 1991) by six central heads of state is a good beginning.

The UN could involve itself more forcefully. It has already taken initiatives on one of the worst killers-land mines;

(ii) Defuse tensions around the globe: Since opposition parties and domestic public opinion may treat peace alliances as unrequired interference, it would be better to involve the United Nations in major problems. We should bear in mind that these problems may arise from economic, social and natural causes. A former UN Secretary-General has said in his 'Agenda for PEACE' :

> "Drought and disease can decimate no less mercilessly than the weapons of war. So at this moment of renewed opportunity, the efforts of the organization to build peace, stability and security must encompass matters beyond military threats in order to break the fetters of strife and warfare that have characterized the past."

To conclude, the role of the UN in development must be strengthened;

(iii) Phase out Military Assistance: Military bases, which contribute to the militarization of developing countries, should be phased out;

(iv) Regulate the Arms Trade: Commercial arms traders have no regrets about making profits out of poverty – selling "High-fidelity" jet fighters or nuclear bombs to nations in which millions struggle to survive each day in their lives. Not only this, arms are supplied to 'Potential' trouble areas, leading to further conflict. We must design a concrete policy framework for regulating the arms trade. Both industrial and developing countries should cut down on their arms production.

Chemical weapons and land mines (which cause such terrible suffering to civilians: globally, millions of land – mines remain buried in unsuspected locations) should be emphasized. Land mines kill and maim civilians even when wars are over. Clearing them is very cumbersome and costly.

The UN should make a list of sophisticated arms, maintain regional (Asia, Africa, Europe and Latin America) registers of armaments, tax the sales of arms and establish more innovative methods of peace-keeping;

(v) Design a new aid policy dialogue: The need of the hour is to make allocations of aid subject to a "Military: Social Spending Index", or giving positive incentives in the form of greater aid to those countries that are working towards **PEACE**;

(vi) Agree on criteria for UN mediation in conflicts within nations: The UN has always intervened in conflicts between nations – through cease-fires, sanctions and more permanent solutions. However, intricate questions arise when the UN is called upon to intervene within nations, with regard to the form of intervention to be made – UN forces, temporary assistance or long-term development aid?

(vii) Create more effective information systems: We need to build up more effective information systems to follow the movement (s) of arms;

Finally, we need to bear in mind that a genuine improvement in human security requires the complete harnessing of that one most important world resource – Peace, Peace and only Peace.

- (Source: Human Development Report, UNDP, 1994)

Wish the rich, industrialized countries could cut down on their extravagant consumption patterns, waste dumping, greenhouse gas emissions, etc, to help **CHILDREN** in the South (as well as those in the North) enjoy better lives. Call it "Feeding Minds, Fighting Hunger".

I remember what Oscar Arias, winner of the 1987 Nobel PEACE Prize had to say:

"..I would like to propose the establishment of a global demilitarization fund..Let the nations of the world, both rich and poor; commit themselves to at least a 3% a year reduction in their military spending levels over the next five years...

The actual numbers are not important...

Only global cooperation can foster the security, which we have sought for so long, but which has eluded us so frequently. Let us make a definitive effort to use the Peace dividend for the construction of just, prosperous and demilitarized societies. And let us capitalize on the benefits of disarmament to promote and guarantee the rewards of Peace."

29

A Just, Prosperous and Demilitarized Global Order

FANTASY WORLD: POOR PARENTS DON'T NOTICE ELITIST CARS. BUT POOR CHILDREN DO.

INNOCENT FRUSTRATIONS, SOCIAL FERMENT and THE PEACE DIVIDEND: REPARATIONS FOR A NEW ORDER

Can we build a global order based on justice? Perhaps we can one that will be less hegemonic than the international relations of the Cold War. We don't have a choice, if we wish to minimize large-scale violence and maximize social and economic well-being.

The Cold War was concentrated on concepts of geopolitics, military strategy and ethnocentric ideology, causing much pollution, overpopulation, poverty, and proliferation. Now with the demise of the Soviet Union (the loss of some ideology) and the end of the Cold War, mankind hoped that things would change for the better.

9/11 changed the scenario completely. Washington overreacted to this terrorist attack in the name of the war on terror and in the guise of preemption, proving once again that the world is still in a process of transition, characterized by instability, fluidity and uncertainty without adhering to a morally accepted international code of conduct.

Human beings have forsaken their morals. The results of man's obscene patterns of material consumption have been disastrous, reading out like an inventory-from poverty,

underdevelopment, insecurity, ethnic conflict, forced occupation, wars and threats of war, terrorism, the list is endless.

Power has been exercised and power has been abused, with two major contemporary manifestations: one economic with a generic trend called 'economic globalization', the other political and coercive, more pronounced post 9/11, something I would call 'coercive globalization'.

By placing unnecessary value on mega trends such as power, success, glamour, superiority and fame, by worshipping power, whether economic or military and as both as an end and a means, man has sinned. That wealth is the only road to happiness, that extravagance ensures success, that comfort ensures security, that opulence will guarantee dignity, and that greed is ultimate fulfillment for oneself, the nation and will eventually lead to global order and security are all false preemptive notions that man carries in his mind. The truth is that only Jesus forgives opulence. And man is paying the price.

(The attacks in Kuta, Bali in October 2002 exemplify how man has already started paying the price)

It is to be noted that in exercising power, both economic and political especially as by the dominant powers and particularly by the US, man has forsaken the chief element that is responsibility with the inevitable result that while human conditions in certain parts of the world have been improved by economic globalization, in certain others, there is now a mammoth gap between the 'haves' and the 'have-nots', forced dislocation, cultural alienation, political instability, and the emergence of a selfish and irresponsible economic and political elite, who remain disconnected from local and national needs, and their common humanity.

Only a sense of justice is what binds power and responsibility together.

What we need is a fundamental shift from the Cold War international relations to global ethical knowledge. By this,

hopefully, we may be able to minimize large-scale violence, maximize social and economic well-being, realize our fundamental human rights and conditions of economic and political justice, and achieve ecological stability.

The poor parent would very often not notice the elitist Jaguar parked outside the slum, but the poor child who lives in a fantasy world of stars would. The rich beware, ostentatious displays of wealth will only add to the frustrations of the innocent child and indeed more social ferment and discontent.

The world goes on for these children (and the children of poor parents will often continue to grow up into cooks, farmers and chauffeurs)

And globalization goes on..there is no sense of right and wrong.

Directly and indirectly, it is affecting the sovereignty of states by transcending conventional political boundaries—changing and even reducing the roles of governments. Even more importantly, it is affecting human beings and the relations among us. The global market place treats human beings as objects and, most often, as obstacles and will result, *if unchecked*, in more poverty, more hunger, more civil strife and armed conflicts and the denial of the right to food for millions (Spitz, 1996, emphasis added).

These risks are real. They can and must be checked.

Consider this:

"If someone says, 'I love God',
and hates his brother, he is a liar;
for the one who does not love his brother
whom he has seen
cannot love God
whom he has not seen."

(The Bible)

I shall say I DARE
Disagree with God.

GOD (in humble faith)
'O Krishna, Thou Loving Shepherd
of the people,
Buddha, Lord of infinite compassion,
Jesus, Thou lover and Saviour of the soul,
Ramakrishna, Thou face of the Divine
Mother, and
Vivekananda of the mighty heart,
May Ye and all the nameless Masters
of the spirit,
Receive and save this soul!
('An Indian Study of Love and Death',

From Sister Nivedita, Miss Margaret E. Noble, the Irish disciple of Swami Vivekananda).

Its all about relating- how you relate- is that major question-

So, Why would I (or, for that matter, anyone?) be a Liar? Why? O Why?

I (WE ALL) have learnt to RELATE...

To the extent that

I have "Special love for Ghana"-

Ghana! In that traditional tone (so very typical of us 'earthly', mortal beings) one would say-

I Have "Special love for Ghana"-

Not Because Ghana Forms Part Of 'Emergent' Africa (O! Africa My Love!)

But because of those rather Contagious Cocoa Beans.

30

A Free Trade, A Fairer Trade

THE FAIR TRADE/BACK-TO-BRETTON WOODS AGENDA

There have been major influences behind the expansion of the global trade network. Major reductions in world tariffs have given the post-Second World War expansion in world trade a big boost! These cuts largely occurred through GATT and its successor, the WTO. The Kennedy Round of world trade negotiations and the Uruguay Round of trade talks completed in 1993, led to further reductions in rich-country tariffs. During the 1980s-1990s poor countries followed up with implementing rapid reduction of tariffs. Added to this, rising transport and communication capacities have led to the emergence of a global 'factory' where components can be sourced from several countries around the world and then assembled in yet another country, now a rising trend!

And now global manufacturing remains dominated by what we would call 'transnational corporations' (TNCs) that control world trade to a large extent. INEQUALITY remains largely a product of misguided free-market economic globalization ideology and plenty of opportunism, both of which have indeed failed to take into account either the global scenario or our long-term future. All this calls for a New Global Order!

FREE TRADE REPLY TO HUNGER:

The World Food Summit goal of merely halving the number of hungry humans has been shaped by a free market ideology that argues that the way to fight global

hunger lies in deregulation, privatization and increased foreign investment. On the WFS's opening day, US Secretary of Agriculture Dan Glickman declared: "Domestic market reforms have unleashed the full potential of American world demand instead of for government programs."

What Glickman called "our farmers" are really the US-based transnational corporations that dominate global food production and commercialization. "Free and fair trade promotes global prosperity and plenty," Glickman proclaimed. "The private sector is the great untapped frontier in the world war on hunger." Driving the point home, the US insisted that "Commitment Four" of the Rome Declaration be written to read: "We will strive to ensure that food, agricultural trade and overall trade policies are conducive to fostering food security for all through a fair and market-oriented world trade system". The objective is to strengthen the hegemony of the World Trade Organization (WTO) over the world's production and distribution of food.

World Bank President James D. Wolfensohn backed the US position with a call for governments to "reduce heavy intervention in the rural economy and concentrate on creating an economic regulatory environment that fosters agricultural growth."

31

Poverty and Hunger (The Food Crises)

WORLD DEVELOPMENT REPORT / THE HUMAN DEVELOPMENT INDEX (HDI) THE THIRD WORLD Vs THE FIRST WORLD

Food: a fundamental human right

At the 1996 World Food Summit, leaders from 185 countries and the European Community reaffirmed, in the Rome Declaration on World Food Security, "the right of everyone to have access to safe and nutritious food, consistent with the right to adequate food and the fundamental right of everyone to be free from hunger." They further pledged to cut the number of the world's hungry people in half by 2015.

Eradicating hunger is not merely a lofty ideal. Ensuring the right to adequate food and the fundamental right to be free from hunger is a matter of international law, specifically enshrined in a number of human rights instruments to which states around the world have committed themselves.

Without adequate food, people cannot lead healthy, active lives. They are not employable. They cannot care for their children, and their children cannot learn to read and write. The right to food cuts across the entire spectrum of human rights. Its fulfillment is essential to the fight against poverty, and it is at the heart of FAO's mandate to ensure a world free from hunger.

What is the Human Right to Adequate Food?

The right to be free from hunger and malnutrition is a

fundamental human right of every woman, man, youth and child. Universal and sustainable food security is part and parcel of reaching the social, economic and human development objectives governments agreed upon at world conferences in Rio, Vienna, Cairo, Copenhagen, Beijing, Istanbul and elsewhere. The right to adequate food is also enshrined in legal terms in the most basic international human rights treaties, including the Universal Declaration of Human Rights, the International Covenant on Economic, Social and Cultural Rights, the Convention on the Elimination of All Forms of Discrimination Against Women, the International Convention on the Elimination of All Forms of Racial Discrimination, and the Convention on the Rights of the Child.

The Human Rights at Issue

The human right to adequate food includes:

The human right to be free from hunger.

The human right to access to safe drinking water.

The human right to access to resources, including energy for cooking.

The human right to the highest attainable standard of physical and mental health.

The world has recognized that human rights are universal, indivisible, interconnected and interdependent. The following human rights are indispensable if the right to food is to be fully realized:

The human right to work and receive wages that contribute to an adequate standard of living.

The human right to a safe and healthy environment.

The human right to freedom from discrimination based on sex, race, or any other status.

The human right to equality between men and women.

The human right of the child to an environment appropriate for physical and mental development.

The human right to education and access to information.

The human right to social security.

The human right to development.

The human right to peace.

The human right to enjoy the benefits of scientific progress.

SOURCE: PDHRE

32

Back to the Future

"Developments in the present decade have underscored that Human Rights are inherent to the promotion of peace, security, economic prosperity and social equity...

A major task for the future will be to enhance the Human Rights Programme..."

- Former UN Secretary-General **Kofi Annan**, in a report to the 'General Assembly', "A Program for Reform".

Human Rights, Human Rights, Human Rights!!! Dated the 4th of April 2003, Reuters reported from Hanoi that as on this day, Communist Vietnam had denied US accusations that "it violates human rights" and tartly suggested "America should not be making such allegations while it leads the war against Iraq..." In its annual review of human rights around the world, the US state department said a couple of days earlier "the southeast Asian country continued to have a poor record. It practiced arbitrary detention, sometimes beat suspects and was reported to be responsible for the disappearances of numerous persons..."

And, these statements were coming from a country, which has itself flouted the United Nations by resorting to aggression, and, should I call it "destructive behavior", against a country which has already been reeling under 10 long years of sanctions, and consequently a breakdown in infrastructure, malnourishment, infant and child mortality and child labor, among other things. Given my keen interest in humanitarian issues, I would be in a position to recall that the then UN humanitarian coordinator in Iraq, Mr.

Denis Halliday, had resigned in protest against what he was to later describe as "genocide against the people of Iraq.."

And, today, dated the 4th of April, 2003, as American and British troops march on Baghdad, I would myself condemn such pre-emptive action, which has already claimed so many innocent lives, and will probably claim many more, including those of soldiers on both sides..the very fact that that we have a war raging, points to the failure (although I wouldn't call it 'utter failure') on the part of the international community to prevent such gross violation of the Universal Declaration of Human Rights... I would call it the "rape of civilization"...

And, civilization has indeed??? Come a long way..from, for instance, the days of the "suffragettes", racism, sexism and economic, social and political authoritarianism, should I say, "imperialism"... gone are the days of Adolf Hitler, Benito Mussolini and the likes of the Nazis... yet, we still have a long way to go...

First and foremost, there are "islands of prosperity surrounded by a sea of poverty"..globalization has brought in its wake, greater inequality within and among nations..instead of achieving lower poverty levels, we now have a global mass of the destitute, the poor, the defenseless, the malnourished, the lean, and the wasted or emaciated, especially children in the developing world, whose rights must be respected if we are to achieve any progress..for some, largely hungry stomachs, life would mean struggling endlessly, day after day, to obtain food, clothing, shelter, clean water, education, medical care, jobs, and freedom from conflict, among others. "Freedom from fear and freedom from want"..must be guaranteed globally...

"Development" (the right to) must respect peoples...

War and conflict leads to millions of political refugees as well as many internally displaced people.

Then, there are child soldiers, forced to serve in war and/

or conflict as a result of adverse circumstances, including, though not limited to, poverty; and social exclusion ..what must life be like for a soldier, and for a child soldier, that too?

We're living in a world filled with violence, poverty and illiteracy, hunger and ignorance, perverted sexuality, sleaze and pornography, sex work, murder and mayhem, stress, and technology that confuses rather than educate...

It is only appropriate that we went back to the future..!

33

Development as Freedom

(THE FUTURE OF INTERNATIONAL DEVELOPMENT)

One has to see development in terms of major and substantial freedoms of masses, with far-reaching implications! One must not reduce development to GNP and/or individual incomes..One must ensure access to facilities for health care and education as well as political and civil rights...

I wish to quote ***Amartya Sen (1999):***

> *"What people can positively achieve is influenced by economic opportunities, political liberties, social powers, and the enabling conditions of good health, basic education, and the encouragement and cultivation of initiatives..."*

Further, Sen opines that Development calls for eradication of major sources of barriers to freedom: poverty and tyranny, poor economic opportunities and systematic social deprivation, neglect of public facilities and intolerance of repressive state..particularly so in the developing countries..while sometimes, violation of freedoms may be a consequence of a denial of political and civil liberties, to some extent more common in the North, though not an irregular fixture in the Southern Nations either...

Assessment of Progress must be carried out in terms of whether people's freedoms are enhanced... The major challenge to development in many developing countries include the need to **"free poor labor from bondage"**, *explicit and implicit- that denies access to open*

markets..market economics is and ought not to be however the single largest determinant, one must pay more attention to the very inherent 'Worth' and 'Dignity' of a human being!

Article 1 *states: "All human beings are born free and equal in dignity and rights. They are endowed with reason and conscience and should act towards one another in a spirit of brotherhood" (UN/GA 1948)*

One ought not to Violate **Human Rights**, *or simply, the rights of Human Beings!*

Further, people need not be viewed as passive recipients of development programs. They must be seen as active participants in the process with options..This is the ultimate kind of freedom!

Millions all over the world suffer from various constraints- lack of freedoms! A great number of **disadvantaged** *human beings, including the elderly, the disabled, women and children, remain affected by Famines and under-nutrition;*

Have little or no access to affordable health care, clean water and sanitary conditions...They are compelled to spend a major part of their lives wasting time and energy fighting avoidable morbidity often succumbing to premature mortality, very common in the **Third World**...*What is less known to most people is that the* **First World** *also has its share of deeply disadvantaged people who lack basic access to health, education or opportunities for economic gains and social security, many live homeless, in abject poverty or on the streets...*

An important development in several economies involves replacement of bonded and forced work..The sensitive issue of **Child Labour** *also relates to the central issue of freedom of choice...There could be no worser violation of Human Rights than the "Virtual slaving" and "Forced Exploitative Employment" of children from disadvantaged families, as opposed to being free and possibly going to school...((Please*

see Juan Somavia: "Decent Work: The Report of the Director-General of ILO;" **Geneva: ILO 1999**; *also Myron Weiner (1991))*

Education actually enables participation, social interplay, and psychological enhancement, broadening of horizons, off course formal education and the ***"Right to Livelihood"****...*

*(And, modern-day sex-workers are sending their children to school, thanks to the fact that their work has still not been accorded the status of "*__Decent__ *Livelihood"...Reminds me, greater literacy can empower and equip to resist* **oppression** *and to get fairer deals by organizing politically...talking of "Civil Rights"...*

(Dreaming! And I can get a letter or pamphlet read..and I can see my community develop..through some of our very own educated activists...)

We come to the Maasai..some parts of Africa are yet to see light in their lives...

What made the Maasai infamous once upon a time?

Traditionally, the Maasai diet consisted of meat, milk, and blood from cattle. The mixing of cattle blood, obtained by nicking the jugular vein and milk is done to prepare a ritual drink for special celebrations and as nourishment for the sick. However, the inclusion of blood in the traditional diet is waning due to the reduction of livestock numbers. More recently, the Maasai have grown dependent on food produced in other areas such as maize meal, rice, potatoes, cabbage (known to the Maasai as goat leaves), etc. The Maasai who live near crop farmers have engaged in cultivation as their primary mode of subsistence. In these areas, plot sizes are generally not large enough to accommodate herds of animals; thus the Maasai are forced to farm.

The Maasai are truly in my opinion the "nomads of civilization" yet to see light in their lives at a time of unprecedented global change. One is yet to see whether the

light of knowledge has actually reached those remote locations that are outside the periphery of modern civilization.

There can be no greater inequality than this discrepancy..between an information society on the one hand and utter ignorance, illiteracy and neglect on the other...

Well, only time will provide an answer...

34

Education, Culture and Society

Brahma, Vishnu, Maheswara. ...The creator, the perpetuator and the destroyer, as per Hindu mythology....there is a lot to learn..and, that is where education, culture and society come in...

Actually, education, culture and society are three tripods of a triangle with the human being at the centroid. The paradox is: Where to begin, where to end? Does it start with the society, go on to culture and end with education? Or is it education that culminates in the culture of a society? There is no definite answer; there is no definite right or wrong. All are right, all are correct!! The myth continues.

Are cultured societies, in general, more educated? Or, for that matter, are educated societies more cultured? These are but difficult to answer..however; an attempt can be made to examine the exact correlation, starting with the meanings of the terms "education"; "culture" and "society"...

Let us look at the Oxford dictionary to understand what they all mean!!!

The term "education" refers to "giving intellectual, moral, and social instruction", with the development of character or mental powers being an integral part of the human system... "culture" means "intellectual and artistic achievement or expression", further, an improvement by mental and physical training..and "society" meaning "the system and organization of an interdependent community", suggesting thereby that this society may or may not approve of men and women who do not wish to "conform" to the

system..as are those who may be uneducated and /or uncultured...

It may be safely asserted that the following aspects deserve our utmost attention, namely, early childhood education, education of the masses, alternative education, mass media and education, the arts and education and education for the future (Silverstein, Dr. Louis), if we, the people of the world are to make any progress in our thinking, and consequently, social change. Dr. Silverstein has pointed out the importance of "the forces that are at play in the course of human events that affect our relationship to self, family, work, social justice, spirituality, and the nature and purpose of human existence.."

May I point out that illiterate people cannot do practical things as read or write a letter, read a bus plate or keep accounts. In developing countries, there is often strong resistance to female education..child labor is prevalent..an illiterate person remains ignorant of his rights, poor and vice-versa. Most people then discard the underprivileged as being a part of the "culture of poverty." I am trying to drive home a point, that, education is, perhaps, the most important factor in social change as a goal towards the attainment of culture...education may be hampered by a system, in which there are irregularities such as teachers absconding from school, or the withdrawal of children from schools by parents who cannot afford it, or the exploitation of child laborers by "uncultured" employers..and, indeed, in most such cases, it is the society that is to blame..we need to make social responsibility more forceful...

Andrew Sandlin in his article: Culture: Do we abandon it, join it, or change it, says:

"…. By culture, I mean the external manifestations of the inward, guiding impulse of a society: Its education, arts, politics, technology, economy, and so on. This impulse is always religious. Culture, in the words of Henry Van Til, is 'religion externalized.' Each religion produces a particular

kind of culture; Christian culture is different from Islamic culture, Buddhist culture, Satanist culture, New Age culture, Secular culture, and so on.

Today, the religion of western culture is secularism. Therefore, our politics, education, entertainment, and technology are predominantly secular. This is our root problem. Getting this particular candidate elected or that particular law passed won't solve it. The problem lies much deeper. We need an entire cultural root excavation..."

To build up a society, it is important that value systems are built into culture, and education must also be imbibed as a culture. A multi-pronged strategy to integrate one with the other will lead to a society, which shall be the backbone for a better tomorrow...

Let us examine, in brief, a few case-studies from Japan, which is a forerunner as far as human progress (the underlying theme in the relationship between education, culture and society) is concerned:

Japan's senior citizens(largely, the elderly) are growing active, turning to more unconventional lifestyles and values, and a new culture is beginning to emerge, and all this, thanks to growing 'information' among people, the result of an ambitious society (survey carried out in March 1999);

More and more men are cooking up daily fare, and the old Japanese adage "men don't enter the kitchen" is becoming a thing of the past, as many cooking schools are teaching men how to cook up ordinary meals like soups and vegetables (survey carried out recently);

More and more people with physical handicaps are heading outdoors to enjoy sports, from scuba-diving to hand-gliding, thanks to changing attitudes and the efforts of volunteers preaching the gospel "I can do it, too!";

In June 1998, the Ministry of Health and Welfare released the results of a national survey carried out every five years to examine Japanese attitudes towards marriage

and childbearing. The results revealed that attitudes are definitely changing, with less than 10% going in for arranged marriages, and most couples now prefer to have a girl rather than a boy;

And, as of 1997- on, more and more companies are acquiring the ISO 14001, an international certification for environment-friendly initiatives.

There are blemishes, however. Any change in society is likely to have its repercussions. It has been reported that violence among young teenagers is on the rise. In each case, it was noted that offenders had absolutely no record of delinquency, and were supposed to have suddenly lost self-control. And this trend is not just confined to Japan. There is a need to devote serious attention to this issue in schools, at home, and among education authorities.

It is clear that a holistic view of the root relation between the three (culture, education and society) would mean that it is "mankind" which is at the centre of the tripod and for which we must all make sincere efforts if civilization is to proceed forward...

I hope I have answered atleast some of your questions...

35

Education in a Social Context- The Importance of Education

CARRYING THE NIGHT SOIL (MANUAL SCAVENGING) /PICKING THE RAGS THE SHAMEFUL STATE OF IGNORANCE IN THE DEVELOPING WORLD (I CAN READ A LETTER/SIGN MY NAME: LIGHT IN THE LIVES OF THE POOR)

"..We have only temporary school buildings made out of bricks and red earth mortar, which can house at the most twenty-five children, and have no electricity and no water. Give us hope.."

- a child school attendee, state unknown

- India.

Again!

"When you are inspired by a great purpose for an extraordinary project, all your thoughts break the bonds, your mind transcends limitations, your consciousness expands and you find yourself in a great and wonderful world. You discover yourself to be a greater person."

We need to look back and learn from our mistakes; and realize that progress has to reach every corner of the world! Even if one tiny part of this universe remains ignorant and neglected, the world will not be a safe place..!

EDUCATING POOR CHILDREN IN INDIA: WHY NOT..?

It's all about...

- Re-branding Education as a career choice-
- Repairing languages education-
- Getting our children about Science-
- Catering to child curiosity-
- Languages at school-
- **BUILDING A KNOWLEDGE ECONOMY!-**

To most Westerners, 'discovering' India seems difficult. Coming to terms with the poverty, the homelessness, the street children who should have been in school and the unacceptable living conditions of so many! Some jobs, example on building sites, dealing with garbage and sewerage that would be done by machines in Western countries are done by hand. Who are these people?

How would they find these children as they taught in a school? Would the Dalit Education Centre be different? How does all this information fit with the current economic view of India as an emerging superpower?

In providing schools, many children who would never have the opportunity to go to school are getting it! An education in English and a job can change the economic circumstances of a whole family! This is the social context of education in india.

Information communication technology (ICT)

Social development for all and e-governance through children's initiatives

There are, in my opinion, two sides of change here. One is 'e-governance' in India. Another is 'Education'. I hope to drive change in society through Children!

- Providing Computer-aided Education for school children as a Model e-governance initiative for local governments-

- Familiarization to computers to all children in Primary schools through simple demos-

- Imparting Proficiency in usage of Microsoft based programs including Google Search-

- Efficient e-administration: In a developing country like India, a number of e-governance initiatives like medical help, legal help, Science Corner and Children's Corner are already underway-

- Smart Cards for children!-

- Community-owned kiosks!-

- These school children can also interact with other schools-

(Talking of creating another "Hansdehar", India's 1st Smart Village!)

A VIRTUAL MASS REFORM PROGRAM IN INDIA

(A) BACKGROUND (e-GOVERNANCE IN INDIA):

"The last couple of years have seen e-governance drop roots in India. IT enables the delivery of services as it caters to a large base of people across different segments and geographical locations. IT can greatly enhance existing efficiencies, drive down communication costs, and increase transparency!

It also gives citizens easy access to tangible benefits, be it through simple applications such as online form filling, bill sourcing and payments, or complex applications like distance education and tele-medicine!

As far as e-gov projects are concerned, the government is gradually changing its role from an implementer to a 'facilitator and regulator'. The time has finally arrived, for greater civil society participation in projects, what I would call "public-civil society participation (CSP) model"!

(B) INDIA (THE ANOMALY):

India's economy encompasses traditional village farming, modern agriculture, handicrafts, a wide range of modern

industries, and a multitude of support services. More than 1/3rd of the population is too poor to be able to afford an adequate diet, and market surveys indicate that fewer than 5% of all households had an annual income equivalent to $2300 or more in 1995-96! On the other hand, India's international payments position remains sturdy, with adequate foreign exchange reserves, reasonably stable exchange rates, and booming exports of software services.

This calls for greater positive social experimentation!

(1) HOLISTIC INTERNATIONAL LIVING- A "VIRTUAL" EXPERIMENT

I intend making sincere efforts to personally add to already-existing e-initiatives that are likely to create a sense of belonging, teach human values, impart (both) spiritual and world education, and create a spirit of service among people of all backgrounds, traditions, and cultures!

My plan includes proposals for some important new measures through a strong program of Reform, and a focus on key priorities. I will primarily though not exclusively give sustained priority to Elementary Education and Primary Health Care; if resources permit, I will also think about sanitary toilets and green houses for eco-friendly living to solve the housing crises among my target populace!

In most of these, I should be a "facilitator" rather than being directly involved. This unique web-based initiative would offer farmers for instance the information, products and services like the latest local and global information on weather, scientific farming practices, as well as market prices at the village level itself through a web portal-all in Hindi (other vernacular). Given the literacy and infrastructure constraints at the village level, this e-initiative will provide support through an interface- in this case, I, between the system and the farmers.

In the future, I intend being a "facilitator" in some of our "state wide area networks" (swans) in education and

health and improvising on a central Community Information Center (CIC). Projects are to be backed by a strong "CSP model" (civil society participation) to achieve long-term sustainability!

A genuine user-facilitator interface!

Deployment and training (online if possible) on e-governance applications!

According to Rajiv Kaul: "..Perhaps the single-largest benefit of e-governance is its potential to give birth to an entire web-based economy..."

Key Priorities of my e-initiatives:-

(a) Growing as a community,

(b) Working for a healthier people, including additional packages for senior citizens and children,

(c) Investing in education and skills, what I would call "information"/knowledge! Also, a virtual academy!

(d) an underprivileged talent promotion program in schools, and the provision of important work to improve literacy and numeracy levels,

(e) developing good international relations through the proposed voluntary program!

(f) supplemental initiatives:

(1) ecology and energy e-initiatives;

(2) farmer kiosks, exclusively for (ideal) farming, the mainstay of the economy;

(3) "ERM" (jobs and extended/lifelong learning);

(4) "KPO" (knowledge process outsourcing to the rural areas)!

Expected Priority Outcomes of my e-initiatives:-

- Equality (social); prosperity (economic) and freedom (democratic)!

- Work on a "happiness index"
- Improved community relations among my target populace
- Reduced poverty and disadvantage among my target populace
- Research into the causes, symptoms and treatment of hunger
- Child sponsorship (CASP) – community assisted child adoption in our target areas
- Safeguarded rights and interests of children in our target populace
- Reduction in preventable deaths and diseases in our target populace
- More responsive hospital services including inpatient and outpatient care in our target rural areas
- Access: an accessible and effective primary care service in our target areas
- Drinking water in schools in our target areas
- Education allowing children in our target areas to reach their full potential (6-14 years)
- A better qualified and skilled workforce in our target areas!

I shall always keep my doors open to other innovation!

(2) A VIRTUAL PEACE FOUNDATION

I intend engaging myself with non-profit, educational, charitable and humanitarian work. I seek to inculcate universal human values in the individual and ultimately a broader society inspiring both to take responsibility in service.

(A) A MODEL VILLAGE

Education and Literacy: A VIRTUAL APPROACH!

OUR FUTURE IS OF KNOWLEDGE ECONOMY!

Only a fraction of children in the 6-18 years age group are enrolled in school/college and employability is at stake.

Unless access, equity and quality of education are ensured, it would be very difficult to fully leverage the demographic advantage of an ever-expanding young workforce!

SHORTCOMINGS OF THE SYSTEM:

- Abundant un-nurtured or under-nurtured talent-
- Lack of timely and easy availability of learning resources/guidance to everyone-
- Consequent loss of opportunity-
- Questionable quality of teaching in rural areas-
- The growing digital divide-
- A complete lack of personalized monitoring and long term evaluation of growth and enhancement in learning, skill and performance-
- A very low percent of digital literacy-
- Complete lack of encouragement to excel-
- Time mismatch between school hours and employment hours for those learners (children) who have to simultaneously earn the livelihood for their families-
- Lack of motivation among teachers-
- Low Salaries-
- Inefficient functioning of the knowledge delivery mechanism-

An overview of to be undertaken 'e-initiatives' in Education in our target areas:

The first step is strengthening the individual by providing holistic self-development programs that will allow the full human potential to blossom!

I will try and devise innovative tools to enable our children and young adults to be effective in their day-to-day lives, like the simple task of being able to read a letter or write one's name. I will also try and devise online/extension/lifelong learning programs that we intend making available to people of all ages, and from all walks of life.

Under this scheme, I intend e-schools, e-colleges, an e-media school, and all distance learning options! Focus will be laid upon – innovative learning processes, teachers who are eternal learners themselves, curriculum for all round development of children, and access to Global Learning through special e-initiatives!

A well-balanced curriculum will combine practical education of languages and arithmetic with moral discourse, Yoga, games and Vipassana, hygiene, cultural discourse, non-violence and respect for the environment.

Through an e-approach, the "Cyber-schoolbus", we will take free uniforms, warm clothing, free textbooks and midday meals to the child's doorstep!

Health and Medicine: A Hospital on Wheels: A Virtual Approach!

I intend a Mobile Medical Dispensary! On each visit, the accompanying physician will attend to alteast about 50-60 patients. Free medicines will be provided. I also intend starting a Homeopathy clinic! And all the above in our target areas.

One experiment I intend applying e-governance to is Tropical Medicine. The hospital I intend tying up with (if possible!) employs tele-medicine to assist doctors in rural areas as they analyze and treat Panchayat residents. This method does away with patients having to travel all the way to the hospital location for treatment. Patients feel better being examined in their own village. Using the power of tele-medicine, the hospital/clinic is able to dispense its expertise to far-flung districts! The patient goes for an examination to the local doctor in the panchayat. This doctor is in contact via a voice and data connection with a doctor at the hospital for Tropical Medicine. Thus, the panchayat resident gets the benefit of being treated by both a local doctor and a hospital specialist!

If this sounds too ambitious to you, then what I can

surely do is facilitate this connection through a databank..my office can surely be a one-stop provider of website information to citizens! They can simply log on and get access to the concerned government department (in this case, health and family welfare)/services (in this case, hospitals/dispensaries/clinics) or even on land, water and taxes!

Energy (Urja!): E-initiatives/e-training in healthy renewable energy options like solar energy, wind and biomass! Organic farming (virtual training!)

(B) Selfless Service:

The second step is building a cadre of volunteers who I intend should be inspired to take more responsibility, and serve the society with love, compassion and care. I intend enabling them be available where the needs are the greatest! In this sense, I am also a Volunteer!

I intend my programs to benefit people from every religion, culture and socio-economic background.

(C) The Ecological Culture Academy- VIRTUAL!:

Is intended to work on health and aging; education; sustainable development including renewable energy to solve the rural energy crises; and peace and conflict resolution.

(d) The e-Research Center:

I intend to encourage research into the causes and symptoms of hunger, and its eventual treatment. I also intend looking into the factors that drive the onset and progression of diseases in the developing world, with specific reference to India. These include, though not exclusive to cancer, HIV/AIDS, to the killer diseases-polio, malaria, TB, diarrhea and cardiovascular diseases that either kill/maim several thousands.

The Center will work closely together with faculties of various agricultural universities and colleges and the Government, with the objective of providing best "e-solutions" to farmers and to access government subsidies!

Since my venture is in the formative stages, I warmly welcome research collaborators and research workers and suggestions from all parties in the process of setting up this initiative. Please write to me!

(3) DARIDRANARAYANSEVA (SERVICE TO THE POOR IS SERVICE TO GOD!)

I aim to achieve the economic upliftment of individuals, families and communities towards a self-reliant society. My long-term goal is far-reaching social transformation, with at least some relief from poverty and disease and eventual elimination in my target areas.

I aim to encourage the 'adoption' of a few villages, train their youth to be our future leaders, set up e-growth and e-transformational approaches, probably plant trees, conduct medical camps, facilitate the building of cost-effective homes, sanitary latrines and bore wells, set up a Micro-finance Program and Self Help Groups and teach energy optimization.

I intend each as separate e-initiatives, harnessing the power of information to reach the masses!!!

I aim, through my program, to raise the standards of living in our impoverished target areas; create a grassroots model for progressive social change; educate both socially and spiritually, give every human being a chance for a disease free body and free from hunger.

(4) Consciousness Studies in schools (a unique e-literacy program for children aged 6-14)

(5) Program 1: Development of stories for children based on the Panchatantra, Birbal Ki Kahaniyan and other Fables (CDs)

E-dissemination of the same!

(6) Program 2: Development of stories for children based on easy translations of the Mahabharata, Ramayana, Aesop's Fables etc (CDs)

E-dissemination of the same!

(7) the "book and a balanced meal/two meals a day" a likely unique experience for underprivileged children

A kitchen that can feed children- several at a time, when needed; long-term objective: Relief from child hunger!

(8) e-vedanta: Inculcating in children a scientific temper and respect for human values

There are certain basic values that unite us as a human community. I believe that incorporating human values into every aspect of life will lead to the development of a more peaceful and just world. I seek to work to foster a deeper understanding of these very values among our target children at the same time imparting them scientific discourse in Mathematics (numbers and symbols) and physics and astronomy and chemistry and the living world. I aim to inculcate basic respect for all of all God's Living Creatures in the minds of our target children.

At these 'heritage schools', the modern 'e-Gurukul', modern science as well as ancient wisdom will be imparted!

I also intend developing "virtual" programs of personal development and value-based education in our target population (rural schools), besides programs of community education and 'hands on' social and educational projects that we will probably entrust to our volunteers.

I have a distant Vision: *"vasudhaiva kutumbakam"- realizing a "One World Family"...*

(9) "E-SEVAK" (THE SERVICE PROJECT MODEL):

I believe that you serve when you love and care! I have a Model in mind that I hope to enlist role models for. Service programs are intended to range from health camps, poverty reduction to educating rural children in our target areas.

Let me give you a glimpse of what I have in mind:

(a) Social Development: Virtual!

Through a process of involvement, my role models (and

we work as a team!) are trained to be in a position to execute service projects to improve the quality of life in their own communities- whether they be far flung areas or large inner cities!

e-health; e-habitat and e-harmony!

(b) e-care! Initiatives for our target child population: Virtual!

- All-Round Education for Underprivileged Children-
- Schools-
- Inclusive e-vocations!
- Trying to enlist support for an orphanage/Ashram!
- E-knowledge on health and hygiene-

(C) tele-medicine and e-health initiatives: Virtual!

(D) a consolidated fund (proposed): To develop long-term strategies to widen community impact!

Health at the doorsteps of the underprivileged! An initiative very close to my heart!

(10) internships/volunteering: A program inviting youth from all over the world (no age bar!) to gain expertise in India's rich spiritual heritage

(11) youth delegates/youth emissaries/youth exchange: A formal exchange program for young people (no age bar!) from all over the world to gain expertise in India's rich service heritage

(12) ERM (e-HRM): A virtual process of matching individual capacities to organizational needs!

This will be a (virtual!) recruiting initiative, with the clear mandate of creating the perfect blend between the talents of these underprivileged children and the needs of the corporate sector, thereby enabling responsible business practice and tackling unemployment!

(13) individual change-agents in e-governance initiatives:

- In order that e-governance brings about required social transformations, all the processes need to be better understood and simplified for all!
- Prioritization should be done based on immediate needs of the people giving priority to education, health and energy-
- Raising awareness-
- Leading the initiative in order to inspire, galvanize, mobilize and implement new initiatives-
- Understanding local needs and delivering in local language and dialects-
- Introduction of computer education Professionals to work on "Virtual Classrooms" to facilitate the children of far flung areas-
- Work on community-owned information kiosks and "Community Information Centers" (CICs) for facilitating citizen services in Rural Blocks-

ANNEXURES

SUCCESSFUL IMPLEMENTATION(S)

- Personal initiative of reform minded citizens like us should be crucial-
- Client-provider interface: Facilitating self-service through a single portal window-
- Requires significant coordination, in this sense, a mass movement based on Gandhian ideals!-
- I am, despite my limitations, willing to provide this centralized leadership for extensive coordination!-

Opportunities on the Horizon

- Edusat available
- The abundance of knowledge on the internet
- Rapidly growing potential for rural cyber kiosks
- Civil society participatory potential
- An underprivileged talent search and promotion program

- Making provision of scholarships and affordable bank loans to needy students
- Convergence of conventional and distance modes of education
- Life long learning (III)

A virtual academy and virtual classrooms (classrooms of the future!)

- For the Arts and Sciences
- For Music and Writing
- For the Performing Arts

My distant dream: A peace university

Along the lines of the United Nations University for Peace, Costa Rica, I will not give up my dreams!

Starting with a virtual experimental fellowship of non-violence and reconciliation-

Motivators and Change Agents

- Taking message to the masses-
- Tackling inhibition, unfreezing mindset, enthusing, and incentivising-
- Role as an infomediary-
- Managing expert network at local level-
- Problem solving and feedback-
- E-health facilitators:
    - Weekly supervision using televideo conferencing facilities at each centre (an e-health community of practice online!)-
    - Telemedicine workshops-
    - E-health associations-
    - Questionnaires and e-surveys of patients and families-
    - Learn about other's experiences-

India's Poverty: Help the Poor Help Themselves

1. While India's growth makes it an economic and

political player to watch in the next decades, the country remains desperately poor. Almost a quarter of India's 1.1 Billion people live on less than $1 a day; 700 Million more live on less than $2 a day.

2. Can India ever overcome its huge poverty problem? It all depends on strategy.

3. (a) 1st Strategy: to abolish the poor, rather than poverty as happened in Mumbai some years ago

(b) 2nd Strategy: trickle-down model, "ignore the poor". Arguing that in the next 2-3 decades, poverty will disappear as market forces go to work

(c) 3rd Approach: Developmental approach that aims to improve the social and physical conditions of the rural and urban poor. This means more and better roads, improvements in water supplies and rural electrification. It also means big steps forward in education and health, together with efforts at microfinance.

(d) 4th Approach: ambitiously seeks to exploit the unused entrepreneurial abilities of the poor.

(e) 5th Approach: 'VIRTUAL'

- Step 1: identify needs: from literacy and training to housing, health care and jobs – and to put them in charge of their own lives;
- Step 2: SHGs, microfinance and loans, micro-enterprises, the government helps them identify opportunities and gives them training in areas like IT and marketing;
- Step 3: IT: the 'VIRTUAL' Approach;
- Aimed to attract service providers for providing free or cheap services to the poor like doctors, cultural institutes and schools-
- We succeed in our "INFORMATION FOR ALL" initiative-
- Consequent building up of a "DIGNITY SOCIETY"-
- Achieving Human Unity-

36

Human Unity - The World is a Global Village

(LESSONS IN INTERNATIONAL UNDERSTANDING) JESUS and KRISHNA – THE IMPORTANCE OF BEING SECULAR

"Through our scientific genius, we have made this world a neighborhood; now, through our moral and spiritual development, we must make of it a brotherhood."

- Rev. Martin Luther King, Jr.

(I wish to add a lesson in Human Dignity)

"If we cannot treat our fellow human beings with respect, then we have no right whatsoever to call ourselves human...

I was born free, I live free

I feel free..."

In the coming millennium, we can optimize the prospects of life on Earth for ourselves and our children...

"Are you a Human Being?
Of course you are...
So am I.
We All agree that we are humans.
But then we forget about it in our daily lives.
We live out of our differences, disagreements and conflicts. This is not satisfactory. The challenges and opportunities of our rapidly shrinking world call for Human Unity.

What should you and I do? We must refocus on agreement. Without being foolish and naïve, we can declare our unity as humans and begin to work together for a better world. Start now, right with yourself..."

There is always sufficient room for a healthy group discussion especially when the topic concerned is "what, in your view, are the prospects of Human Unity, given the ground realities as explained by our guest speakers?"

The ground realities are immense in scope and application. Human Unity is such a subjective and vast issue that not everyone is expected to nod 'every time anyone says anything'..However, let us not deny ourselves. Let us stimulate our intellectual capabilities to the absolute core-

Optimizing the human prospect: *"There lies before us, if we choose, continual progress in happiness, knowledge, and wisdom. Shall we, instead, choose death, because we cannot forget our quarrels?*

We appeal as human beings, to human beings:

Remember your humanity and forget the rest..."

- Bertrand Russell

The events and aftermath of Sept 11, 2001, a most extraordinary time of pivotal events and rapidly accelerating changes propel the world towards either self-destruction or unexpectedly wondrous endowment: security and wholeness of lives and environments, for each and all on earth..."The choices we are making right now- and those we will make- determine the quality of our lives, and even more so, that of our children's lives..."

(Anonymous)

We owe it to ourselves and our children to give *Human Unity* our most serious consideration...

A paradigm shift for all: we have finally emerged, the family, the band, the clan, the tribe, the nation, but not yet to the human. Our *Humanness* we have relegated- to

culture, religion and nation..we do NOT LIVE our common shared humanness...we live our differences, yes, I admit there is a fundamental distinction, yet, there is no denying one fact: that we are all *HUMANS*...Is it not right? Not good? Wherein we all? The Earth lies culturally disconnected, and we are but orphans to the core. We MUST reconstitute ourselves as *Human beings...* Our ultimate fulfillment, as also perhaps survival, depends in pretty much measure to an integral and optimal relationship with the *human whole...*

The advent of united humans : 'A realization is emerging that everything we want, love, value, and hope for- everything that is enduringly important to us- depends on healing all of us into wholeness'- *uniting as humans...*The *essence* of it all would be that in our own relationships, one would prefer a kinder, more humane world...Why then would grow ups take to arguments and wars..?

Human nature: O! We always seem to have a rationale, a reason, an alibi...call them explanations for our failures on Earth...

"It's just human weakness,
Subject to human error,
We are only human,
It's human nature, you know."

There always seems to be a separation from our humanness, we all seem to believe in the *'Human quintessence' of our lives, we all agree that we are humans, then why the disagreements?*

"We are all human beings" : 'In actuality, if brought to the foreground, this agreement is the root that nourishes and supports all the branches of human diversity and would allow us to act in concert."

Former U.S. Senator Sam Nunn once famously remarked: *"The day after a Nuclear Attack, what would we wish we had done? Why aren't we doing it now?"*

The truth is that true security remains possible only

through human unity: *presently, rapid proliferation of polarizing forces, lethality, technical advances in warfare and communication, has made us less distant but certainly more vulnerable...Current measures seem impractical, and latent widespread resentment among groups and individuals pose unprecedented perils and challenges...To achieve human agreement, we need some sort of an "insurance policy" against risks...*

How do we then release and harness our universal human agreement?

We come to the "message of human unity" : in the true "spirit" of freedom(s), let us join the world's six billion human beings...let us embrace our shared innate potential, make sincere efforts to 'unlearn' our learned habits of inhumane and violent interactions, 9/11 was crucial, but there happens to be something more urgent and imperative, our major responsibility, our children, our planet's past, present and future! We need fresh perspectives, because the lives of others, including our very own, are at stake...

The cost benefits of economies investing in highest shared human priorities rather than warfare are enormous..like diverting a percentage of military expenditure to social development, like health and education...

Sri Sri Aurobindo ("Life Divine") has been followed from "the ideal of human unity":

To curb deforestation and reduce our dependence on fossil fuels, to tackle climate change, renewable energy can be used to improve access to food and to light, and to promote enterprise. Projects with potential to play a significant role in offsetting carbon emissions can actually drive policies on climate change...incubating new enterprises, and obtaining subsidies, credit and soft-loans for end-users at micro-credit and institutional levels, and these include Solar PV pumping systems (installation), Solar home systems, solar lanterns... A Renewable Energy Project can generate both profit and employment. Profits include pay less for power, and yield

more reliable and better quality of light besides off course employment-generation and profitable initiatives such as drinking water.

Traditionally, Poverty-alleviation has been linked to schemes offering food, clothing and shelter. There is now a growing understanding that Poverty can be alleviated or even eradicated by providing better and more dependable energy, specifically Renewable Energy. 'Way of the Future' (in India, RE systems are expensive, not widely available, and often unreliable), RE forever remains the best option environmentally, as also for Social Uplift...One has to look for creative ways to provide RE reliably and relatively cheaply to disadvantaged sectors. RE is gender-friendly and easy to operate.

Renewable Energy represents the future...The world needs to take big steps to effect a radical change in energy use...

"AURORE" CEO Hemant Lamba points out: (Lessons in Human Unity):

> *"The biggest motivation for me to get involved in promoting Renewable Energy is not only just good ecological and scientific reasons for doing so, but that there are deep spiritual reasons for changing our energy use. The Mother pointed out that the present form of energy, which is drawn from beneath the Earth, is not an elevated form of energy, and that the future lies in drawing energy from above. This remains my guiding belief..."*

MANAV EKTA DIVAS
(Human Unity Day), April 24, 2006

"A new spirit of oneness will take hold of the human race..."

Towards unity?

Vasudhaiva Kudumbakam, said the ancient Indians: the world is one family. The ideal of human unity, which was

already present at the dawn of civilisation, has never appeared so close to realisation, but paradoxically the closer we come to it, the more it seems to elude us. It is as if at the onset of the 21st century the need for human unity has never been so great, and yet quite often this very unity, seen as inevitable, is perceived as somewhat threatening.

World in crisis

We speak of globalization, and in the same breath we deplore the dangers of uniformity... We speak of democracy as a universal ideal and of the progress of all nations towards it as irreversible, and yet at the same time this democratic model is perceived as a system imposed by some nations on others. We are facing environmental problems which threaten the very survival of our planet. We are aware of 'global warming' and a decrease in the finite resources of the planet, and we know that in order to tackle these common problems the individual nation-state is not an adequate institution anymore. But the very concept of a supra-national body is perceived as a possible infringement on the sovereignty of the nation-state, won in numerous cases after many decades - or longer - of struggle and pain.

Erasure of cultures

We claim that today's world is a global village, because technological progress has made our earth very small, and news can instantly reach every inhabitant of the earth through the highroad of information. But there is the fear that this global village culture may erase the diverse cultures of the earth; indeed it is argued that there is already an immense drive towards uniformity of life habits and uniformity of knowledge.

Economic front

On the economic front, the much-talked-about liberalization process is seen by many as an attempt to impose everywhere a model only suited to some countries, and to spread everywhere a culture of consumerism. A

computer for everyone and bread for only one quarter of the world population; is this the goal towards which we are advancing?

Science

In the 19th century, intellectuals saw the progress of science as the great factor which would lead to the unification of mankind, since science was a thing common to all men in its conclusions and was international in its very nature; but we know now that science can be misused, and is being misused, to discover more and more means of destruction. We have lost faith in science as a panacea for all evils, but what is there to replace it?

Biggest obstacle

We know that egoism is the biggest obstacle to a life of harmony and peace on earth, but after so many centuries of civilisation no amount of religious preaching or moral teaching has been able to convince the ego to forego its claims, as to speak to him of fraternity is to speak to him of something fundamentally contrary to his nature.

It all started with God..He created nature, and then He created man. Was He aware of the consequences? Pray, have we forgotten how to think deep? And though the consequences may have been somewhat, if not entirely disastrous, in our efforts to preserve nature, and restore harmony to mankind, let us endeavor to walk the common path of existence...this global oneness is truly the very essence of the concept of human unity!

But, how do we, pray my beloved friends of the world, achieve this human unity? The possibilities are immense and man's mind as also the very power of human existence (with some wallowing in luxury, while some others plain existing on the fringes of civilization..) unduly incredible! We, do, however, have a major problem here- the Problem of *'EGO'*, which though differing from state to state (one's inner as well as one's external state) has permeated into and caused

massive erosion to the mind and consequently with matter overruling the mind, to human existence, and we, instead of practicing ourselves as a thinking, rational, emotive and reasoning society, as our great seers and saints had envisaged (nee envisioned) for us, have only managed to achieve an egocentric, rather base, carnal and selfish, should I say, society- A 'Video-camera Society'! I am sorry I ever said this, but under the garb of terms such as 'Sustainable Development' and 'Jobs for the Poor' etc, we have only managed to *keep people where they are (rather than where they ought be), an extremely sorry state of affairs of humankind in as much as lessons in human dignity...*

Let us start with ECONOMICS..AS HUMAN UNITY...

Persistent inequalities exist, glaring disparities, if I may, both within and among Nations..and we are too much subsumed by national and racial and cultural Pride...There arises a strong Need to restore equilibrium, especially in as much as it might relate to Child Poverty. It is our marathon, an Egalitarian World Order..We ought not to fritter away this golden opportunity in the History of Nations...We ought to run! Economic Science is really not necessarily helping in the removal of disparity...And we're pessimistic about growth rates as they are simply not happening, but hopeful nevertheless..!

To my mind also comes a thought about "The Economics of Welfare"- Famine, Hunger and Entitlements, the Human Condition, Health and Education and so on and so forth, and off course, Professors Jean Dreze and Amartya Sen. This was, in fact, Prof. Amartya Sen's primary involvement and consequently, what led to him being awarded the Nobel Prize for Economics in 1998. Prof. Sen's mind also led to some pioneering work in and consequent establishment of the "Pratichi" Trust in Gurudev Rabindranath Tagore's Shantiniketan, in the deep and extravagant rural confines of the state of West Bengal in India.

Santiniketan..the name would surely conjure up images of the great Nobel Laureate, the erstwhile Rabindranath Tagore...and his life is perhaps the most outstanding lesson in human unity...and I quote Professor Uma Das Gupta: Rabindranath Tagore's thoughts on the *"universal man"*...

-"I am trying hard to start a school in Santiniketan. I want it to be like the ancient hermitages we know about. There will be no luxuries, the rich and poor alike shall have to live like ascetics. But I cannot find the right teachers. It is proving impossible to combine today's practices with yesterday's ideals..."-

-"There are men who think that by the simplicity of living introduced in my school I preach the idealization of poverty which prevailed in the medieval age...should we not admit that poverty is the school in which man had his first lessons and his best training? Even a millionaire's son has to be born helplessly poor and to begin his lesson of life from the beginning. He has to learn to walk like the poorest of children, though he has the means to afford to be without the appendages of legs. Poverty brings us into complete touch with life and the world, for living richly is living mostly by proxy, thus living in a lesser world of reality..."-

-"The school was conceived as a state of creative *unity* where the student's minds would be free from blind superstition, where they would respect human beings irrespective of caste and creed"-

-"There was a *unity* among us when the Indian mind was actively engaged in thinking. But now there is division. The large branches no longer find themselves connected to the root. The separation of limbs is dangerous for the body. Likewise, the Indian mind is now divided into the Hindu, Buddhist, Jaina, Sikh, Muslim and Christian branches. They are unable to receive anything from the composite whole or give back anything to the composite whole. Our ten fingers must necessarily be together to make an offering or to receive an offering. Therefore Indian education must be a collective of the Vedic, Puranic, Buddhist, Jain and the Islamic minds

to fill the Indian heart. We must find out how the Indian mind has flown along these different streams from the past. That is the only way India shall realize its unity within its diversity. We must understand ourselves in this connected way..."-

-"...in every nation education is intimately associated with the life of the people. But for us modern education is relevant only in turning out clerk, lawyers, doctors, magistrates, munsiffs and policemen, the few favourite professions of the gentle folk. This education has not reached the farmer, the oil-grinder, the potter. No other educated society has been struck by such disaster. The reason for this is that our universities have not been a growth from the soil...When a truly Indian (or, for that matter, of any other nationality, I should add) is established it must from the very beginning implement its acquired knowledge of economics, of agriculture, of health and all other everyday sciences in the surrounding villages. Then alone can the school become the centre of the country's way of living. This school must practise agriculture, dairy-keeping and weaving on the most modern methods. And to obtain its own financial resources it must adopt cooperative methods bringing *together* students, teachers, and the people living around..."-

-"*I have proposed to call this ideal school* Visva-Bharati..."-

Seedlings of universality, to be nurtured with care...the tide must be allowed to rise...

In the context of religion ..as human unity..we talk of "spirituality", we talk of religion..the question uppermost on our minds is: "Is religion helping (achieve Human Unity)?" The prospects are immense, the limitations rather obnoxious...Fundamentalism is rearing its ugly head, religious fanaticism and bigotry the order of the day...And yes! We have most certainly forgotten our great seers and saints! However, as I said earlier, the prospects are undoubtedly immense; religion can certainly act as more

than a binding force in times of calamity, and this given the fact that almost everyone these days has surrendered to... well, I realize that I am writing for some very enlightened, elite readership, students of international understanding, if I may! And God save India, my bread, my corn, my beloved, brilliant example of unity in diversity (nee a plethora of faiths and beliefs, a syndicate of religions, for God's sake, may not there be a repeat of 1992 demolition and very recent Godhra)..!

The political aspects are equally important...at this point of time in the history of nations and perhaps "world civilization", we stand besieged by the retrogressive forces of political exploitation on the one hand, and obscene war and conflict on the other...they call *Africa* emergent, but look at the way *she's suffering*?

Calling it the entire leadership question..! (faulty leadership and bad regimes, if I may!)...haven't we seen it all...in *Afghanistan, Iraq, and who knows, we may extend our "cooperation" to Teheran and Pyongyang as well! I wouldn't know for sure but the Northern nations could be at least partially responsible...*

What is the world coming to? *What is it that we are passing on to our children...? Poverty, illiteracy, malnutrition, war, child conscription, sex and violence- the list is endless...*

It should take, (and especially as science is the truth), the cultivation of a scientific temper (and may I be allowed to call it "Western technology") and its optimum amalgamation with Eastern wisdom..we're certainly diverse, but that shouldn't prevent us from complementing (nee supporting) each other...

These days most people are brought up and educated to regard most matters mainly from a relatively individual viewpoint. Even when we are taught to identify with and protect the best interests of one party against another, be it our group, our society, our nation, our culture...the perceived

self-interest, even of a very large grouping, is indeed not always compatible with the universal good. Such a clash of apparent interests - the individual against the common good - almost always lies somewhere at the root of human conflicts and also those between man and environment. All taken into account, however, the true, long-term interests of the individual cannot conflict with what is best for all.

This is doubtless due on the one hand to the principal differences between nature and man, on the other to the facts of deep social and cultural differences that affect all aspects of human life at some level throughout the world.

Every question, every matter about which we wish to know the truth, can be regarded from the individual viewpoint or the universal viewpoint. Between the two extremes lie the viewpoints that are adopted by any amount of groups, institutions, schools of thought, traditions, national or world cultures etc.

We're talking about unity despite diversity...(utopic) harmony that we might have dreamt of! Nation-states and the world community, people the entire world over (we all speak different languages, practice different faiths and beliefs, cultures, food and attire, my color of skin and gender differs from that of yours, but that's the way God has made each one of us, wherein the question of discrepancy, or, for that matter, questioning the Creator, the very essence of our being, our existence, the beginnings of life?) ..(and the universal cup of joy floweth over!)...

Need for real unity

Therefore it appears that although we are moving somewhat reluctantly towards a kind of unification, this is not a process likely to solve the many acute problems of the Earth, nor will the envisaged unity answer the deeper needs and aspirations of the human being. In fact, we have begun to understand that if we want to preserve the freedom for man to develop and grow in all liberty; this unity cannot be

built through mechanical means. It cannot be achieved as long as man does not recognize a real unity between man and man; it cannot be arrived at through social and mechanical devices; and we have even started to realize that if its aim is not to bring about a fairer, brighter and nobler life for all mankind, this unity is hardly desirable.

These are, what I would consider, the simplest *lessons in International Understanding for human unity, love,* because that's what the world is in dire need of, because that's the most beautiful thing that God has ever made..!

Love - the key to human unity

Jesus grew up at Nazareth till he reached thirty. After Joseph's passing, Jesus sought his mother's permission to embark on his Divine mission. He got baptized by John, the Baptist and spent forty days in penance in a forest. During the penance, he prayed to God for three things: One—He should be blessed with the quality of loving equally everyone; Two—He should have the strength and forbearance to suffer patiently any indignity or persecution that he might be subjected to by anyone; Three—He should be enabled to use his God-given body wholly in the service of God.

After forty days Jesus emerged from his penance with the faith that his prayers had been granted. Jesus encountered the fishermen, at Galilee, who became his first disciples. He told them that he had come to establish the reign of love on earth and that they would be his helpers in his mission. He spoke to them about preciousness in human birth and urged them to seek the Kingdom of God within themselves.

Without **faith in God one cannot experience bliss...**

Without any knowledge of **Vedanta**, if one is blessed with God's love, he can surmount all problems of life. Without faith in God, all scholarship, wealth or name and fame are of no avail. He cannot experience bliss.

Christ also taught that the body should be used for recognizing the Indwelling Spirit and not to protect itself. It is the mark of ignorance to pamper the body and ignore the Spirit within.

Likewise, man should seek to distinguish between the permanent and the transient and realize what is everlasting. Man is endowed with the capacity to discriminate between the permanent and the evanescent, but unfortunately instead of using this capacity he is caught up in the delusions of the phenomenal world and is wasting his life.

"You must adhere to truth and not succumb to falsehood or unrighteousness. You must face with courage the vicissitudes of life. You must love even your enemies. Universal love transcends all other virtues. Love is the supreme virtue", declared Jesus.

Only Love of God is real Love

Jesus taught that God is Love. Instead of recognizing this basic truth, men are allowing hatred, envy and other evil qualities to pollute their love. Man is gifted with the quality of love not to express it for selfish purposes but to direct it towards God. Jesus declared that they should do good even to those who harm them.

As Jesus went on with his preaching and drew multitudes towards him, some of the priests and those in authority grew envious at his popularity. This happens in all countries. They started persecuting him and charging him with treason. Jesus however continued up to the end to carry on his mission of Love and Righteousness, first, as the Messenger of God, and later as the Son of God. Only the Divine knows the real purpose. Everyone should regard himself as a Messenger of God and try to lead an ideal life. This means that one has to give up selfishness and self-interest. This may not be easy. But with God's Grace, it should be possible to progress towards Self-realization gradually.

Love is the means of developing devotion and achieving liberation, apart from other things. Only the love of God is real love. It is the royal road for man to realize the divinity in him and in everyone.

Sai Love unifies all from different countries

Here is an example of the power of love. Today, in this hall are gathered people from many countries. They speak different languages and adopt different religions and culture and have different dresses, manners and customs. Forgetting all these differences, they are all moving here as brothers and sisters because of their love for Sai, which has unified them. They are expressing the joy of oneness because of the love in their hearts. When there is no love there is hatred. Faith in God promotes love. Love leads to peace. Peace prepares the way for truth. Living in truth, man experiences bliss, which is Divine.

Where there is faith there is love
where there is love there is peace
where there is peace there is truth
where there is truth there is bliss
where there is bliss there is God.

The Divine manifests Himself in many forms. God is worshipped in many forms for the joy to be derived from it. In ancient Rome, many Gods were worshipped as in *Bharat*. At that time there was no belief in one God. Then came Christianity. The concept of unity in diversity came to be accepted. In ancient Greece, Plato, the disciple of Socrates, was the first to point out the immanence of the Divine in everything in the Universe.

Truth is one, regardless of the nation or religion. Truth or Divinity cannot change according to place or circumstance. That is why it is said: Truth is God. That Truth is within us.

Embodiments of Divine Love! Strike down the walls that separate man from man. Get rid of differences based on caste

and creed. Develop firm faith in the oneness of humanity. Cultivate love in your hearts. Only then will the nation be united, prosperous and happy.

Look at the state of things in Bethlehem, the birthplace of Jesus. Christmas could not be celebrated there this year, because of the ill feelings among the people. How unfortunate that while the rest of the world is celebrating Christmas there should be no celebration in the place where Jesus was born.

God belongs to all. He is Universal. All of you have to give up differences of every kind and give no room for narrow parochial and national loyalties. Consider yourselves as the children of one God. You may worship God in any form of your choice, but recognize the truth that God is only one. The observance of holy days like Christmas is an occasion for realizing the importance of love and harmony among human beings.

Remember the Lord with love. Worship Him with love. Sanctify your life with love...

Today's challenges include primarily building up a *humane and enlightened society based on love, compassion and respect* for everyone of God's lovely creation...(Jesus Christ, our savior, teach us lessons in forgiveness and compassion..)

If the society of humankind is to pursue its aim it must not only seek to unify humanity, it must then maintain social conditions in which each and every individual member of that united mass achieves the full development of whatever diverse potentialities they may have. That is the only way to ensure that human knowledge, in all its forms, grows continuously. In short, the society must foster, support and demand individuality both among its membership and in the human population at large in all its forms; consistent, of course, with the continued infinite survival of our species.

The answer to the question with which this topic began is therefore to be found in a full understanding of the

treatises on the individual and on peace , coupled with the conclusions drawn from those treatises in the Essay on Equality. From those sources in its founding literature it can be seen that the society of humankind reconciles unity with diversity in human affairs because it must have both if it is to have any realistic chance of achieving its aim. Indeed, the society goes so far as to identify diversity as both the cause and the purpose of human unity, as well as being the most valuable quality and characteristic of any viable human group. As the Essay on Childhood makes clear, '..it is the duty of the Society to teach all its children that variety in humanity without unity is purposeless, while unity without variety is valueless..'.

"International understanding for human unity" ...are and ought to be *lessons in forgiveness, love, understanding and respect: by each one for everyone else..!*

The need for holistic understanding is emerging as the process of globalization extends itself further and further and human relations extend across old divides. Growing recognition of the inter-dependence of environments, societies and nations has accentuated the need to assert the unity of mankind and to develop understanding of a kind which forwards this both in theory and practice. The chief motive and guiding principle of understanding and of meta-science is therefore to discover unity in diversity.

The chief assumption is that, just as the human being is essentially the same the world over, so is the essentially human faculty of understanding universal.

The overall principle of unity is the guiding principle of holistic understanding. Human understanding moves towards the unitary whole..eventually to include all aspects of life.

Diversity characterises everything that makes up the natural world, not excluding human beings or our societies. Without the millions of species of different organisms, plants

and animals, the ecology of nature becomes impoverished and can suffer serious breakdowns. Without the many sorts of human activity, the ever-changing pattern of occupations, enterprises and pastimes, the present level of world development could not have been achieved. The importance of diversity is seen in almost every kind of endeavor. Thus, variety is clearly 'the spice of life'.

The fact of diversity can teach us is to perceive everything for what it is and to respect and enjoy its uniqueness. Each moment is an unrepeatable historic event. Each thought, word and deed has specific meaning and consequences in its specific context. Each person is a special individual acting in a private drama. Life's richness comes from this profusion of nature and life and is experienced best through wonder and expanding one's vision all the time to include others and to appreciate their otherness for what it is, not liking them for what we want them to be. Without this basic experience of diversity, one cannot see how the unity of all beings is realized...

Understanding, the Common Good and Values

In question where values are involved, the result of looking at things exclusively or even mainly from the individual end of the spectrum is eventually to invite disharmony and disunity. Most human problems remain insoluble until the various contrary views are brought together under the universal standpoint so as to hammer out an overall solution. 'Holistic' understanding arises when all partisan interests are viewed as parts of a greater whole, and that can be defined in terms of the 'common good'.

It has through the ages repeatedly been objected that the idea of the 'common good' tells us nothing for it depends on how each individual interprets what is good, and this will be a subjective judgement conditioned by individual taste, interests, beliefs or politics etc. Yet the ideal of the 'common good' itself implies something worth striving for. That it is meaningful is seen in the universal conviction that some circumstances are better for humanity and some are worse...

All understanding aims at some higher unity of purpose. We understand each thing and action in terms of what it is all for. The nail and the hammering are 'part of' the building process, itself a step on the way to making a school. When the school is built, we again see this as an integral part of a whole system of education (which itself may teach various ideas having to do with human unity). Education may, for example, be seen as a good serving national unity, or also for world peace (unity) or unity at yet more universal levels.

The chief repository of holistic understanding is not in books or other media but in the mind of each individual, where it is generated and regenerated through learning processes. This occurs through sound upbringing and education tempered by broad and positive life experience, illumined by concentrated reason, intuition and by constructive understanding in relating to others and the world we share in.

This fact also strongly accents the greater importance to the human community of persons with mature holistic understanding than technological innovations that would replace them and the greater overall security their decisions would ensure than most kinds of specialist expertise operating on its own.

For the humanities, understanding must take place within the perspective of our highest aspirations and deepest motivations, including our visions of the purpose of our lives in relation to God and the Cosmos...

The written or spoken truths of the major religions have been passed on to us, often at several removes from the source. Successive translations, loss and suppression of parts of the original and of the relevant historical facts often occurred even before the question arose of how to interpret and apply crucial points that are unclear to us in our situation.

Where there are conflicts of ideas, policies and cultures, the aim must always be to discover shared human values,

the underlying agreement - the common interest - that unites. Without the guiding faith that we can experience increasing unity with all that is, it is hard, or perhaps impossible, to see how unity of purpose in human society can be understood and generated.

The basic faith that lies behind the ideal of unity is that the existence of life and humanity has meaning; it is not a blind accident of some unknown physical cause. This is a fact, for it is only some kind of faith that gives people a reason to live. No cosmic reason can be invented, either, for then it would not be cosmic. This does not mean that there is no cosmic reason... on the contrary we cannot invent or simply choose a faith for ourselves. It arises as a result of a process of living and understanding. Some kinds of faith are more limited and dependent - e.g. investment of all one's faith in a lover or in friendship, in a political ideology, in doing science to find truth, while others are more expansive and inclusive in their aims. Only very few are really universal. Those who grow up in a sphere of living spirituality, as many Easterners still do, learn the spiritual meaning of life from an early age as being self-realization through faith both in the inherent Divinity. As fragments of divinity, we are a complete microcosm within God. The meaning of life is then to merge fully with this identity. This teaching is as old as the Veda, the most ancient mother of religion. The principle of unity here is inspired by the same Vedantic insight.

Universality in Understanding

One essential test of holistic understanding is the degree of universality of one's basic conceptions.

Since universality can mean various things in different contexts, some further qualification of it is required. Universality of understanding must be inclusive of all human beings, regardless of national or other origins, race, colour, creed or class, without negative discriminatory biases.

One may well believe that there is unity in the essential

nature or ultimate purpose of humankind, yet the cultures of the world still exhibit amazing diversity, not least on these questions. There is not only a divergence between different world cultures; it increases in volume and quality, if not in essence, the more closely one examines doctrines and beliefs within any given culture. How, amid all this in our newly-globalised but fragmented world culture, can one talk seriously about unity of understanding?

One does not only have to be a religious bigotist or a totalitarian censor to qualify, for many Western intellectuals also wish to ridicule and eliminate ideas foreign to the widely-indoctrinated logico-scientific world view that is inherent to Western materialism.

Where understanding lacks, the thoughts, words and actions of the human being are in conflict. The consequence of this is disharmony and further conflict. Above all, understanding naturally aims at seeking to penetrate to the universal kernel of truth in divergent cultures and their products and the common ground for reconciling conflicting values.

"Imagine... a better world..." May God bless the world...

37

A New Global Order

A BRAVE NEW WORLD

Lets listen to what just a few of the World's many non-religious experts have to say, some of the HIGHEST-RANKING members of this planet's managerial class, who have the weight of scientific data and statistics to back them up:

Dr. George Wald, Nobel prize-winning scientist, Harvard University, said, "I think human life is now threatened as never before in the history of this planet! Not just by one peril, but by many perils that are all working together and coming to a head at the same time. And that time lies very close to the year 2,000. I am one of those scientists who find it hard to see how the human race is to bring itself much past the year 2,000."

(Well, we've survived past 2000! Now, this should be a time for us to introspect!)

"We are abroad a train which is gathering speed, racing down a track in which there is an unknown number of switches leading to unknown destinations..most of society is in the caboose—looking backward!"—Scientist member of the prestigious "Club of Rome" socio-economic group.

Kurt Waldheim, while Secretary General of the U.N., said, "I do not wish to seem overdramatic, but I can only conclude from the information that is available to me as Secretary General that the members of the United Nations have perhaps 10 years left in which to subordinate their ancient quarrels and launch a global partnership

to curb the arms race,
to improve the human environment, and
to supply the required momentum to
World development efforts.

The alternative is a situation beyond our capacity to control!"

But most people never seem to sense impending doom or things that are about to happen until it's too late.—most people just go on business as usual, no matter what is happening!...and knew not until the flood came and swept them all away, — most people today are just going on with business as usual!

(Just thinking of Malthus and Hitler and Marx)

Who are these people anyway?

No wonder they fly business class (not at all concerned about the economy!)

Welcome on board (those high-ranked, resourceful dignitaries! Flying!!) to Human Dignity and Humiliation Studies

Please fasten your seat (of power) belts!

We are ready to take off (to Stockholm)!! (To Copenhagen)!! (To Tromso)!!

We will finally touch down at (Nobel) Medicine/Literature/Economics/whatever! "Peace"! Oslo!!!

Dream...

..Continue dreaming, children of the world, youth of the world...

It's your moment...

It's your day...

It's your life...

Of which you are the chief executive officer...

These are your seconds and minutes and hours...

These are your days and months and years...

It's your life, lead it the way you wanna do (Oh! I love

*America!)..you are born free, so, breathe free and live free and stay free..*as free as the wind blows, as free as the grass grows...

If you have a dream, work towards it and live it each day of your life..and you will find yourself moving steadfastly towards your goal...

Swami Vivekananda says:

'To succeed, YOU must have tremendous perseverance, tremendous will,

"I will drink the ocean," says the persevering soul,

"At my will mountains will crumble up."

Have that sort of energy, that sort of will; work hard, you will reach the goal.'

'Ye are the Children of God, the sharers of immortal bliss, holy and Perfect beings. Ye divinities on Earth- sinners? It is a sin to call a man so; it is a standing libel on human nature. Come up, O lions, and shake off the delusion that you are sheep; you are souls immortal, spirits free blest and eternal; ye are not matter, ye are not bodies; matter is your servant, not you the servant of matter..'.

(Swami Vivekananda)

Consider the 'Dream rulers':

Former South African President Nelson Mandela was voted the choicest person to lead a fantasy World Government (in a Power Play game conducted by BBC) from among 100 of the World's most powerful leaders, thinkers and other high-profile people...

World Governments exist for fantasy anyway...

And contemporary International Politics is all about games of power being played in a global arena...

Our powerful Leaders and thinkers..how much do they Lead, if at all, and Think..?

That's me, the **angry young woman** *for you!*

But I have a heart...

And I can feel...(unlike a few of our leaders and thinkers)...

And sometimes some little things...actually touch my heart...*(like out-of-place community health systems; schools and drinking water)*

Think about all those that were affected by 9/11, the BALI and the LONDON BOMBINGS, and the TSUNAMI... Gosh! It takes all of the above to ever...

Strike a chord of compassion in the minds and hearts of men...

To **stir them out of complacency,** *one would say...*

How deplorable, how pathetic..!

(Humanity is now a concept of the past..*it would seem!)*

(Dreaming: Gunter Grass was a man of great humanity, he always spoke for the masses..)

Well, the fact that he was German..takes my mind to Germany...and I can feel...

The Hanover and the Frankfurt and the Hamburg and the Cologne and the Karlsruhe and the Mittenwald and the Munich (from 1972 ethnic gunning down to the Oktober Fest!) and (the Nuremberg! Those trials, those concentration camps and the Gestapo) and the Düsseldorf and the Leipzig and the Stuttgart and the Berlin in me

Yes, I love Germany and German...

(Dreaming!) I make it a point to travel by the Deutsche Bahn (German railways) rather than by air as and when I'm visiting the Bundestag...

(Dr. Angela Merkel would surely invite me over!)

-Who me? Someone who professes...

-Who professes?

'I was born free...I breathe free...

So let me live free..I feel free..'

I do not have any, not much for world society, at least I do not profess to, and it's my lifestyle and thinking that has always landed me in troubled waters!

It seems I shall have to "sacrifice my essence, my ideals, my very being" at the altar of world society, whatever that means to most people!

So, this is what **world society** *is all about?*

It's about professed ideal living, with fairness, integrity, honesty and human dignity- *principles that give us the security to adapt to change, and the wisdom and power to take advantage of the opportunities that change creates..(anonymous)*

The 'anonymous possibilist' is talking about enhancing the human resource...

I guess that despite contemporary responsibilities and demands of time, travel, work and families, one can try and square inner thought ('one thinking man is worth more than a 1,000 none') and outward behavior, resulting in private as well as public integrity..and consequentially, managing to break cycles of humiliation.

As William George Jordan says: "Into the hands of every individual is given a marvelous power for good or evil- the silent, unconscious, unseen influence of his life. This is simply the constant radiation of what man really is, not what he pretends to be."

(And, Stephen Gould wrote in the New York Times following 9/11..)

It's about "empowering" to achieve true "empowerment"...

"We are not our feelings. We are not our moods. We are not even our thoughts...self-awareness..affects not only our attitudes and behaviours, but also how we see other people.

It becomes our map of the basic nature of mankind...

Until we take how we see ourselves (and how we see others) into account, we will be unable to understand how others see and feel about themselves and their world..."

(Stephen R.Covey: 'The 7 habits of highly effective people', 1992)

Covey calls it the "social mirror"..we are largely conditioned to behave...

The way our predecessors did to us...our DNA's...

The way our experiences did to us..they settle into our psyche...

38

Affirmative Action (An End or the Beginning of Inequality?)

DISCRIMINATION may manifest in a 'general form' as in Racism, Sexism, Ageism, Religious intolerance, Reverse discrimination or as Xenophobia, or 'specifically' as Social discrimination, discrimination against ethnic groups or discrimination against beliefs.

Common manifestations include Slavery, Racial profiling, Lynching, Hate, Hate speech and Hate Crime, Genocide, Ethnocide, Ethnic cleansing, Race War, Religious persecution, Blood libel, Paternalism and Police brutality.

There could be a "Discriminatory" Movement or an "Anti-discriminatory" Movement.

There could be discrimination on the basis of Race, religion or sex. Sometimes, such segregation may be pronounced, as happened in South Africa in the form of Apartheid. Sometimes Group rights become important as well. One example of a notable discriminatory policy is the Ghetto benches, and Wake Up! Calls have been given.

Anti-discriminatory Policies may include Emancipation, Civil Rights, Desegregation, Integration, Equal opportunity and Gender equality.

I see every point in practising "diversity". Oppression must be rooted out and so must prejudice! It is in the end always politically correct to practice tolerance versus intolerance!

Because all men (and women) are created equal in dignity and rights, so the question of supremacism and discrimination does not arise...so, is this an end or the beginning of inequality?

39

Capital Flows and Inequality Hurts Contemporary Casino Economy

"... there is unquestionable evidence of a mammoth divide in income, the great unmentionable..."

Today among rich countries, and increasingly among poor ones, there are few barriers to global transfers of enormous amounts of money. Huge amounts of money can be transferred these days at the mere press of a button on the keyboard! We live in an era in which hot, speculative money chases short-term profits. This enormous availability of cash has had a major effect on both rich and poor countries.

For many rich countries, the global casino economy has made it easier to have the luxury of continually borrowing from the rest of the world while at the same time lecturing poor countries about the sins of over reliance on debt and the virtues of free trade. For poorer countries this casino economy has also had many downsides. There is on the one hand a Third World Debt crisis and on the other following economic growth much speculation and investment by rich-country companies, banks and financiers. It is as if multinational corporations have taken over in countries otherwise besieged by heinous poverty...

Contemporary world governments seem to be complying more and more with the forces of globalization, thereby aiding and abetting its spread. Also crucial has been the technology that allowed globalization to happen in the first place, and I would talk particularly about transport and

communications. While on the one hand, we seem to see all the political decisions of globalization getting all the headlines, it is actually a skewed world order that powers it along.

Firstly, we have the world's transnational corporations (TNCs) wielding tremendous influence. One would seem to think that many of our governments have fallen under their influence! The second group is the International Monetary Fund (IMF), the World Bank and the World Trade Organization (WTO). These are in effect mostly headquartered in and as a matter of fact shaped by the United States, the post-Second World War Global Superpower.

The United States began the modern era of economic globalization and most governments around the world have progressively reduced their trade and capital controls ever since. We have already lost some important ideology following the collapse of the Soviet Union and in the post Cold War period, the free-market ideologies of Milton Friedman, Margaret Thatcher and Ronald Reagan have become the order of the day.

Further, it may be stated that poor countries get hit hard when these so-called world 'bureaucracies' impose pro-globalization, free market conditions on loans taken by them. We have, in effect, created a 'corpus of debtors' accounting for about 40% of the entire world's economies. Meanwhile the World Trade Organization has increasingly pushed the boundaries of trade globalization through harsh trade rulings and new areas- such as patents, investment and services trade- included in the Uruguay and Doha Rounds. Eventually, WTO trade talks at Cancun in Sept 2003 collapsed over many new issues!

We need to encourage greater poor country participation in international trade negotiations that very often lack the resources to be able to participate in them properly. Roughly

1/4th of all the poor countries can't even afford to maintain delegations at the WTO's base in Geneva with only one or two representatives from Sub-Saharan Africa while rich countries send a small army!

To prevent the mushrooming of the WTO as an international trade regime, world governments ought to encourage more regional trade blocs such as and including the EEC (European Economic Community), the NAFTA (North American Free Trade Agreement), the ASEAN (Southeast Asian) and the South American Mercosur.

Like the WTO, the IMF and the World Bank have always been frequent targets of the anti-globalization movement. Protestors have often taken to the streets during annual general meetings of the Bank. Indeed, over time, the Bank has applied the same free-market prescription to every poor-country crisis, regardless of its cause. Several World Bank officials have indeed resigned, including one-time Chief Economist Joseph Stiglitz, Herman Daly, the 'World Development Report' (2000) probing editor and one-time head of the World Development Task Force, Ravi Kanbur.

Economists feel that because Bank loans often touch on areas of government activity that are crucial to the human and economic health of poor countries, their one-size-fits-all prescriptions frequently has devastating consequences. These consequences have included:

- The outbreak of bubonic and pneumonic plague in India in 1994 as a direct result of Bank loan-mandated budget cuts in 1991;
- The bankruptcy of small and medium-sized farmers in Bangladesh in the early 1980s as a result of IMF-mandated elimination of agricultural subsidies;
- The fuelling of the war in Bosnia as a result of IMF/World Bank-driven budget cuts in the amount of federal government assistance the central government in Yugoslavia provided to its provinces;

- The escalation of a recent severe drought in Malawi through the sell-off of its national grain buffer stock stipulated by the IMF in 2001.

Now that Economic globalization has been around long enough, it has developed powerful vested interests, in the form of those transnational institutions that power it along, in addition to the powerful new technologies that enable its operation and expansion. These ensure that there is enormous self-perpetuating force behind the global economy in these times, which only means that the anti-globalization and ***anti-inequality*** movements are up against indeed an extremely powerful foe!

40

Corporations, Commodities and Currencies—The Engines of Inequality

INEQUALITY BREEDS INEQUALITY! THE ANTI-GLOBALIZATION PROTESTS

The rise and spread of inequality around the world has been fed by many factors. Most importantly, world governments have always complied with pro-globalization decisions. Globalization has created certain institutions, and the 'devil' in them has had an ever-increasing vested interest in the ongoing expansion of the world economy. Technology, particularly transport and communications, has added to the work of the devil!

Two groups of institutions have relentlessly pursued the promotion and expansion of economic globalization leading to a situation in which more than half the planet goes to bed hungry every night while the other half continues to splurge and indulge to a point of abominable and loathsome greed, opulence, extravagance and luxury! Obscene material consumption patterns and waste dumping continue to dominate the day!

The world's transnational corporations (TNCs) wield enormous influence! They control most of trade, investment and employment decisions and their influence often exceeds that of many governments. Our international financial institutions like the IMF, the World Bank and the WTO, though answerable to the world's governments, have in practice each become major global 'bureaucracies' wielding enormous, largely unaccountable influence!

TNCs have always done well out of economic globalization, companies that operate across borders, based in several countries at once. Reduced trade and investment barriers have created vast new markets and these companies have expanded limitlessly. In the 1970s there were about 7,000 TNCs in the world, with the number going up to 53,000 by 1997. Today a major share of all global investment remains in the hands of the largest TNCs.

Like every other aspect of globalization, TNCs are very much a creation of the rich parts of the world, nearly always owned by rich country shareholders, managed from rich countries and with very Western/hierarchical structures. Most are headquartered in the rich world-Western Europe, the United States and Japan. Very few are headquartered in poor countries.

Today the area where these TNCs wield some of the greatest influence is trade. Nearly 70 per cent of global trade is controlled by them, including trade in information technology, the world's raw materials, the world's grain, the world's ***coffee,*** tea, cocoa and bananas.

The power of these corporations and of rich countries in general, is further augmented by their domination of the world's ***patent research and development.*** Rich nations account for 97 per cent of the world's patents, and roughly the same proportion of international research and development spending, with 40 per cent spent in the United States alone.

FEUDALISM..ALIAS AMERICAN CAPITALISM

"..there is overwhelming evidence that masquerading behind a democratic façade, an economic elite comprising less than 1% of the population is quietly and cunningly ruling America"

Economic differences between rich and poor countries are considerable.

A study by the World Institute for Development Economics Research at United Nations University reports that the richest 1% of adults alone owned 40% of global assets in the year 2000, and that the richest 10% of adults accounted for 85% of the world total. The bottom half of the world adult population owned barely 1% of global wealth.

The major component of the world's income inequality (the global Gini coefficient) is comprised by two groups of countries (called the "twin peaks" by Quah [1997]).

- The first group has 13% of the world's population and receives 45% of the world's PPP income. This group includes the United States, Japan, Germany, France and the United Kingdom, and comprises 500 million people with an annual income level over 11,500 PPP$.
- The second group has 42% of the world's population and receives only 9% of the world PPP income. This group includes India, Indonesia and rural China, and comprises 2,100 million people with an income level under 1,000 PPP$. (See Milanovic 2001, p.38).

When we draw Comparisons

Some of the economic disparities among nations can be better appreciated when rich and poor countries or societies are contrasted. For example, with regard to income inequality, according to some estimates by Branko Milanovic from the World Bank:

- "An American having the average income of the bottom US decile is better-off than 2/3 of world population." (Milanovic 2002, p.50)
- "The top 10 percent of the US population has an aggregate income equal to income of the poorest 43 percent of people in the world, or differently put, total income of the richest 25 million Americans is equal to total income of almost 2 billion people." (Milanovic 2002, p.50)

With regard to wealth inequality a 2006 report with data from 2000 concluded that:

- "India dominates the bottom third of the global wealth distribution, contributing a little under a third (27 per cent to be precise) of this group."
- "for the world as a whole the share of the top 10 per cent was 85 per cent in the year 2000 and the Gini equalled 0.892 using official exchange rates" (Davies et al. 2006, p.32)

James Davies, Professor of Economics at the University of Western Ontario, and one of the authors of the report, said: "Income inequality has been rising for the past 20 to 25 years and we think that is true for inequality in the distribution of wealth." "There is a group of problems in developing countries that make it difficult for people to build assets, which are important, since life is so precarious."

Other disparities can be better appreciated when rich individuals (or corporations) are compared against poor individuals. According to some estimates, for instance:

- "The richest 1 percent of people in the world receive as much as the bottom 57 percent, or in other words, less than 50 million richest people receive as much as 2.7 billion poor." (Milanovic 2002, p.50)
- The *three* richest people possess more financial assets than the poorest 10% of the world's population, combined.
- As of May 2005, the three richest people in the world have assets that exceed the combined gross domestic product of the 47 countries with the least GDP, (calculation based on data from list of countries by GDP (PPP) and list of billionaires) (Annan, 1998)
- As of May 2005, the 125 richest people in the world have assets that exceed the combined gross domestic product of all the least developed countries (calculation based on data from list of countries by GDP (PPP) and list of billionaires).

41

Global Inequality-A Defining Influence of the Era

This arises as a defining influence of our era. In the post-Second World War decades of the 1950s, 1960s and 1970s it was technology. We then spoke of the Sputnik; man's landing on the moon, the Aswan Dam in Egypt, the 'green' revolution, Thalidomide, birth-control pills and mainframe computers!

In the 1980s, the 1990s and in our contemporary era, we are talking about money-particularly global money! Everyone knows about the NASDAQ and the Dow Jones indexes. We've had a brush with Enron! Most of us have an idea about exchange rates! Post-9/11, there were huge stock-market gyrations played out on our TV screens! This is all the influence of economic globalization! We are all caught up in it now!

A larger church is what we would call the 'anti-globalization' movement. I would prefer to call it the 'anti-inequality' movement. We see widespread activism in the form of Peace and non-violence, the gender debate, poverty, the rights of indigenous people and the climate change movement to name a few. And now we have the war on terror! These are all to be perceived as distinct and yet synonymous aspects of the fight for greater equality. Why the word 'greater' cannot be removed to make it a 'fight for equality' is something beyond the best of comprehension in as far as I am concerned!

It is said that 'there is something for everyone's needs,

but not for everyone's greed..'. I strongly believe this persistent inequality may have indeed arisen out of the irrepressible greed of transnational corporations. I remember what former British Prime Minister Tony Blair said in 1998, "globalization is irreversible and irresistible". I ought to say it is not! Economic globalization has never really been an inevitable part of human evolution and is therefore eminently reversible and hugely resistible. I am trying to give hope to those that are indeed fighting to achieve a new global order sans 'inequality', both within and between nations, for a more 'sustainable' future for particularly our children-not a naïve hope but one actually based on real and viable alternatives!

I believe that such a future is indeed possible! A future that can be achieved by the common and indeed combined efforts of all-global planners and policymakers, world governments, international organizations particularly the United Nations, academicians and civil society..I also believe that we must indeed give greater opportunities to the poor in decisions affecting their lives, for the world can be a better place if at all with prior consultation of the poor in policy, for it is their lives that we are trying to improve and no one but the poor should have the final say...

Inequality hurts! It does indeed! That a child in Kalahandi district of Orissa state in my home country India should die of malnutrition is as painful is as perhaps that several innocents lost their lives when the World Trade Center collapsed! But while 9/11 made it to the front pages throughout the world, seemingly very little may be made of the former. It is more often categorized as just 'another malnutrition death'.

42

KBK - India's Poor (Kalahandi, Bolangir and Koraput)

*The way our **National Policies** did to us... sheer discriminatory humiliation...*

((We are talking about the IT-Sector, the Pharmaceutical Industry and Bio-Technology, a knowledge base economy characterized by fishermen and taxi drivers with mobile phones and universal ownership of motorbikes and scooters! And, Flyovers will crisscross the city! And, multistorey offices and residential structures surrounded by car parks and inner City Expressways!

And, my Country will become Bangkok and Singapore!

With further expansion in the retail and entertainment sector (more departmental stores and more of someone getting away with buck-lynching and shirt-ripping and someone with strip to 'Murder': Laugh!)

And, there are likely to be tourists from Prague and San Francisco and Shanghai hopping in and out of my country!

More business, more trade links for everybody!

By 2050, India will join the EU, the US and China as economic super power!

And conferences titled 'India- Asia's second giant is waking up' are being held someplace, sometime, not much remote!

And India is still attractive as a business location...

WOW! That's what I call 'National Development'! (Laugh!))

-And the Whatever Chambers of Commerce (and Accountancy and Industry!) will expand further and provide an even better service to its members and everybody interested in Indo-whatever Business and Trade..New whatever Companies will lead delegations to participate in a large number to get a fair share of business in the international market to ensure a bright future for India (and for themselves!)...While they insult our Nobel Laureates on Poverty and Famines and Entitlements...

Noam Chomsky, John Kenneth Galbraith, Mahbub ul Haq, Amartya Sen and Muhammad Yunus

"I will become Chairman in the next election" (the power of micro-finance)/the happiness index

> "Poor people: They are like bonsai. You take a seed of the tallest tree and plant it in a flower pot to curtail its growth. But, if society gives them a larger base with enough nutrients, they will grow like any other tall tree and reach out for the sky..."
>
> - Nobel laureate Prof. Muhammad Yunus

To achieve the "happiness index", one can adopt the following paradigm (though there are no hard-and-fast rules):

(1) shelter and security of tenure must be guaranteed;

(2) livelihood including micro-credit: Micro-credit can play an important role in achieving our millennium development goals. Prof. Mohammad Yunus started with his personal beliefs about the poor to 'feel like an angel' when he lent $27.

I quote Prof. Yunus:

"As a professor of Economics, I returned..after the famine, I felt totally useless when I saw hundreds die outside while I taught...there are thousands of ways to die. But death by hunger is the most frustrating...I went to financial institutions telling them to reach out to people and give loans...by not reaching out to the two-thirds of

the population in the world, they have created financial apartheid..."

(3) health and education:

(4) vulnerable groups: Women, children, minorities, backward communities, persons with disabilities and senior citizens (a revolution in geriatric care needed):

(5) basic services- drinking water; sanitation; transportation; governance (including e-governance and a process of decentralization); ICT etc

(6) disaster management / global climate change strategies:

(7) renewable energy /alternative energy options:

(8) any other: Like linking our rivers and solving for once our problems of famine and drought (but this may not be a viable option); call-centers for farmers; a social sector stock market that would list corporates attached to the social service sector, a virtual one that too but that could be a good beginning.

These are innovative, result-oriented and replicable, easy to scale-up.

This is all about the outstanding importance of the poor, or rather the importance accorded to this class of peoples, something very few could actually come to terms with! It represents a lesson in human dignity.

I see that there is virtually no field of human endeavor that humanity cannot touch! In the process, one can actually touch the lives of the poor!

These are in essence some of the core values I would always cherish:

- Uncompromising concern for the underprivileged
- Human dignity
- Belief in human capacity nee potential
- Gender equity

- Inclusiveness, empowerment and justice.
- A fairness, deep honesty and integrity of purpose, discipline, creativity and innovation, accountability and transparency, quality products and services, ecological sensitivity among others-

In brief, it is a utopian paradigm in sustainable human development that I believe in!

Let us state a clear mission statement: "The visible and invisible objectives should include, among other things, higher aspirations for the ultra poor, higher need responsiveness, a scientific temperament in the process of changing lives, sustainability, and off course a cathartic training of trainers towards helping the poor empower themselves..."

43

Giving Voice to the Poor

(IN DECISIONS AFFECTING THEIR LIVES-A NEED FOR GREATER GLOBAL DECENTRALIZATION)

"I'm not an actor, I'm not a star,
And I don't even have my own car,
But I'm hoping so much...
..that you will love me anyway"

That *you* will love me anyway...

How do *you matter ..?*

Your decisions have no legally binding force for governments, or in any manner whatsoever carry the weight of world opinion or the moral authority of the world community...

You're not Nelson Mandela *or Wangari Maathai*
Bill Clinton or Hillary Clinton
The Dalai Lama *or Aung San Suu Kyi*
Noam Chomsky or Nafis Sadik
A Greenspan *or Benazir Bhutto*
Bill Gates or Condoleezza Rice
Steve Jobs *or Irene Khan*
Bishop Desmond Tutu or Shirin Ebadi
Richard Branson *or Angela Merkel*
George Soros or Margaret Thatcher
Kofi Annan *or Gro Harlem Brundtland*

(Or, maybe yes, **Kofi Annan**..*you are the change you see in good old me..)*

Kofi Annan...*my mind has already taken me to the imposing (though not an imposter!) secretariat building of the UN headquarters in...well! I guess I'm writing for elite, enlightened readership!*

44

UN Works

(THE UNITED NATIONS WORKS FOR EVERYONE)
(A NEED FOR REFORM)

And, Trygve Lie...and the Nobel Peace Prize goes to **Kofi Annan...***would you stop dreaming, little girl..?*

And, Dag Hammarskjold...you were brilliant on the Congo mission, until we lost you while you were valiantly pursuing your mission...would you stop dreaming..?

And, U Thant..can we restore democracy to Burma..? Now, you are simply trying' our patience..?

And, Kurt Waldheim...I thought 'possible' was actually a word found in the dictionary of Napoleon Bonaparte (and, who might we be, if I may ask?), so. beat the Alps!

And, Javier Perez de Cuellar...of Boca Jr in Argentina, Favelas in Brazil, and, elections in Peru...wouldn't you love living the Latin American experience?...you think you can change the world, try and change yourself first!

And, Boutros Boutros-Ghali...I think I saw him visiting an orphanage in Riyadh, or was it Cairo...what rubbish! Said my friends ...you're always imagining! Let me see, or, perhaps, I was just looking at a picture of him in Time/ Span...some American magazine!

And, **Kofi Annan!** *And,* **the UN at 60!** *And,* **the UN marathon, its everybody's marathon!**

Somewhere deep in the confines of the forest, a little girl is reading and writing because the light of education has reached her...because the UN has intervened...

Doesn't matter, time to make some fun (of the world body) ...(big laugh!)... I don't guess the UN would collapse!

And, ***UNESCO****...and, education, science and culture and tolerance, peaceful co-existence, international co-operation and global un-der (their)-standing;*

And, ***UNHCHR****...and human rights, from food on our tables to (Saddam and Milosevic and Abu Ghraib and Guantanamo) genocide, war crimes and international war crimes tribunals for and against former Yugoslavia and Rwanda and crimes against humanity;*

And, ***UNICEF****... and our children..and those undernourished, emaciated, laboring in those football and carpet and fireworks factories and simply out of school, our world's future and those people just sitting there tight..pathetic! Deplorable;*

And, ***UNHCR****...and the world's 'no-one's': Our refugees, asylum seekers and internally-displaced persons, I have complete sympathy for their cause, we, the peoples of the world have put such our (unable to) 'able' representatives in "power"!*

And, ***WHO****...and 40-km away nearest health clinics ('centers' of dollar-paid doctors!) and pregnant women allowed to die in labour, and no preventive measures but epidemics and quarantine and sanctions and utter collapse and vaccines for typhoid and polio and measles and pox and Denis Halliday resigned in protest!... (I'm taking you back, it's the "time machine": Well, that's my gene!); and the scourge (read Sub-Saharan!) that is HIV+AIDS!*

(And, dreaming! ***UNDW****...United Nations whatever for drinking water..)*

And, ***UNEP****...and climate change and global warming... (and Tuvalu and Bangkok sinking!), earthquakes and tsunamis and forest fires! And, floods in the Philippines and Midnapore (India)and post-disaster restructuring and reconstruction, but no constructive pre-disaster warning*

systems or assessment or audits or whatever..and, no systematic renewable energy plan...and, Maurice Strong's "strong"words to humanity but more in number and style elaborate cars! No heed to greenhouses and HFC's and polar ice caps melting...

*(**UNCC**... United Nations Commission to Ensure Comfort: Pray! How much more comfort do we greedy mortal beings need when at this moment, a little flower called a 'child' is* scavenging *for subsistence out of a trash can, and another child is being born as a* cretin *because his mother's diet lacked iodine)*

[I must say that discrimination begins before birth]

*And, **UNICAO**: United Nations conference / convention attending organization! All they need do is 'fly' to attend..those glamorous conferences and conventions and workshops and meetings...and God knows what others!*

(And, maybe we could form some sort of a "conglomerate of cows") (laugh!)

*And, **INSTRAW and UNIFEM**..I beg to reserve my comments, I am a woman after all! I must confess that nothing much is clear to me...*

*And, **FAO**...the "food attempting organisation"..and, malnourished or undernourished children, parents selling their 'estates'and 'bodies' in a sincere attempt to ensure a 'one-time meal' for their families, it hurts!*

*And, **UNDP**... 'dreaming'...Mark Malloch Brown and Baaba Maal and the **"millennium development goals 2015"**...*

*And, **ILO**..."in the name of dignity of labor and labor specialization, we seriously intend to keep people where they are...these I would call not labor standards, but double standards.."*

*And, **UN Maritime and Space**..its '**world contact day**', who cares about our millennium development goals 2015..lets call all occupants of interplanetary craft..practise*

*the moon, the stars and the galaxy..***how do they matter,** *those* **earthly starvation deaths?**

And, IMF and the World Bank (IBRD)... *'dreaming'..forget about famine and entitlements, the Dow Jones is more important...(what indecisive indices!) let money seep through (let there be corruption, Transparency International aghast!), let us dictate terms..let us also ensure that families get displaced in the wake of dams and other multi-purpose projects...*

And, ***UN—HABITAT****..."dreaming"...green (houses) for the poor, low-cost sanitary latrines and a place to live a decent life...'Habitat for Humanity scandalized...'*

And, **IAEA***..spends its time supporting people that chase WMDs...*

And, finally, **UNU***..churns out every year..."thesis brains with very little or no capacity towards constructive action..."*

Cryin' "we need to reform ourselves"...talking of ***UN reforms...***

(1) We need to **sensitize** *ourselves towards greater awareness of the UN;*

(2) We need to prove to ourselves that the world body is of continued ***relevance;***

(3) **We need to educate** *ourselves about the role of the UN in global futures;*

(4) We need to look afresh at the work, particularly, the **achievements** *of the UN not only in having averted a Third World War, something we would call "peacekeeping", but also, development, democratization, human rights and humanitarianism, and ecological sustainability, to name just a few;*

(5) We need to and perhaps could assess the organization in terms of the ***"lives it has touched"*** *(worldwide) and in however insignificant a manner;*

(6) We need to deepen our ***understanding*** *of the UN particularly among children and the youth;*

(7) We need to realize that following the **Cold War** *period, the world lost some important ideology...and now is a less safer place, thanks to some indeed very negative ethnic overtures, some catastrophic disquietude arising from serious inequities of wealth and income between and within nations, also some major depletion of the earth's resources thanks to unhealthy exploitation and consequent grave ecological concern, poverty and hunger and armed conflict again within and between nations;*

(8) We need to ***revamp*** *the world body to the extent that every member of the planet ought made feel important, from the brick-kiln laborer to the night-soil picker to the sex-worker to those that are disabled or in any way disadvantaged or dysfunction, even if that should involve either shifting of HQ's and/or* ***decentralization****...*

(9) I often wonder whether or not I should concentrate on ***reforming myself*** *rather than 'dreaming' about reforming the UN, things that are really not of much consequence to most people...*

(10) "Inconsequential"...but the UN is 'determined to save succeeding generations from the ***scourge of war****..and to reaffirm faith in fundamental human rights,* **in the dignity and worth of the human person**, *in the equal rights of ..nations large and small,...and to promote social progress and better standards of life in larger* **freedom**,*..and to practice tolerance and live together in peace with one another..'.*

45

The World Social Forum Agenda

SOCIAL AND ECONOMIC PROGRESS OF NATIONS-THE THIRD WORLD

A MORE TOLERANT GENERATION, A MORE PEACEFUL GENERATION

Organizers called one event the largest gathering of world leaders in history. In early September 2000, more than 150 heads of state converged on New York City for the United Nations' "Millennium Summit." During three days of meetings, the leaders tried to address the most pressing problems of the new century. At the end of the 20th century—inarguably the bloodiest in human history—the summit was remarkable in that conflict and war did not dominate center stage. Instead, the heads of state focused their rhetoric on the problems of widespread poverty, the AIDS epidemic, environmental destruction, and the lack of education for millions of the world's children.

"The statistics of poverty and inequality in our world are shocking and shameful," Prime Minister Bertie Ahern of Ireland said. "Half the world's population struggling on less than $2 a day, over half a billion on less than $1. A quarter of a billion children of 14 and under working, sometimes in terrible conditions. Death from preventable and treatable diseases—10 people will die of malaria in the five minutes I take to address you."

As each speaker came before the UN General Assembly, one after the other noted that the increasing interconnectedness of the world means that—questions of morality aside—the wealthy nations cannot afford to ignore the world's deepening social injustice.

"The wishes of the developing world are simple," Nigerian President Olusegun Obasanjo, Chairman of the Group of 77, a forum for developing nations, said. "We are all living in the same house, whether you are developed or not developed. What we are saying is that some of us in this house are living in superluxurious rooms; others are living in something not better than an unkempt kitchen where pipes are leaking and there is no toilet. We are saying, 'Look, in the interest of all of us, let us living in the superluxurious rooms pay a bit of attention to those who are living where the pipes are leaking, or we'll all be badly affected."

Magnitude of the problem:

Human Rights is for the people, by the people, of the people. Our world's future hangs precariously..Lopsided development and rampant consumerism have widened the chasm between the world's rich and the world's poor. We have witnessed a gross violation of human rights across the globe. Millions of the world's CHILDREN still cling precariously to life. About 40,000 of them die every day due to preventable causes-hunger, disease, war and neglect. Women in the developing world face gross inequities in food and nutrition, income (s) and opportunity. Terrorism is devastating large parts of the globe. Millions of the world's people lack access to safe drinking water, decent health care, shelter, education, and means of communication and jobs. The task of ending world hunger remains formidable. Increasing population pressures, deforestation and desertification are eating away our precious natural resources. Many countries face the 'darker' side of development, "Debt". War and disease are forcing millions to flee their home countries. And, indigenous people all over the world are becoming fast endangered under pressure from the forces of global expansion. Also, there are those innocent people being sexually abused, raped or mutilated (as in war). Drugs, alcohol, poor mental health, juvenile delinquency and HIV/AIDS are taking a heavy toll. Pollution is now a

major health hazard. The ozone layers are getting depleted. And the Earth is warming up...

What we need today is sound vision coupled with forceful, efficient and effective policies and a firm commitment to the eradication of POVERTY and its attendant ills. The time has come in the history of nations to liberate their peoples from centuries of illiteracy, ignorance, POVERTY, disease and war.

Concerns leading to this global issue (>>as to why there is food insecurity, why such state of affairs, “Garibi Hatao” changes sarcastically to “Garib Hatao”, why inequality is growing complemented with wider eliticism, why there is economic inequality and rural poverty, is population explosion the only reason, what is the responsibility of the Govt., why there is a discrimination between a boy child and a girl child, why female infanticides are rampant in some parts of our country, why there is under nutrition and high death rate among children, what is poverty line and endemic hunger, is shortage of food produced- a cause or an effect, why store food grains and allow food to rot or get eaten away by rodents, who controls the pricing, is the public distribution system ineffective and corrupt because of connivance, why major initiatives like “food for work”, “mid day meal” fail, what are the employment opportunities amongst the rural poor, why social awareness thru media coverage is not made mandatory, what are the current challenges facing mankind, what legal experts and social activists have to say on these etc. etc >>) are endless.

Why, who, when, what, where??? Really mind boggling.

But still there is hope!!!

Socio economic rights

Socio-economic rights: Food, shelter, education and health >> how they all are bound to uphold dignity

Socio economic rights >food and health:

«In a world overflowing with riches, it is a outrageous scandal that more than 826 million people suffer hunger and malnutrition and that every year over 36 million die of starvation and related causes. We must take urgent action now.»-

—Jean Ziegler, April 2001, UN Special Rapporteur on the Right to Food.

Food: a fundamental human right: despite the fact that the right to food is recognized directly or indirectly by all countries in the world, hunger, whether caused by war, drought, natural disaster or poverty, continues to cause widespread suffering. And poverty, one of the causes of hunger, is also a consequence of it. Hunger dulls intellects and thwarts productivity, keeping entire societies from realizing their potential. For poor families in developing countries, hunger-related illness adds to household costs and increases the burden of care for healthy family members often already struggling for subsistence. When this hardship is multiplied by millions of families worldwide, it creates a devastating ripple effect that imperils global development. At the 1996 World Food Summit, leaders from 185 countries and the European Community reaffirmed, in the Rome Declaration on World Food Security, "the right of everyone to have access to safe and nutritious food, consistent with the right to adequate food and the fundamental right of everyone to be free from hunger." They further pledged to cut the number of the world's hungry people in half by 2015.Eradicating hunger is not merely a lofty ideal. Ensuring the right to adequate food and the fundamental right to be free from hunger is a matter of international law, specifically enshrined in a number of human rights instruments to which states around the world have committed themselves. What is the right to food? Since its inception, the United Nations has identified access to adequate food as both an individual right and a collective responsibility. The 1948 Universal Declaration of Human

Rights proclaimed that "everyone has the right to a standard of living adequate for the health and well-being of himself and his family, including food?" Nearly 20 years later, the International Covenant on Economic, Social and Cultural Rights (1966) developed these concepts more fully, stressing "the right of everyone to adequate food" and specifying "the fundamental right of everyone to be free from hunger". So, what is the distinction between the right to be free from hunger and the right to adequate food? The right to freedom from hunger is fundamental. This means that the state has an obligation to ensure, at the very least, that people do not starve. As such, this right is intrinsically linked to the right to life. In addition, however, states should also do everything possible to promote full enjoyment of the right to adequate food for everyone within their territory — in other words, people should have physical and economic access at all times to food that is adequate in quantity and quality for a healthy and active life. For food to be considered adequate it must also be culturally acceptable and it must be produced in a manner that is environmentally and socially sustainable. Finally, its provision should not interfere with the enjoyment of other human rights — for example, the acquisition of sufficient food for an adequate diet should not be so costly as to threaten the satisfaction of other socio-economic rights, or be fulfilled to the detriment of civil and political rights. The rights connection and the civil, cultural, economic, political and social rights proclaimed in the Universal Declaration are considered interdependent, interrelated, indivisible and equally important. To be able to enjoy the right to food fully, people need access to health care and education, respect for their cultural values, the right to own property and the right to organize themselves economically and politically. Without adequate food, people cannot lead healthy, active lives. They are not employable. They cannot care for their children, and their children cannot learn to read and write. The right to food cuts across

the entire spectrum of human rights. Its fulfilment is essential to the fight against poverty, and it is at the heart of FAO's mandate to ensure.

Cuban President Fidel Castro says "..Hunger is the offspring of injustice and the unequal distribution of the wealth in this world.... What kind of magical solutions are we going to provide so that in 20 years from now there will be 400 million instead of 800 million starving people?... Let the truth prevail, and not hypocrisy and deceit."

Sustainable development must be achieved at every level of society.... Governments ... should ... [promote] food security and ... food self-sufficiency within the context of sustainable agriculture.... All countries need to assess ... the impacts of [economic] policies on ... food security.... The major thrust of food security ... is to ... increase ... agricultural production in a sustainable way and to achieve a substantial improvement in people's entitlement to adequate food.

Socio Economic Rights >Education:

The first Minister of Education, Mr. Zalman Shazar, who later became the third President of Israel, eloquently addressed the Knesset upon the enactment of the *law (the* Compulsory Education Law, 1949 *which guaranteed all citizens and residents of Israel the right to a free education until twelfth grade, and compulsory education until tenth grade within the public school system).*

"In reality, the Government is introducing a law, which is, in principle, already in effect in Israel. The majority of the Jewish localities in Israel are already accustomed to compulsory education, notwithstanding the absence of any laws on the subject. ....and already statistics indicate that 90% of our children attend schools. I believe that such a situation is extremely rare, namely, that a nation can say about itself that 90% of its sons and daughters are enrolled in schools without any compulsory education laws compelling them to be there."

What a noble approach to Human Rights!!!

Constitutions of many countries around the globe prohibits both the State and private parties from discriminating unfairly against anyone on a range of grounds, including race, gender, sex, pregnancy, marital status, ethnic or social origin, colour, sexual orientation, age, disability, religion, conscience, belief, culture, language and birth.

In order to make this right real and effective, the Constitution requires the State to enact national legislation to prevent or prohibit unfair discrimination.

We need to introspect whether this is true at all places. We need to ponder only on educational front and no other ground. Women and girl children are prohibited from going to schools to have basic education. It is ONLY the boy child who has the right and prerogative to have education. But why??

Experience in several countries has shown that a good general education, which the formal school system should be able to provide, considerably increases the ability of the individual to benefit from later training. It is also an essential factor in development of human being .Even concept of organizing, leadership, ability to take decision, upholding the high level of integrity and value system and management within the limited resources depends on the quality and level of formal education received by individuals. Education opens up the "inner eye" and has an important bearing on thinking, attitude, happiness, enjoyment and quality of life.

Studies have shown that the benefits of increasing education and training to rural women are abundant and far-reaching. In patriarchal societies, this is a taboo and always a deterrent factor. Hampering the potential or skill of women and girl children is a step backwards from the goal of poverty alleviation. Education does not mean imparting knowledge at the masters or PhD Level. This means at the

grass root concepts for improving the quality of life. Some of the areas which need to be looked into are, if the society at large is to progress:

1. **General Educational Skills:** Literacy, arithmetic, local/national language (reading/writing), name signature, communication, an elementary understanding of science and the importance of the immediate environment.
2. **Community:** local and national institutions and processes, local and national governments, cooperatives, organizing community projects, being aware of rights (free association, access to land and other natural resources, etc.),bank operations as deposit and withdrawal etc.
3. **Agriculture and Farming:** more modern, efficient and environmentally sustainable farming practices, simple financial management, basic economics (assessment of market trends and consumer needs).
4. **Family Health**: nutrition, food security, family planning, HIV/AIDS prevention.

The education process takes a community effort and in turn is communally beneficial. Enriching women's general skills opens up the channels of communication, allowing knowledge to spread throughout the community and to the younger generation. Studies have shown that this community education to women and children have enhanced the "self esteem and ego" of each one of the members of the community and is working as a new and rejuvenated energizer.

Releasing Untapped Potential

According to a World Bank study, when female farmers were allowed access to a primary school education, farming yield increased by 24%. Allowing women to enrich their skills in farming implies an improvement in farm operations and productivity. They are taught to enlist more efficient procedures and technologies in crop selection, storage,

processing, animal husbandry, etc., permitting more time for other responsibilities such as family care, home maintenance and off-farm income generating activities.

More knowledge of market demand and the economy allows for more economically sound decision-making in terms of crop selection, technology selection and capital allocation. The result is less waste following a harvest and the more efficient allocation of time and of farm resources (labour, raw materials, machinery). Enhanced storage and processing skills will further reduce waste and help make the most of crop surpluses.

Additional benefits have come in the form of:

Food Security and Family Health

Advancing Rights, stimulating Sustainable Growth

Communication: For today and for the future

Fuel the engine of change through collective efforts

"We must realize the infinite results that can be achieved through the investment in the female rural community."

(Source: Article from IFAP Standing Committee on Women in Agriculture Mrs Victoria Kakoko Sebagereka, a woman farmer from Uganda. More information: http://www.ifap.org/issues/womeninag.html)

Unquote

Socio economic rights >shelter:

Homeless and isolated in a cold world

Shelter for all

An international coalition for the homeless

The world today is still grappling with unmet basic housing needs of millions and millions of its citizens who still live in sub-human conditions on pavements, in squatter settlements, railway platforms, metro tunnels, foot paths, bastis, parks, gardens, jhuggies, buildings under

construction or unauthorized slums and are under constant threat of being evicted/battered/raped/killed/sexually abused and what not with out the slightest concern of the authorities concerned. The picture is the same in developed countries as well as in developing/underdeveloped and Third World countries across the globe and also be it in cities like New York, London, Cape Town, Shanghai, Mumbai and Dhaka.

In India, one of the first, and perhaps most important, housing rights cases to go up to the Supreme Court in India was the Olga Tellis case in 1985. This petition to the Bombay High Court was in the form of public interest litigation by thousands of pavement dwellers of Bombay city. The petitioners argued that they could not be evicted from their squalid shelters without being offered alternative accommodation. They further argued that they had chosen a pavement or slum to live in only because it was nearest to their place of work, and that evicting them would result in depriving them of their livelihood. The petitioners (living in around more than 10,000 hutments) were to be evicted under the Bombay Municipal Corporation Act, which empowered the Municipal Commissioner to remove encroachments on footpaths or pavements over which the public have a right of passage or access.

In South Africa, in 1998, Mrs Irene Grootboom and many other households were living in Wallacedene, an informal settlement in the Western Cape Province, under deplorable conditions. All the households in Wallacedene lived in shacks without water, sewage or refuse removal services; only 5% of the shacks had electricity and the area was partly waterlogged. Most of the residents of Wallacedene had apparently applied for subsidised low-cost housing from the municipality and many had been on the waiting list for as long as seven years.

In September 1998 Mrs Irene Grootboom and 390 adults and 510 children could no longer tolerate the conditions they lived under in Wallacedene and, in

desperation, moved out and occupied vacant land that was privately owned and had been earmarked for low-cost housing. They erected their shacks and shelters on the land, which they called "New Rust" (New Rest). Like many similar unlawful occupiers of land, Mrs Grootboom and her community were evicted through a court order and their homes were bulldozed and their possessions burnt: conduct reminiscent of apartheid-style evictions, according to the Constitutional Court.

However, this was followed by a landmark judgement.

The decision of the Honourable Court was considered a land mark in "Socio-economic rights for shelter to uphold dignity to Mrs Grootboom and her community in provision of permanent accommodation, or basic nutrition, shelter, healthcare and social services for the children of the affected community. The order granted by the court was that the children should be provided with shelter and should be accommodated together with their parents until the parents are able to provide appropriate shelter for their children."

Legal Aspects/Responsibility of Nation/State

On December 10, 1948 the General Assembly of the United Nations adopted and proclaimed the Universal Declaration of Human Rights..Following this historic act the Assembly called upon all Member countries to publicize the text of the Declaration and "to cause it to be disseminated, displayed, read and expounded principally in schools and other educational institutions, without distinction based on the political status of countries or territories."

4.1 Responsibility of Nation/State >>

After the *"preamble"*... **the General Assembly proclaims this Universal Declaration of Human Rights** as a common standard of achievement for all peoples and all **nations**, to the end that every individual and every organ of society, keeping this Declaration constantly in mind, shall strive by teaching and education to promote respect

for these rights and freedoms and by progressive measures, national and international, to secure their universal and effective recognition and observance, both among the peoples of **Member States themselves and among the peoples of territories under their jurisdiction.**

Article 1 starts with "..All human beings are born free and equal in dignity and rights. They are endowed with reason and conscience and should act towards one another in a spirit of brotherhood" and ends with Article 30 "..Nothing in this Declaration may be interpreted as implying for any State, group or person any right to engage in any activity or to perform any act aimed at the destruction of any of the rights and freedoms set forth herein..".

Food /Health /Housing >> *Article 25.*

(1) Everyone has the right to a standard of living adequate for the **health** and well-being of himself and of his family, including **food**, clothing, **housing** and medical care and necessary social services, and the right to security in the event of unemployment, sickness, disability, widowhood, old age or other lack of livelihood in circumstances beyond his control.

Education >>*Article 26.*

(1) Everyone has the right to **education.** Education shall be free, at least in the elementary and fundamental stages. Elementary education shall be compulsory. Technical and professional education shall be made generally available and higher education shall be equally accessible to all on the basis of merit.

(2) Education shall be directed to the full development of the human personality and to the strengthening of respect for human rights and fundamental freedoms. It shall promote understanding, tolerance and friendship among all nations, racial or religious groups, and shall further the activities of the United Nations for the maintenance of peace.

(3) Parents have a prior right to choose the kind of education that shall be given to their children.

Based on Universal Declaration, how to address local issues agreed Globally

Work by Organizations:

Currently there are thousands of organizations across the globe at the International and National level and NGOs working towards these goals addressing Human Rights issues, be it in the areas of food and food security, education, health and health care, housing, safe drinking water availability, sanitation, personal and community hygiene, HIV/AIDS and other disease prevention, women empowerment, HR violation issues and redressal, counseling, child abuse, gender discrimination, female infanticide ,economic upliftment, sexual abuse of innocent people, rape or mutilation (as in war), drug abuse and alcohol, poor mental health, juvenile delinquency ,pollution, global warming etc and myriads of such issues however trivial which in some form or the other violates the "RIGHT TO LIVE DECENTLY". It is a Herculean task no doubt but all of us in the individual capacity have a role towards this and as the poet said>>>

The woods are lovely, dark and deep,
But I have promises to keep,
And miles to go before I sleep,
And miles to go before I sleep.

- Robert Frost

Soft Human Rights Issues

As has been said, enough work has been done but still a lot of work needs to be done on many softer issues, some of which are as:

- Are Legal Rulings Enough for Victims of Food and Shelter
- Psycho-Social Effects of gender bias on education
- Mental Health Effects on sustained fights against food security

- Socio economic impact on adverse sex ratio
- Refugees >What impact it causes on existing food system
- Street Children>Are they social parasites??

LOOKING TOWARDS SUSTAINABILITY

Some opine that Human Rights is a closed system. The author is of the opinion that it is neither a CLOSED nor an internal system. New problems and new circumstances require new solutions and interpretations. It may very well be that we need to improve the net of human rights conventions with new strands. Most importantly, we need to supervise the existing conventions more efficiently. This means, for example, that people need to be better informed about human rights and the possibility of protection they bring with them. We also have to make sure that the international organization dealing with individual complaints can continue their work.

One dimension in the credible control of the human rights is the identification of the quarters that are responsible for human rights violations and making these quarters confront the legal consequences of their actions. As states are the contracting parties in human rights conventions, it is clear from the view point of the international monitoring organs that if a regional or local self-government organization or an individual official has violated human rights, the state is responsible. The state is equally responsible for the neglect of its positive obligations to act if it, for example, delegates its duties to private enterprises and this results in the decrease of human rights protection.

The division of responsibility may turn out to be different at the national level. This is often called the horizontal effect, which means that responsibility is focused on individuals and their relations.

The primary means by which a state can ensure the realization of human rights in individual relations, is by enacting laws which prohibit violations. But maybe even

more important than the criminal responsibility is to consider if an individual should be at least liable to pay damages if he intentionally impedes the realization of another person's human rights.

Apportioning individual responsibility for the most flagrant human rights violations is being considered and put into practice at the international level, too. Successfully setting-up functioning machinery for establishing responsibility for flagrant human rights violations would be proof on the part of the international community that human rights are being taken seriously.

CONCLUSION

"Humanity is indeed a family...I hope that people all over the world... Will realize they share similar experiences. Then they might think, this is our world, we better take care of it."

- Ken Heyman

"We shall require a substantially new manner of thinking if mankind is to survive."

Albert Einstein

"The development of a kind heart (a feeling of closeness for all human beings)... Is for anyone who considers himself or herself, above all, a member of the human family and who sees things from this larger and longer perspective".

The Dalai Lama, from "A Human Approach to World Peace".

46

Kennedy, Eleanor and King, Marx and Engels

GANDHI REMAINS RELEVANT - LESSONS IN NON VIOLENCE

"..What difference does it make to the dead, the orphans, and the homeless, whether the mad destruction is wrought under the name of totalitarianism or the holy name of liberty and democracy..?"

MAHATMA GANDHI

Writes Pierre Zanre, a 18 year old girl student from Burkina Faso, Africa-

"When people no longer buy weapons,
When people no longer sell weapons,
When society parties are no longer held,
When hospitals are less full,
When school attendance rises,
When children know the joy of living,
When parents can procreate without worrying,
When people give to receive,
When people receive to give,
When people work for other people...
Then I can say that I am in a humane society."

Gandhi's words, ideas, actions and vision have always meant a lot to people around the world, and so to me! I always use them for guidance in my daily life!

Gandhian Economics and Gandhian Futurism: Gandhi espoused an economic theory of self-sufficiency and simplicity. He envisioned an India that would focus on meeting the needs of a democratic citizenry prior to generating wealth and industrializing!

To practice Gandhi today: one must set upon the same personal journey to seek the truth and build one's life around it. It is not necessary to be austere! But undergoing personal challenges, travails (and I have gone through some life difficulties myself!) and the testing of one's spirit, resolve and fundamental values is a definitive element.

Relevance of Gandhian trusteeship as an "instrument of human dignity": Gandhian ideals are most certainly relevant to modern polity! Gandhi is relevant!

The great man had perspicacious understanding of the Indian countryside, and strongly felt that the key to the country's progress lay in the strengthening of the decentralized self-sufficient village economies! Gandhi is meant to be carried forward!

47

I Do Not Know Much About Albert Luthuli

BUT I HAVE BEEN CERTAINLY INSPIRED BY THE WORDS OF NELSON MANDELA

"..But as long as injustice and inequality persist in our world, none of us can truly rest. We must become stronger still...

Like slavery and Apartheid, poverty is not natural. It is people who have made poverty and tolerated poverty, and it is people who will overcome it.

Overcoming poverty is not a gesture of charity. It is an act of justice. It is the protection of fundamental human rights.

Everyone everywhere has the right to live with dignity; free from fear and oppression, free from hunger and thirst, and free to express themselves and associate at will.

Yet in this new century, millions of people remain imprisoned, enslaved and in chains.

Massive poverty and ***inequality*** are such terrible scourges of our times – times in which the world also boasts breathtaking advances in science, technology, industry and wealth accumulation.

While poverty persists, there is no true freedom...

People living in poverty have the least access to power to shape policies – to shape their future. But they have the right to a voice. They must not be made to sit in silence as 'development' happens around them, at their expense.

True development is impossible without the participation of those concerned.

Take the right to housing. Three million people in Africa have been evicted since the turn of the century from informal settlements.

We have also seen in Africa the scourge of HIV/AIDS, decimating the lives of our people, especially those living in poverty. All of us – rich and poor, governments, companies and individuals – share the responsibility to ensure everyone has access to information, means of prevention, and treatment. And our starting point must be respect for individuals' rights.

We know that it is the already marginalised who are most affected by HIV/AIDS. And we know that within this group, women are marginalised yet more and bear the most significant burden. As daughters, mothers, sisters and grandmothers, every day they experience and live out the reality of this pandemic.

Women are also being killed by other preventable causes. One woman dies every minute from deaths relating to pregnancy. And where do almost all these women live? In the developing world – in poverty.

This balance of power, and the broader one it represents, must be shifted.

There is a need for a turning point. What I want to see is an environment where the young people of our country have a real chance to develop the inherent possibilities they have to create a better life for themselves..That is what development is about..."

48

Eaters of the World, Unite

THE IMPORTANCE OF HUMAN DEVELOPMENT

"Out of each dollar you spend on groceries, only 19 cents goes to the farmer, with corporate middlemen grabbing the rest"

Excerpts from Jim Hightower Article about where the food industry is going

Mother Teresa had said, **"A family which eats together, prays together, stays together".** This may sound simple but has the basis ethos of Human development - the very purpose of existence. She talked of the basic needs ***(eats together)*** which is physical. She talked of the sublime needs ***(prays together)*** and talked finally on the most important social needs ***(stays together).***

The greatest challenge globally to all of us in the 21st century lies in the quest for an understanding and a cure of the issues confronting mankind: Human development. Is human development a problem or a solution???

What ever it is, the magnitude of it is enormous and vast... But if the attempts bring about smiles on a few faces on this earth, we, the current generation, have done a bit. The issues and the realities of survival of the poor and the marginalized are very touching and therefore even the deep concern for the humankind on these are but a small step towards this larger issue.

Every day, around the globe, thousands of people go

through the traumatic circumstances of one or the other. Lopsided development and rampant consumerism have widened the chasm between the worlds's rich and the world's poor. We have witnessed a gross violation of human rights across the globe. Millions of the world's children still cling precariously to life. About 40,000 of them die every day due to preventable causes-hunger, disease, neglect. Women in the developing world face gross inequities in food and nutrition etc. Millions of the world's people lack access to safe drinking water, decent health care, shelter, education to name a few.

The task of ending world hunger remains formidable. Increasing population pressures, deforestation and desertification are eating away our precious natural resources. War, disease, terrorism are forcing millions to flee their home countries. And, indigenous people all over the world are becoming fast endangered under pressure from the forces of global expansion. Innocent people are being sexually abused, raped or mutilated (as in war). Drugs, alcohol, poor mental health, juvenile delinquency and TB/HIV/AIDS are taking a heavy toll. We need to act urgently on some of the most pressing issues like massive population growth, poverty, hunger and human rights abuses.

The time has come in the history of nations to liberate people from centuries of illiteracy, ignorance, poverty and disease as a step towards: ***Family Nutrition and Human Development.***

The World's underprivileged need food, shelter, medicine, education, peace, sympathy, empathy, economic rehabilitation for the middle aged and social rehabilitation for aged people and above all LOVE ...

We all share a responsibility for the planet on the above thought provoking and challenging, global issues and concerns. There is a challenge for all of us–individuals, policy makers, governments, civil society and the corporate sectors.

And so they all sing...

"It is better to light just one little candle than to stumble in the dark......

All you need is a tiny spark...

And the world will be free..."

Let us all start with a vision of a sustainable world leading to human development. Let us relegate poverty to history! Let us work towards a future that is economically, socially and ecologically viable for all, in other words "sustainable".

This is not just a step towards "family nutrition and human development" but in my view, shall bring about the "New Human Revolution"...

49

My Millennium Development Goals – My MDGs

WHY SET GOALS WHEN WE CAN ACHIEVE THEM OUTRIGHT?

Our global challenge

The Millennium Development Goals are an ambitious agenda for reducing poverty and improving lives that world leaders agreed on at the **Millennium Summit** in September 2000. For each goal one or more targets have been set, most for 2015, using 1990 as a benchmark:

1. Eradicate extreme poverty and hunger; establish an international Coalition for the Homeless (the vast international mass of the destitute, the vulnerable, the ill and street children):

Target for 2015: Halve the proportion of people living on less than a dollar a day and those who suffer from hunger.

More than a billion people still live on less than US$1 a day: Sub-Saharan Africa, Latin America and the Caribbean, and parts of Europe and Central Asia are falling short of the poverty target.

The goal of halving the proportion of people living on less than a dollar a day has been set for long. We ought to be more ambitious.

2. Make it mandatory for countries to divert a part of their spending on arms to health and education. Give incentives to cut down on small arms production.

Sometimes, violence can escalate into war, the beginning of arms and armies...

3. Achieve universal primary education

Target for 2015: Ensure that all boys and girls complete primary school.

As many as 113 million children do not attend school, but the target is within reach. India, for example, should have 95 percent of its children in school by 2005.

Set up goals to ensure that children are not out of school; establish a fund to give incentives to poor parents to send their children to school. Child labor should be high on the agenda.

4. Promote gender equality and empower women

Targets for 2005 and 2015: Eliminate gender disparities in primary and secondary education preferably by 2005, and at all levels by 2015. Reduce the incidence of trafficking.

Two-thirds of illiterates are women, and the rate of employment among women is two-thirds that of men. The proportion of seats in parliaments held by women is increasing, reaching about one third in Argentina, Mozambique and South Africa.

Birth control and reproductive rights and technologies; HIV/AIDS; gender and sexism

"..Enlighten men and empower women. Then you will truly achieve..."

A few of these issues merit our attention:

- **Abortion:** I am reminded of the massive debate in America and the Catholic Church;
- **Pregnancy and childbirth:** For many women in the developing world, this is a difficult proposition;
- **Living with HIV/AIDS:** Consider the stigma and pain that is a part of this condition;
- **Scared at school:** Human rights organizations

have reported widespread sexual violence against girls in South African schools;

- **Sex education:** Has always got sacked;
- **Sexual harassment:** Has become the order of the day in the corporate world;
- **The sexual victimization of women:** Is something I would associate with corporate globalization;
- **Slavery and human trafficking:** In young girls and women must be put an end to;
- **Domestic violence:** Is sometimes the silent ordeal millions of women go through;
- **Women with disabilities:** The stigma is dual, being a woman and being disabled;
- **Violence against women in times of war:** Rape has continually being used as a weapon of power by the male species, this is again what I would term 'serious inequality in gender', trying war crimes, genocide and crimes against humanity helps but the root causes of gender-based discriminatory violence have to be addressed;
- **Male bashing on TV:** Article "warning for our male readers: The following article contains big words and complex sentences. It might be a good idea to have a woman nearby to explain it to you"
- **Male rape in U.S. Prisons:** This HRW report charges that indifference and even feigned ignorance on the part of prison authorities are responsible for the widespread existence of male prisoner-on-prisoner violence in U.S. Prisons
- **Survivors First:** Is someone in the neighborhood a convicted child molester?

Living with HIV/AIDS

I am human, a person first,

And, fallacy (of fallacious reasoning)

Thy (my!) name is human,

So what if I err?

Because to err is (absolutely) human!

"So, what do you tell a bride in an arranged marriage, whose husband confesses he is HIV-positive and whose in-laws still expect grandchildren? ..It is recommended that they opt for in –vitro fertilization using sperm from an uninfected donor so the husband will not infect his wife..It is often wiser to match HIV tests than to match horoscopes..You are saving the next generation...

Protecting the unborn child is most important..like if the mother took a course of Active Retroviral Drugs (ARV), before delivery and by going in for an elective Caesarean section..."

Wise Choice, and somewhat close to the truth!

"Every time I say 'right' (instead of wrong) to a human being, I confer upon him an inalienable right, actually, enable him assert something that already exists for him! I 'free' him to choose for himself, his choice...

Endorsement of the other person's "right to make his choice" is, I believe, the best thing one could ever do for one's fellow human beings..it would save mankind all that trouble...food for thought, right?"

And, I'm taking your minds back (or, rather forward!) to the year 1948...

5. Reduce child mortality

Target for 2015: Reduce by two thirds the mortality rate among children under five.

Every year nearly 11 million young children die before their fifth birthday, mainly from preventable illnesses, but that number is down from 15 million in 1980.

Give priority over space exploration to chronic child poverty research.

6. Improve maternal health

Target for 2015: Reduce by three-quarters the ratio of women dying in childbirth.

In the developing world, the risk of dying in childbirth is one in 48, but virtually all countries now have safe motherhood programmes.

7. Address the global threat of new and re-emerging diseases

(Health care and health care reform)

8. Combat HIV/AIDS, Malaria and other diseases

Target for 2015: Halt and begin to reverse the spread of HIV/AIDS and the incidence of malaria and other major diseases.

Forty million people are living with HIV, including five million newly infected in 2001. Countries like Brazil, Senegal, Thailand and Uganda have shown that the spread of HIV can be stemmed.

Achieving the (UN) Millennium Development Goals for all Living with Disability (The Biwako Millennium Framework)

'Unless disabled people are brought into the development mainstream, it will be impossible to cut poverty in half by 2015 or to give every girl and boy the chance to achieve a primary education by the same date- goals agreed to by more than 180 world leaders at the United Nations Millennium Summit in September 2000'

James Wolfensohn, former President, World Bank

I start with a statement of the UN Millennium Development Goals:

- Eradicate Extreme Poverty and Hunger
- Achieve Universal Primary Education
- Promote Gender Equality and Empower Women

- Reduce Child Mortality
- Improve Maternal Health
- Combat HIV/AIDS, Malaria and other diseases
- Ensure Environmental Sustainability
- Develop a Global Partnership for Development.

For the differently abled, I would re-state the Millennium Development Goals as follows:

- Eradicate Extreme Poverty for People with Disabilities and their Families
- Achieve Inclusive Education
- Promote Gender Equality for Women with Disabilities
- Reduce the Mortality of children with Disabilities
- Achieve the Rights of Children and Families
- Combat HIV/AIDS
- Ensure Environmental Sustainability
- Develop a Global Partnership for Development.

I would also strongly advocate a global initiative called "Building Inclusive Futures" (BIF), linking knowledge at all levels (local to global) to support policy dialogue and development around disability and inclusion.

The UN MDGs are a set of eight time-bound and measurable goals for reducing poverty, hunger, disease, environmental degradation, illiteracy and gender equality, agreed upon by world leaders at the United Nations Millennium Summit (Sept 2000). The UN MDGs provide an international focus on reaching specific targets, offering a framework for advancing inclusive policies and practices for people with disabilities.

There need be provision of an agenda for inclusive policy and programming in education, maternal and child health, poverty reduction, human rights, gender equality, HIV/AIDS and global partnership substantiated by clear targets that we are committed to working towards by the year 2015.

To realize this commitment, we must work through

- Knowledge and Data Collection
- Resource Development and Knowledge Sharing
- Policy Engagement.
- Bringing the disabled into the development mainstream.

IN GREATER DETAIL, WE TALK ABOUT:

- Advancing a global initiative called Building Inclusive Futures (BIF), linking knowledge at all levels (local to global) to support policy dialogue and development around disability and inclusion-
- The UN MDGs are a set of eight time-bound and measurable goals for reducing poverty, hunger, disease, environmental degradation, illiteracy, and gender equality, agreed upon by world leaders at the United Nations Millennium Summit (September 2000)-
- The UN MDGs provide an international focus for advancing inclusive policies and practices for people with disabilities-
- Let us examine our revised Development Goals now:

1. Eradicate Extreme Poverty for People with Disabilities and their Families-
2. Achieve Inclusive Education-
3. Promote Gender Equality for Women with Disabilities-
4. Reduce the Mortality of Children with Disabilities-
5. Achieve the Rights of Children and Families-
6. Combat HIV/AIDS-
7. Ensure Environmental Sustainability-
8. Develop a Global Partnership for Development.

Provision of an Agenda for inclusive policy and programming in education, maternal and child health, poverty reduction, human rights, gender equality, HIV/AIDS and global partnership substantiated by clear targets that

we must commit to working towards by the year 2015.

To realize this commitment, we must work through:

1) Knowledge and Data Collection;
2) Resource Development and Knowledge Sharing;
3) Policy Engagement-

Two important areas for action:

- Comparable data on disability in each of the Millennium Development Goals-
- Create a capacity to link the knowledge and expertise of people with disabilities, their families and organizations to decision-making processes-

'The rights of disabled people need to be better incorporated into our poverty reduction work and the achievement of the Millennium Development Goals'

Gareth Thomas, Parliamentary Under Secretary of State, DFID (DFID Spotlight 29 September 2004)

Disability is recognised by DFID as one of several factors, such as gender, age and caste, which interact to impoverish people and keep them poor.

- *Disabled people are typically among the very poorest, they experience poverty more intensely and have fewer opportunities to escape poverty than non-disabled people*
- *Disabled people are largely invisible, are ignored and excluded from mainstream development*
- *Disability cuts across all societies and groups. The poorest and most marginalised are at the greatest risk of disability. Within the poorest and most marginalised, disabled women, disabled ethnic minorities, disabled members of scheduled castes and tribes etc. will be the most excluded.*

9. Ensure environmental sustainability

Targets:

- *Integrate the principles of sustainable development into country policies and programmes and reverse the*

loss of environmental resources.

- *By 2015, reduce by half the proportion of people without access to safe drinking water.*
- *By 2020 achieve significant improvement in the lives of at least 100 million slum dwellers.*

Give incentives to nations to cut down on their carbon emissions.

Give livelihood incentives to the poor, to prevent deforestation for instance.

Address and monitor the following important issues-air quality; carbon monoxide; chemical agents as well as such emerging threats such as bioterrorism; chemical weapons; hurricanes, tornadoes and earthquakes; Global Warming and Ecological Debt. The Kyoto Protocol ought be every nation's priority.

More than one billion people lack access to safe drinking water and more than two billion lack sanitation. During the 1990s, however, nearly one billion people gained access to safe water and the same number to sanitation. BUILD A WORLDWIDE CONSORTIUM FOR WATER.

10. Develop a global partnership for development

Targets:

- *Develop further an open trading and financial system that includes a commitment to good governance, development and poverty reduction – nationally and internationally*
- *Address the least developed countries' special needs, and the special needs of landlocked and small island developing States*
- *Deal comprehensively with developing countries' debt problems*
- *Develop decent and productive work for youth*
- *In cooperation with pharmaceutical companies, provide access to affordable essential drugs in developing countries*

- *In cooperation with the private sector, make available the benefits of new technologies – especially information and communications technologies.*

In the process of developing a "global partnership for development":

11. Develop an official development assistance indicator.

Make aid more sustainable and reliable. The way aid is meted out to the developing world is deplorable. Is it just, I ask you? One's human dignity should not be compromised in the process of receiving aid.

12. Develop an international consortium of debtors. Also, an insolvency fund to solve once and for all the debt crises.

13. Abolish the death penalty. Also, abolish slavery in all its forms and torture.

14. Establish a morally-accepted international code of conduct.

15. Switch to renewable energy.

16. Establish fora for Water and Sanitation.

17. Devise strategies for Urban Poverty (rural migration, proliferation of slums and forced demolition of urban poor habitat)

18. Establish fora for youth participation.

19. Establish norms for fair trade practices.

20. Set up social security standards.

21. Establish norms for the protection of refugees, migrants and internally displaced persons.

22. Set up equitable labor standards.

23. Set up fora to encourage NGOs and civil society working in development.

These are global issues that affect everyone. Formulating norms or setting goals on them will restore justice to the poor/ go a long way in reducing the have/have-not chasm.

50

The Tragedy of Being the World's Poor

The tragedy of being the world's poor

Justice for the poor/the have/have-not chasm

Buckminster Fuller would have readily agreed!

(Peacekeeping; humanitarian aid and global poverty – health and education; water; shelter for all and renewable energy)

"What the world has to eradicate is fear and ignorance..."- Jan Masaryk

("The mightiest works have been accomplished

by men who have kept their ability to dream great dreams..."

-Walter Bowie)

So!

("Do not fear to pioneer,

to venture down new paths of endeavor..."

-Ralph J.Bunche)

(1) Renewable Energy: We do get wonderful opportunities to learn about the cost-effective technology being used in the renewable energy sector in the Netherlands or Germany, for instance, but we are too busy exploring collaboration possibilities with their companies, but what we actually need to do is to explore ways and means towards achieving our rural electrification targets, for instance, through an Application of this important option! These would include Wind, Solar, Biomass/Biogas and energy recovery from waste options, to name just a few;

(2) Humanitarian Aid: We're just releasing Drums of tonnes of EU/E-Currency towards helping in the time of natural catastrophes, like floods for instance, wherein then training the local folk in tackling natural calamities..The Tsunami was lesser-known and therefore lesser-feared, until things happened..Well, we could always study the formation of Tsunamis, potential areas of occurrences, its effects and the likely near-future areas of assault..Oceanographers stand perplexed as to the causes of the Tsunami, or for that matter, the Sumatra earthquake of Dec 2004: We need to have Science promising us conduction of awareness programs among coastal communities..which could go a long way in reducing casualties in case another Tsunami struck..Forestation with several types of coastal vegetation, depending on the environment suitable for their growth, could also be a significant remedy, among other things...

(3) International crisis management: I must confess that NATO (the North Atlantic Treaty Organization) has done really well in maintaining security and stability, for example, in the Balkans and in Afghanistan, with over 5000 troops taking part in NATO operations in Kosovo and Kabul (May 2005)..I must also sincerely add here that this is certainly no way to address Global Security Issues, the key lies in what I would call "The Food on the Tables Syndrome": Child Poverty, Hunger and Malnourishment; or the "Health Center Syndrome": Happy and safe Motherhood and an elaborate Health Intervention System in place; or "The Books and Classes Syndrome": Schools and Colleges and Clean Drinking Water and Textbooks and Blackboards and Pencils; etc, finally, harnessing of that one most important resource: ***Peace, Peace and Only Peace!***

(4) IBM (International Business Management!): It's important to understand that in a place like Germany, the business community simply puts its correspondents to study trends in various zones across the world and write about

them..The other major thing I wish to talk about is "Corporate Social Responsibility", known elsewhere as ***"Corporate Philanthropy"****..I wish to quote B.C.Forbes on this one, when he talks of 'humaneness in business'..With all thy getting, get understanding..to inspire a philosophic mode of life, broad sympathies, charity towards all..he further goes on to say:*

'I have faith that the time will eventually come when employees and employers, as well as all mankind, will realize that they serve themselves best when they serve others most..'

(5) Global Poverty: *is THE ISSUE we need to address..Surely, the death of a child by Malnutrition ought to merit more attention compared to say the launch of a space-vehicle from NASA..The death of a woman in labor is surely catastrophic, and reflects on the sad issue of a Community Health system entirely out of place, globally, there are an estimated several million HIV+ orphans largely in Sub-Saharan Africa, and there is the dangerous trio upfront largely in countries very low on the HDI, such as Bangladesh, Malaria, TB, Cholera also Diarrhea, and women in post-Apartheid South Africa are presumably trading their bodies for a decent supply of drinking, or should I say, 'drinkable' water, the pathetic, I should say, deplorable, condition of schools and related facilities merit our immediate attention, the state of affairs are the same everywhere, from India to South Africa, if there is a Dharavi in Mumbai city of India, there are Favelas in Rio so there are the Ghettos in America, if little children are being assaulted here, an elderly man could be mugged in downtown Los Angeles, and the media as usual chases those with fame and money and lifestyles...*

The human rights scenario is also rather bleak..and countries are struggling to put their records in place...

Global Warming has assumed menacing proportions...it wouldn't be long before temperatures have risen, our ice caps

could melt and our oceans have consequently risen, flooding, storms, famine, death and hunger have actually devoured us and our species could become extinct!

Under these circumstances, global polity merits stronger and more effective regimes, we need more efficient leadership, a more focused attention on global poverty and related policies and concerns, greater attention to each one's needs and no hunger for more, optimum allocation of the earth's finite resources and last but definitely not the least, attention to the principles and resolutions of the United Nations with emphasis on human rights, and inherent "dignity and worth of the human person..."

This is certainly not a prescribed agenda, but...

Talking about possible futures for this our beloved planet!

51

Tsunami (Swept Away by the Ocean the Child Learns to Survive, there Cannot be a Greater Disaster!)

Disaster management (leaving the poor to die)

What kind of a world is it anyway that we are passing on to our children?

"Everyone expects to go further
Than his father went;
Everyone expects to be better
Than he was born
And every generation
Has one big impulse in its heart-
To exceed all the other generations of the past
In all the things that make life worth living..."

On the concept of "**human dignity**"

Further,

Every individual has a place to fill on earth; everyone is in some respect important...

So, you need to have courage..the most sublime courage is perhaps the one that the class too poor to know they possess it possesses, and something the world hasn't discovered as yet! There can be no alleviation for the sufferings of mankind without courage...

Let me impart to you a lesson in courage..in the face of adversity...

"I am tsunamika's mother.

I have no other name now. Not since the ocean that lived outside my village, and gave me and mine food and sustenance, claimed everything in one fell swoop...

I have lived my life by the ocean. I was born, married my fisherman husband here. It was here I bore him children, my two girls. We lived in a house we had made with our own hands. He had two boats..the ocean took it all...

I was not made homeless alone. There were 11,000 people, of which 500 were families like ours. All of them lost so much. Most, everything...

The entire community was devastated. For days, weeks, we could not think of lighting home fires. There was no home left, no light in our lives, no desire to eat...

I knew the end of our lives was near. There was nothing to live for. Nobody could understand the extent of my despair, that of my family, my other fishermen sisters and brothers. Each had lost so much. What was there to live for?

But God moves in mysterious ways. We found a new life in an unexpected way, through tsunamika, who was born of the fury of the ocean...

She taught me to **live** *again!*

Today, we make so many dolls.

We earn money from them. ***We use it to help children of the village go to school, study and become big men and women.*** *We helped the men buy new nets. Others have now started repairing their broken huts.*

But, most important, we have found **life.** *Each of us is now a mother of a new child. The little dolls have a name. They are no longer just pieces of cloth.*

They have a meaning. And they have given us **life.**

Our beloved!"

(Text courtesy: www.tsunamika.com

C/o Auroville/tsunamika,

Upasana Design Studio, Auroville, Tamil Nadu, India)

*(**Childhood** is indeed one of the most fascinating stages of our life..the child is innocent of artifice and evil. His needs are limited and focused. He sometimes asks for the moon, but can be diverted..to something more real...*

Think: Walk down any maternity ward with newborns in their cradles, and try and identify their caste, creed, religion, or faith..every newborn is a perfect creation, a symbol of mankind's will to survive...

Every saint and criminal was as helpless, as tiny and as innocent of worldly ways as any child that has just opened its eyes to the brand new world around it...

*Mythology celebrates the child...every religion has its stories of God-like children and our Gods as children..the infant **Jesus**, the child **Krishna**, the baby **Rama**: Poets and painters have immortalized their attributes, sung their praises, and painted their exploits...*

*The infant Jesus, whose birth was heralded by a star, even as a boy, was a fount of **wisdom, tolerance, love** and **piety** (**virtues** lacking in the world today..)*

Little wonder, we believe that the child is father of the man...(Wordsworth 1770-1850)

And this is how Gerard Manley Hopkins (1844-1889), a modern day poet, reacted to Wordsworth: How can he be? The words are wild..the man is father to the child. The child is father to the man! How can he be? The words are wild...

I am sorry! I can feel for you..children of the mortal species!

Dreaming!

(What kind of a world is it anyway that we are passing on to our children!)

52

Climate Change and Global Warming – Our Children are Paying the Ecological Price of World Trade

ECOLOGICAL DEBT

(A Convenient Truth for the Rich)

The explosion in world freight has had an adverse impact on the global environment. Nearly all global freight is powered by fossil fuels. A study in 1997 by the Organisation for Economic Co-operation and Development and the International Energy Agency found that the transport sector accounted for between 20 and 25 per cent of the world's total carbon emissions.

The steep rises in global fossil fuel use since World War II have meant that annual global carbon emissions are now nearly four times what they were in 1950, leading to a 16 per cent increase in world carbon dioxide concentrations over the same period. These increased greenhouse gas emissions may eventually see world temperatures rising up to 4 degrees centigrade by about 2070. 'Global Warming' may cause our polar ice caps to melt, leading to rising sea levels flooding many coastal areas. Other regions may see disease and famine and/or extinction. In no small measure, the world's environment is paying the price of the spread of economic globalization.

Aircraft and shipping also have alarming specific pollution effects. Aero planes produce large quantities of carbon dioxide as also significant quantities of nitrogen

oxides, both of which are significant greenhouse gases, while nitrogen dioxide causes acid rain. Aircraft emissions of nitrogen oxides are predicted to double between 1996 and 2010. In shipping they use a low-grade type of fuel that produces nitric oxide and nitrogen dioxide that can cause acid rain and photochemical smog. Global shipping's pollutant emissions equals about half of the land-based emissions of the same generated by the United States. Shipping also produces nitrous oxide, a potent greenhouse gas, as well as sulphur oxides that cause acid rain. It is to be deeply regretted, however, that pollution from world freight is exempt from the Kyoto greenhouse gas protocol.

Mindless consumerism, trade and GATT, waste dumping, slumps and collapses, inflation and changing fashions in policy; an international monitoring mechanism; the anti-globalization movement

The World Economic Forum (Davos)

Post-Second World War Dominance by the United States:

The United States was economically very dominant after the Second World War and utilized this dominance to shape the International Monetary Fund (IMF) and the World Bank, as also global trade agreements, in the form they desired. America's clout also ensured the IMF and World Bank were headquartered in Washington.

Technology:

Modern-day transport and communications systems have contributed to massive reduction in the costs of moving goods and capital around the globe and have definitely made world business information more available than it has ever been before.

Compliance of governments:

The modern era of economic globalization began when

the United States floated the US dollar in 1971 in a panic move induced by post-war trade competition from European economies and loss of competitiveness caused by its spending on the Vietnam War. Most governments around the world have progressively reduced their trade and capital controls ever since. The free-market ideologies of Friedrich von Hayek, Milton Friedman, Margaret Thatcher and Ronald Reagan have become the order of the day.

The strong influence of the IMF, World Bank and WTO:

The onset of the Third World debt crisis in 1982 gave the IMF and World Bank enormous power, which gave them free rein to impose pro-globalization, free-market conditions on their loans to poor countries. Past or present IMF and World Bank debtors account for about 40 per cent of all the world's economies. In the interim, the WTO has more and more pushed the boundaries of trade globalization through harsh trade rulings and new areas – with patents, investment and services trade – included in Uruguay and Doha.

Corporations, speculators and global investors:

Corporations have perpetrated the influence of economic globalization through their domination of world trade, investment, and research and development. The largest corporations wield enormous control not only over world trade but also over global foreign investment and world output. Currency speculation is now rife.

Poverty; Mindless Consumerism; Waste Dumping and Slumps and collapses:

They say inequality breeds inequality! I can foresee another French Revolution considering the widespread social discontentment...The chasm between the rich and the poor has deepened. The haves are literally splurging, indulging in luxury and opulence and extravagance to the point of nausea, while those at the other end of the spectrum

have nothing to eat! Child malnutrition is a major cause of deaths of children in the developing world. Then there are the debt crises, and industrialized nations are using the developed world for dumping waste...Recently, there has been a slump of sorts, and many people have lost their jobs. It seems that the bureaucracy that is the UN is worried, but is not the UN supposed to continue with its work? Is the UN so meek and powerless that it had to call a meeting at headquarters?

There is so much heat that the refrigerated climate of ***DAVOS*** cannot perhaps provide an answer!!!

There is no answer. We have lost our reason.

53
The Global Loss of Democracy

Globalization, economic

Globalization, opulence, extravagance and luxury

(Diamond yachts, ornate jewellery, sleek convertibles and Fashion-TV)

(Disturbing trends in global material consumption)

And one would say

(Talk of 'the cream you choose to apply on the face for glowing, resilient skin'...talk of all those worthless, destructive beauty pageants...talk of Armani and Peter 'England': O! The British and their councils and a comprehensive increase in programme (d) funding for India; a consequent larger number of programme (d) directors, officers and assistants and malnourished South Asian societies!) and their DFID's! (decide first for international development, laugh!) and Allen Solly and Oxford and Harvard and DAKS London and Forbes magazines and brand ambassadors and the EU (and their 'cultural weeks' in impoverished South Asia or whatever) and the 'OSCE' (how much cooperation there is in Europe that they should be divided on Iraq...create "morgues of orphaned residue..."who gives them the right anyway?...(and OPEC) and Santa Barbara and the Bold and the Beautiful...and Moschino and Regen hair vitalizers..talk of our 'vital' issues and Elizabeth Arden and Chanel Paris and L'Oreal and Estee Lauder and wrap-a-rounds and camisoles and jackets and dinner jackets and a pair of Levi's jeans and innerwear and footwear!... And Audi and Porsche...and camcorders and

cookies!... And spaghetti and macaroni and broccoli and some mustard!...and Charlie's Angels and La Femme Nikita...and pornography and perverted (piracy) labels and records..winding it all up with either a Bacardi or a Cappuccino..!)

O! The Western World..!

(The IELTS goes online and payment by credit cards and the cash-rich, the pound-sterling moneyed ones get to go to the London and the Wharton business schools without batting an eyelid! While the "Heavily-Indebted Poor Country Initiatives" are forced into remote with low-paid professionals' cataract camps!)

(Dreaming..!)

The Western world, do they really care about us... treating us with pity, do we actually need them...I wish for once that they could appoint me some sort of a 'Goodwill Ambassador to the Western World', maybe I could fix their minds, hearts and heads and come back! (Big laugh!)

(Dreaming...'Lessons in International Understanding..'.

And, who might give me the right to blame them anyway? An entire species of peoples! They're such lovely peoples, giving away so much to us, sacrificing so much of their time and energy for us... With such lovely littles in shorts Johns and Jacks and Toms and Michaels and lovely littles in skirts Natalies and Carols and Peggys and Janets..they're draining so much on their state exchequers and acoustics and percussions (never mind the repercussions!) in the process of giving away!... They're trying to 'imagine' how to 'heal the world'...not an amazing feat!... And spending so much of their time working as 'volunteers' and 'interns' with the Peace Corps in Guatemala and Oxfam in Mogadishu and SOS-Kinderdorf International in 'very-low-on-the-HDI' Bangladesh...it would

be very unfair on our part to call them (actually, each other) "foreigners"..they're (we're) certainly not 'aliens' from outer space!...we're (all) the world, we're the children..and 'it's a small world after all'..love..we're all friends...

Together(yes, all the Oxfams and the Plans and the Villages of Hope and SAARC and the ADB's (both Asian and African) and the EU's and the UNICEFS and the UNDPS and the WHOS and the Habitats for Humanity!), we can do it!

Dreaming..! With a bit of fun thrown in!

((Why on earth are these coveted UN/non-UN positions (nee missions) reserved only for "stars"- Hollywood, Bollywood, Tollywood and Lahore's Lollywood, are they really the best for these missions? Mega/giga success is surely no index of missionary potential;

And, some of us ordinary folk are really so much better at it than most of these commercial bigwigs! Work ought to count! Mass appeal is and ought not to be enough! They actually don't do anything beyond celebrity cause endorsement...has the world in any way changed because of them...please tell me...I would appreciate that! Thanks very much indeed, 'deciders of the world..I know your voice counts'! (Laugh!)...

Not everyone can be a Meg Ryan or an Angelina Jolie or a Bob Geldof or Bono ...and why would anyone be excluded from or in any way denied an opportunity to do some good work for mankind? Most of us ought to be enabled instead!

With such 'terrific' goodwill ambassadors, youth emissaries, international peace and security spokespersons and whatever, we have collapsed! (Laugh!)

I find the whole system flawed on this one! Except perhaps for Baaba Maal!

Actually, why can't we have 'dream' missions to our neighbours as a regular fixture, if cricket, soccer, baseball

and NBA's and MBA's and cinema can always happen (and with all that exotic expenditure!), so can those that the world is truly in need of?); and Grammys and Faith Hill and Norah Jones (celebrity daughters!) and Emmys and 'Desperate Housewives' (well, if I were a Nobel Laureate, I would include them in the GDP and GNP of nations!) and Immys and American and Indian 'idol-worship' and Michael Johnson and Michael Schumacher (and AIDS and cancer research) and Sarah Jessica Parker (as Carrie Bradshaw-God alone knows where she parks her car, where they all do- O! These celebrities and their private lives!))

54

What they Don't Teach you at the Kennedy School of Government

That South Asia is the world's largest mass of destitute

Where opulent private lives co-exist with hopeless destitution

"..How large developing countries such as India handle farm sector reforms has important implications for the well-being of people not only in India, but worldwide.."

- Per Pinstrup-Andersen, Director General, International Food Policy Research Institute, December 1997.

Many poor countries including India and Pakistan have millions of undernourished people without basic amenities such as food, clothing, shelter, sanitation and hygiene, clean drinking water, jobs, education and health care, among others...

According to the World Development Report 2000 / 2001 ..a majority of the world's poor live in South Asia and Sub-Saharan Africa... And of these, India has the largest concentration of poor people in the world, a tremendous moral challenge for our planners...

Too many children in India, "innocent flowers", die of hunger and malnutrition (the "true terrorism" of our times) daily..added to factors like gender discrimination and inadequate infrastructure...

Wish the rich, industrialized countries could cut down on their extravagant consumption patterns, waste dumping, greenhouse gas emissions, etc., to help children in the South (as well as those in the North) enjoy better lives. Call it "feeding minds, fighting hunger".

Poverty alleviation in India calls for greater commitment towards sustaining the growth rising from economic liberalization, a process initiated in 1991, as well as better local governance (including a deeper understanding of democracy among the rural poor). This, in turn, would, in my opinion, call for increased investment in India's vast human resource potential, including food and nutrition security, primary health care and education, clean drinking water, subsidized housing, a change in the lifestyles of india's elite, jobs (including strategies like "job-sharing"), land reforms, a "social safety net" for all those whom markets exclude (like insuring farmers against agricultural yield shocks through public works programs and food grain distribution), increased (state) transparency, and last but definitely not the least, making children in India a top priority in actions on poverty. I suggest that a part of military spending in India (Oh God! India and Pakistan!) be diverted to human development..we have to learn from the experiences of Southeast Asia...like, for instance, emphasizing maternal health care..and applying science and technology, to, for instance, famine and drought management.

We must all realize that poverty pressurizes the ecosystem; therefore, there is a need to work towards "sustainable development." Given the fact that most of India is agricultural, there is a need to give priority to the same through proper irrigation facilities, optimum use of technology and by diversification. And, an extremely urgent issue would be "population crisis intervention", with India all set to overtake China... including making education free and compulsory and phasing out child labor. In all of these, the corporate sector as well as NGO's has to play an important role.

Only then can India achieve progress; so, let us put in our best efforts...after all, we have all agreed to halve the number of the world's poor by 2015!! And, India's performance would be critical! Remember Rio, Copenhagen and, more recently, Johannesburg???

55

Today's Thoughts for a Better Tomorrow...

(Can We Predict India's Future????)

It is exciting to imagine what our world will be like in the 21st Century. Futurologists are busy predicting possible future developments..We are all hoping for a better world..However, for a developing country like India, the population will have to put up with the challenging task of providing infrastructure, food, education, housing, medical care and many other facilities on a massive scale...

The country's number one problem is its teeming Population, which is the root cause of innumerable other problems..We are already a country with more than 100 crores of population and the population clock is constantly ticking every second, every minute, every hour and so on... We have no doubt been spending enormously on family planning, and yet a burgeoning population confronts us. Statistics would only show that problems on account of the above have been increasing exponentially as compared to the solutions being provided. At the current rate, India is all set to become the most populous country in the world in another three decades...

There is lurking danger of damage to the health of millions of young men, women and children due to inadequate nutrition. Besides, our hospitals are unable to provide adequate treatment to the underprivileged. Moreover, the rural areas are devoid of dispensary and hospital facilities. It seems that in this century, a large number of our poor will die without the adequate provision

of medical facilities both in our rural as well as in our urban areas. Can they hope to afford the enormous expenditure on medical care? Time for sociologists, policy makers, decision makers to start thinking..Time also to take a reasonable notice of this aspect as far as it applies to us...

Adding further to the problem are the strong rural-urban divide and consequent mass migration from the villages to the cities. This is leading to social rift and tension followed by urban overload. Serious crises in the realm of housing, water supply, growth of slums, etc. have arisen...

More than ever before, there is now excessive demand for energy, but our current scenario of hydro and thermal potential does not seem to be inspiring. On the contrary, it is worth pointing out that India can become an important source of solar energy in the world, given its immense potential, both in terms of availability of high technology and the climatic conditions in this part of the world. Surprisingly, we have not seen much application of solar energy research and development to India's rural development programs. Policy makers need to have a closer look at this.

At the same time, policy must address the continuous environmental degradation we have seen in terms of forest depletion, soil erosion, climatic changes and floods. This is bound to have serious repercussions on poverty, as the poor are directly or indirectly dependent on nature for their sustenance... With increasing environmental pollution, the ecological balance is being seriously threatened..In fact; the large-scale automobile emissions would very soon be giving rise to innumerable pollutants like carbon dioxide and carbon monoxide, with the result that there is likely to be a spread of diseases like lung cancer, TB, asthma and bronchitis, etc in 21st Century India.

Our old social problems are far from being solved, while new ones are being added with increasing rapidity..like rampant consumerism..We have had a Green revolution but

without the power to purchase foodgrains for a majority of our population..A revolution in telecommunications enables us to talk to our friends at the other end of the planet but does not facilitate our talking to the village next door. What an anomaly? Our literacy rate continues to be the lowest in the world. A large majority of our population is still illiterate. 50 million children in the age group of 6-11 either do not go to school or drop out after a few months or so. It has been predicted by sociologists that in the early part of the 21st Century, India would be having the largest number of illiterates in the world..Children are living under deplorable conditions. Many child laborers are wasting their childhood washing dirty dishes, cleaning tables, manufacturing fire-works, weaving carpets and stitching footballs with their nimble hands. Juvenile delinquency is on the rise!!! What about street children and child beggars? Female infanticide still exists- a phenomenon that demonstrates how Science and technology can be misused to enlarge social evils...

Our educational system hardly prepares our students to learn to cope with present challenges and opportunities. Are "value" systems imbibed in the innocent minds? Besides, 60 percent of India's population lies outside the scope of the education system comprising our universities, institutes of advanced learning, colleges and schools..This century will generate millions of educated unemployed youth..Due to an acute shortage of job opportunities and a serious lack of vocational training and self employment opportunities, the frustrated youth will be involved in anti-social, criminal and terrorist activities. Drug abuse and trafficking, large scale alcoholism, immoral traffic, violence, murder, sexual abuse, terrorism, anti-social activities, hooliganism, HIV-AIDS, corruption, degradation of social and moral values shall now be new menace.

All these years of development have been years of missed opportunities..as management gurus...say, "The 20th Century has been a management of mismanagement.."It's

a shame that we are yet to pull 300 million households out of abject poverty. Some parts of the country like Kalahandi and Bolangir in Orissa, to name only a few are best known for their starvation deaths.

The greatest challenge facing Indian planners and policy-makers is to convert the vast Indian population into an asset and a resource towards future development... Increased application of Science and Technology to progress can actually help pull India out of poverty and backwardness and sort out imbalances in the system..Our education system should be made future-oriented. It should be such that it prepares our coming generations to participate in development work. We are running against time. We need to have a national dialogue so that a long-range perspective can emerge for poverty eradication, at least in 'basic need' areas..Economic performance has to be made accountable, our planning has to be monitored and corruption has to be weeded out from the system. India has enormous agricultural, industrial and technological potential, which can be utilized for achieving economic self-reliance in the 21st Century. The country needs strong and honest leadership, motivation towards progress, an efficient administration and brilliant vision...

India has a great future (provided we learn how to make it great) if only we dare dream...

We can do it...

A dream...for a better tomorrow with a vision...

A vision with action...

May God bless India...

May God Bless Every Other Nation...

56

God's Blessings: The Buddhism of Nichiren Daishonin Explains

WORLD HUNGER: THE POLITICAL ASPECT AND THE RIGHT TO HUMAN DIGNITY

Buddhism of Nichiren Daishonin explains >>"***Hunger*** is a condition characterized by an insatiable desire for food, power, wealth, fame, pleasure and so on. In this state, one is tormented with relentless craving and the inability to satisfy it, even when the desire is achieved. Looked at positively, *HUNGER* is the driving force behind most human activity. Put simply, without the desire to do some thing, nothing would get done.."

This philosophy gives a bird's eye view of both the magnitude of problem as well as the "unfinished agenda" for a global strategy. It cannot be denied that there have been remarkable advances made on many issues but it is also true that many areas of our society are still left untouched by whatever development has taken place. This raises a series of haunting questions.

Keeping this point in view, I would be constrained to address briefly on only one facet of this global monster called "Politics of Hunger of food and the Right to Human Dignity".

«In a world overflowing with riches, it is a outrageous scandal that more than 826 million people suffer hunger and malnutrition and that every year over 36 million die of starvation and related causes. We must take urgent action now.»

Jean Ziegler, April 2001,UN Special Rapporteur on the Right to Food

The Universal Declaration of Human Rights emphasizes "...everyone has the right to a standard of living adequate for the health and well-being of himself and of his family, including food, clothing, housing and medical care and necessary social services". But for most of humanity, these rights are increasingly inaccessible.

Nelson Mandela in his Nobel Lecture stated "..the children must, at last, play in the open field, no longer tortured by the pangs of hunger or ravaged by disease....this must be a world of democracy and respect for human rights, a world freed from the horrors of poverty, hunger, deprivation and ignorance..."

"Politics has a major hand in what can go wrong and right in this world, and if food or poverty or the basic necessities for survival are not secured for everybody in the world, then the world is not at peace." —Anonymous.

Studies show that high levels of child hunger are linked to population pressures created by high fertility levels and rapid growth in populations. "This suggests that improving women's status through education and employment opportunities should be central to improving both food supply and child hunger rates."

Studies have also shown that reducing hunger throughout the world is more than just a question of agricultural and economic development. "Hunger is also a distributional problem, and the obstacles to improved distribution are primarily political. Conflict regulation, violence prevention, the reduction of international arms trade, and the protection of civil and political rights should be central to policies that address hunger."

Researchers point out that food is not in short supply. In fact, food products have never been so abundant. There is enough available to provide each of the Earth's

inhabitants with at least 2,700 calories a day. But production alone is not enough. Then where is the issue then???

Prof. Amartya Sen, winner of the Nobel Prize for Economics, has shown how government policies can cause famine even when food is abundant. He contends that greater responsibility for the well-being of society must be given, not to the market, but to the state. A state that must be sensitive to the needs of its citizens and, at the same time, concerned with human development throughout the world.

Prof. Amartya Sen argued that public action includes not only what is done ***for*** the public by the state, but also what is done ***by*** the public for itself. World hunger is extensive in spite of sufficient global food resources. Therefore increased food production is no solution. "The problem is that many people are too poor to buy readily available food". Therefore measures solving the poverty problem are what is required to solve the world hunger problem.

Many insist that revolution, green or otherwise, must be undertaken in partnership with the peasants and the local society. The color of the revolution is **not** important. What is important for sustainable development is the revolution of the human mind which has no color, no religion, no caste, no boundaries...

Cuban President Fidel Castro says "..Hunger is the offspring of injustice and the unequal distribution of the wealth in this world.... What kind of magical solutions are we going to provide so that in 20 years from now there will be 400 million instead of 800 million starving people... Let the truth prevail, and not hypocrisy and deceit."

Sustainable development must be achieved at every level of society.... Governments ... should ... [promote] food security and ... food self-sufficiency within the context of sustainable agriculture.... All countries need to assess ... the impacts of [economic] policies on ... food security.... The major thrust of food security ... is to ... increase ... agricultural production

in a sustainable way and to achieve a substantial improvement in people's entitlement to adequate food.

A very poor farmer in Mustang district said to the IFAD-financed Production Credit for Rural Women project member in Nepal: "Before the project we felt our hunger and poverty were for ever and nothing could be done about them. We do not fear to starve any more during the winter months. We now have hope and, as a woman, I have acquired *izzat* [dignity]."

The journey has begun. Rays of hope are shining. Civil and political rights should not be divorced from social and economic ones. Investing in the right to food through the promotion of groups and associations, with the participation of the most deprived - women and men - in decision-making, so that they can voice their demands and exercise their freedom of speech, is investing also in human dignity.

57

Will Wear their Hair Short... and Dress Like Men

(THE GENDER DEBATE)

AS WOMEN EMANCIPATE THEMSELVES...

"..There are many kinds of emergency situations that can impact your family's well-being- whether the problem is a natural disaster like a tornado, snow storm, hurricane, drought, etc. or a personal emergency such as a job layoff, major illness or death in the family..Many people (men and women alike) don't know how to handle the possibility of something happening outside their control ..Given all the demands of a hectic lifestyle, thinking about what could happen is often overwhelming so you don't even feel like starting...

..I know that when there is a crisis, WOMEN are the first to help and encourage one another. No matter what happens, whether you face a crisis or just minor inconveniences in living life, there is always hope. We need to pray and ask for God's strength to handle whatever happens together..."

- **Karen Anderson's Y2K Women Today...**

Phoenix, AZ 85029, USA.

Information for Women on Living Life Simply, Safely and Securely in the Year 2000 and Beyond.

And I wish to add here, that as long as there are women, there is more than enough hope for the world...

Beatrix Potter, a mycologist, catalogued the entire Fungi family of the British Isles. Yet, she could not get the recognition she deserved as a scientist, after which she turned her skills to write books for children...did I not say that as long as there are women, there is hope for the world? And, for our children?

After all, life begins in the womb... Unfortunately, many children, especially girl children, remain deprived, or, should I say, bereft of the joys of childhood, with much-needed love, attention, nutrition and health-care being denied to them..but are women to blame? Certainly not. In fact, women are often the last ones to eat in the household... A stark fact this one...

Indeed, talking about women's empowerment, it is sad that a majority of women in the developing world have not an iota of reproductive choice on themselves..I wish to quote Ana Maria Pizarro of Nicaragua, quoted from a Latin America public hearing...

"Health policies only see women as reproducers and mothers. Existing programmes provide only prenatal care, institutional care during birth and nursing, postnatal care and care for the baby's development and growth..the first cause of death among women is clandestine abortion in the cities and haemorrhage during childbirth in the countryside."

Barbara Klugman from the Southern Africa public hearing feels that "the sole function of health-care services must not be the reduction of fertility rates, because the quality of life of a population is global.."

We cannot isolate child-bearing from an understanding of sexuality...however, it is sad that today's generation remains obsessed with sexuality, and adolescent pregnancies and sexual abuse of children and teenagers are issues which we simply cannot ignore..free choice in the context of reproduction policy remains constrained by social

norms..what is important is that women in all societies be treated as full citizens, at par with men. I'm sure that once women have been provided with information and education to manage their own reproductive rights, they could and invariably would communicate the same to others in the family, work place and community. In the main, women would ideally be the (right) ones to take into account the impact of their choices on future generations and environmental sustainability..it is indeed unfortunate that the so-called sexual revolution might have occurred in behavior but not in knowledge...

Sex and reproduction apart, I've often wondered as to why there be a skewed distribution of women in power, worldwide..it is ironical that the United States has never had a lady president. I guess, most, at least some people feel that women may be incapable of running the Presidency, especially as it relates to defense matters. This is just not done, even a country like Pakistan, has had a lady at the helm of affairs...

The major problem is that men and women do not decide or act in isolation from society, but are influenced by what they see, read or hear..and, this is an extremely unfortunate fact, for instance, you may know that very few or no women will want to train as pilots when all that they are seeing, reading or hearing of all the time is that aeroplanes are manned by men...

Yet, have you or have you not heard of our women scientists? We all know of Madame Curie. And then, there was Maria Goeppert-Mayer who discovered the Shell model of nuclear structure, for which she was to later receive the Nobel Prize...Rachel Carson went on to establish the Environmental Protection Agency. She investigated the effects of pesticides (like DDT) on humans during the 2nd World War, and succeeded in getting many of them banned from use. The Environmental Protection Agency now works with and for governments and pressure groups worldwide.

Dian Fossey in the seventies and other women naturalists came up with some very new interpretations on gorilla interaction, while studying and conducting research in Africa, and many of their ideas simply did not conform to traditional "masculine-feminine stereotyped gorilla behavior"...Lise Meitner was among a handful of scientists that refused to work on the Manhattan Project that developed the first nuclear bombs...Rosalind Franklin's work on the structure of DNA should never be forgotten...

Now, what is science without computers, you might say. "Daring – Do for Digital Daughters", does this remind you of something? It should. It's all about "computer confidence for women". And, Rachel K. Adelson writes, quoting Advertising Age: "It would be beneficial to show girls that their moms have no trouble handling computers." Further, she writes: "Promoting a certain fearlessness, whether it be on the soccer field, in the study hall, or at the silicon-sparked workstation, can make the difference between floppy ambitions and a charged career drive..." A male friend of hers adds: "Many girls did not get the skills needed to take things apart when they were growing up. The forces and motions needed to do this have to be learned. It's not some magic male skill." After all, we've had some brilliant women in this field, talking about previous recipients of the prestigious 'Lovelace' Awards, namely, Adele M. Koss, who developed the first compilers; Betty Holberton, one of the six original programmers of ENIAC; Margaret H. Hamilton, founder of Higher Order Software; Amy D.Wohl, pioneer of office automation and Ergonomics; and, more recently, Dr. Frances Allen, the first woman to be named an IBM fellow, the company's highest technical honor.

Bravo!!!

Women have really achieved in the past, at times, under impossible conditions..and difficult circumstances..under conditions in which being a woman was considered a liability..under circumstances in which there were absolutely no role models ..accolades for all those women who finally went on to conquer..despite everything...

From womb to tomb, from cradle to grave...society shapes our thinking, actions and feelings. Even play time is time for gender-stereotyping..Barbie-dolls, skipping and cooking for the girls, and construction toys, soccer and science for the boys. Society gives us absolutely no scope to take our own decisions..and the vicious cycle continues..at times, I wonder why Mills and Boon does what it actually does to perhaps millions of girls worldwide..and why must emotions like love and affection continue to remain sultry and gospel-like R and B and girls' talk, while, some men are to be found screaming at the top of their voices and smashing their guitars...(that is really not a very good thing to do) come on women, Tina Turner, Tracy Chapman, Aretha Franklin and Alannah Myles, you too can be like them!!!

All this is only a process of conditioning..today, women are to be found in almost every walk of life-auto rickshaw driving, truck driving, bus conducting, railway ticket-collection, gas-station work, army/navy/air-force cadetship and officialdom, adventure and rough sports like boxing, soccer, hockey, cricket, martial art, freestyle wrestling (China!!!), high-adrenalin sports like bungee jumping and cross-country running, (so, don't be surprised if you run into a woman lifting 29 kgs or playing rugby, baseball, doing formula-one racing or cross-country cycling, remember the "Battle of the Sexes" match in tennis, in which Billie Jean King defeated Bobby Riggs...)...and, then there are to be found women educationists, bio-technologists, researchers, doctors, film-makers (as Mimi Leder, who directed an action-film 'The Peacemaker'), film-photographers, photo-journalists, writers, social workers and political leaders, and, last but definitely not the least, from homemakers to the primary carers of children..however, women should never remain confined to the kitchen, and, mankind can progress only if women, half of humanity, progress...

And, giving birth, well, that is a right given to women only...however, I would just love to see men doing much the same thing, and I believe, from information that I have on

me, (that's according to the head of a leading fertility clinic in the UK), that it may be possible, given advanced fertility techniques...I mean, why should the contribution of a man in creating life remain confined to a sperm only?

And, women are the ones who really knit, but men should start knitting as well, because, after all, tiny tots (for whom such work may be done) come when papa loves mama...

Mama's rights are important, and her rights have finally been recognized as human rights. This is especially true of the Twentieth Century...and the impact of this global transformation on political, economic, and social life will be fundamental...

Time now for the women's revolution to make them (women) visible as actors, direct participants, and leaders in all walks of life...and make them be recognized as pivotal pillars of change...

The "Convention on the Elimination of Discrimination against Women" (CEDAW), voted on by the UN General Assembly in 1980, led to the accumulation of data on the status of women in many countries, North and South alike, which revealed "an unknown dimension of development: the systemic discrimination and marginalization of women (and their deprivation all over the world) that created a momentum for change..." not all efforts in this direction have been wasted, as can be seen from the results of the first UN Conference on Population and Development, Bucharest (Romania), 1974; the Rio Earth Summit; the Cairo Conference (1994); the Social Summit in Copenhagen (1995); the UN Conference on Women in Beijing, China (1995); and, more recently, the World Summit on Sustainable Development in Johannesburg, South Africa, 2002. Immediate efforts ought to be made to rectify unfavorable situations, such as these: the results of a FAO study in 1979, found that African women made up 80% of the food producers in some countries, yet they received less

than 10% of the visits made by agricultural advisers..and, in some countries, primarily African, women's health continues to be plagued by rituals such as female genital mutilation and absence of education..actually, no war can be won without active participation of us (read "we") women, especially, those from the developing world..decades of struggle by the women's movement finally have been recognized by the United Nations (as laid down in UNDP's Human Development Reports).

This includes the realization that the value of their unpaid, largely invisible work contributes, on an average, $11billion per year to the global quality of life, including work in subsistence agriculture, livestock husbandry, domestic work, child-care, and care for the elderly, the disabled, and the ailing, among others. All future policy should incorporate these aspects, including the provision of something like 'gender auditing' a measure of the conditions under which the girl child lives, including, among others, low-birth-weight babies, illiteracy, the lack of primary education, low social confidence, (the extent of) sexual abuse, forced prostitution, etc, all of the above being yardsticks for the development process. There should not be any more missed investment and lost opportunity. This is the time for action, to enable women to add their experience and their culture to the organization of both society and economics..after all, the futures of half the world's population, (with abilities beyond the ability to procreate) are at stake.

I wish to wind up with a few memorable quotes on a woman's right to choose by some amazing women celebrities:

According to Susan B. Anthony: "The day will come when men will recognize woman as his peer, not only at the fireside, but in councils of the nation. Then, and not until then, will there be the perfect comradeship, the ideal union between the sexes that shall result in the highest development of the race."

"Something which we think is impossible now is not impossible in another decade," so says Constance Baker Motley, first Black woman in the U.S. to become a Federal Judge.

Former ace tennis player Martina Navratilova thinks that women should not set any limits...

Gloria Steinem feels that "the first problem for all of us, men and women, is not to learn, but to unlearn."

Barbra Streisand has this to say: "I am also very proud to be a liberal. Why is that so terrible these days? The liberals were liberators-they fought slavery, fought for women to have the right to vote, fought against Hitler, Stalin, fought to end segregation, fought to end Apartheid. Liberals put an end to child labor and they gave us the five day work week! What's to be ashamed of?"

Finally, this is what Virginia Woolf had to say: "As a woman, I have no country. As a woman my country is the whole world."

58

My Country is the Whole World

The people of Vietnam gave a red carpet welcome to President Bill Clinton when he visited their country.

I have deep commitment to working on issues related to peace and development. In fact, I have decided to make it a lifelong commitment. My primary interest lies in women and children caught up in situations of conflict and/or deprivation. Given your support, I can, in the future, work as a "peace or goodwill delegate" or on a similar assignment, representing my country to peace and development forums, among other things.

Now, let me give you an idea of the kind of issues I am concerned with. It is heartening to note that the world's first permanent "war crimes court" will try war crimes, genocide and crimes against humanity. Former US President Mr. Bill Clinton is said to have remarked: "In taking this action..we reaffirm strong support for international accountability and bringing to justice perpetrators of genocide, war crimes and crimes against humanity." And what more beautiful than the "dividends of peace", that 25 years after the Vietnam War, the people of Vietnam gave a red carpet welcome to Mr. Clinton, when he visited their country...even when they are still suffering from the war's after-effects-the Vietnam landscape hiding thousands of mines that still kill and maim many unaware innocent citizens...

I have indeed deep feelings for women (and I'm a woman myself), and children caught up in difficult situations like war and/or poverty. They are, perhaps, the worst sufferers when it comes to war crimes such as rape

and sodomy, forced conscription (for children) and the vicious cycle of poverty and deprivation. How much I hate to hear of a war rape being committed? And what exactly are world governments doing about this? (It is only when women gain their place as equal and strong members of society, once problems such as reproductive choices and under nutrition are solved, that such demeaning acts against humanity will finally cease to occur, am I right?)

And Behavioral Science of which I am a student has a very important role to play in this regard. I am someone deeply concerned over social injustice. And I understand that one's values can definitely provide immense support to the peace-building process. One's values can surely facilitate dialogue processes in conflict resolution. Is it not common to react to situations of poverty, violence, and social injustice with fear and violence? This is, precisely, what Psychology can do. Examining the correlation between poverty/ deprivation (child poverty, in my case) and conflict would definitely do us good in the long run. I quote the American Psychological Association: "We believe that we must apply and make public our knowledge in order to contribute to human welfare..and work to mitigate the causes of human suffering" (APA, 1992, Principle F).

Now, why is such research important? For the primary reason that it begins to involve a new generation of young people committed to working towards a sustainable, socially just, peaceful world. The crux of the matter lies in developing a culture of love and mutual respect.

I wish to quote someone (anonymous): "I have met the future, and it is us." Let us all give it up for peace and harmony. The world is in deep need of "feeling", among "citizens of this beautiful planet."

59

Rich World/Poor World

The world is in deep need of feeling (Poverty, illiteracy, ignorance, neglect and utter destitution in the developing/ underdeveloped world).

It is indeed a misnomer that everyone grows richer from economic globalization. On the contrary, globalization has created two classes of people on this planet – the "Haves" (who have all the Wealth and the privileges, the so-called 'Rich') and the "Have-nots" (the utterly destitute, the so-called 'Poor'), and a world order in which only the rich benefit. There is what I would call obscene "***Inequality***" between nations, between regions of the world and also within nations. So, for instance, while it may be possible for a child in the United States to enjoy on a single plate several different types/brands of the best cheese from all over the world, it may be impossible for a child in Sub-Saharan Africa or Latin America or indeed in India to even dream of fulfilling his needs for and indeed rights towards clean drinking water in school! The implications of such inequality between children are enormous! They could, possibly in the long-run, offset a bloody revolution as happened in France during the French Revolution of 1789. The world cannot afford to either neglect or ignore this situation for long!

Another widespread global trend that disturbs me is this 'unflinching', I should say, "Material Consumption" in the Developed World for which now the world seems to be paying a heavy price in the form of "Global Warming". Mindless Consumerism following the advent of globalization has led to extravagant consumption patterns and accumulation of

wealth in the 1st World and utter destitution, poverty and hopelessness in the 3rd World, particularly Africa, Latin America and South Asia.

There are indeed significant exceptions, but in general, economic globalization does seem to have mainly benefited the rich. Globalization has led to a situation in which the rich have become richer and the poor poorer. Both the structure and the politics of our globalized world are unambiguously tilted in favor of rich countries; left as it is, indeed instead of a "Global Village" we shall have a global supermarket and a sorry situation in which the rich become richer and the poor poorer with devastating consequences.

WEALTH CONCENTRATED IN THE HANDS OF A FEW THE POLARIZATION OF WEALTH

The wealth record of poor nations, taken as a group, since the start of the Industrial Revolution, does in no way make for heartening reading. The stark truth is that the industrial revolution and economic globalization may have brought a lot to the world, but they definitely have not made it a more financially ***egalitarian*** place! Since the start of the Industrial Revolution the gap between the world's richest and poorest nations has grown wider and wider to the extent of developing into a deep chasm. The United Nations Development Programme (UNDP) estimates that in 1820 the difference between the per capita incomes of the world's richest and poorest countries was 3:1, by 1950 35:1, by 1973 44:1, and by 1992 to a horrendous 72:1.

I quote David Landis, Professor Emeritus of History and Economics at Harvard University: "the difference in income per head between the richest industrial nation, say Switzerland, and the poorest non-industrial country, Mozambique, is about 400 to one. Two hundred and fifty years ago, this gap between richest and poorest was perhaps five to one, and the difference between Europe and, say, East or South Asia (India or China) was around 1.5 or two to one". This does not mean that everyone was rich 250 years ago; they weren't – nearly everyone was poor then. But over the period since only a select few have grown richer and the rest have been relegated to a life of utter misery, hopelessness and destitution.

60

Sprawling Mansions and Personal Private Golfing Estates and Dream Fairytale Like Weddings...the Rich of the World

Famine, disease and hunger, where children die daily..the poor of the world.

Paris-the fashion capital of the world; Kalahandi-the desperation capital of the world.

Our polar ice caps are melting, temperatures have risen, Katrina struck and the Tsunami has grown fiercer.

This day, over 26, 500 children died around the world.

The tragedy is, children do die daily from poverty and other preventable causes, this however rarely makes headline news.

"Around the world, in rich or poor nations, poverty has always been present. In most nations today, inequality - the gap between the rich and the poor – is quite high and often widening. Whether the cause is a lack of individual responsibility, bad government policy, exploitation by people and businesses with power and influence, or some combination, many feel high levels of inequality will lead to problems such as increasing crime and violence, and risks social cohesion.

The latest World Bank figures for world poverty reveals a higher number of people live in poverty than previously thought. For example, the new poverty line is defined as $1.25 a day. 1.4 billion people live on or below that line.

Furthermore, about half the world – over three billion people – live on less than $2.50 a day and at least 80% of humanity lives on less than $10 a day."

From "Global Issues – Social, Political and Environmental Issues that Affect us All" – last updated Sunday, Nov. 30, 2008.

As I write this, somewhere a child is dying of malnutrition. But the rich do not seem to be bothered...

All that Western music, Western culture, the bare torsos, all that nudity...yet another child dies of hunger...

All those Fashion-TV parties..a nation goes hungry...

All that white skin vs sheer native desperation...

All those sprawling mansions and personal private Golfing estates and dream fairytale-like weddings..a nation loses a child of hunger...

Malibu and the rich man's bread, pray how much more comfort does one need?

Paris-the fashion-capital of the world; Kalahandi-the desperation capital of the world...

(The lifestyles of the rich and the famous in Kalahandi, Bolangir and Koraput, Orissa, India)

Paris and Milan fashion weeks, and lifestyle and hairstyle institutes in the West, and Vogue and Cosmopolitan, and Michel Adam, George Michael and the Sex Pistols, and one more child assaulted after a teen pageant, and one more child dies of hunger (calling for a shift in priorities)...

And English as the language of destruction (a polarized world) though I don't mean it literally...

Nina Ricci, Yves Saint Laurent, Dolce & Gabbana and Christian Dior and Giorgio Armani, F-Parties, the Fashion Bar Party in Singapore, an exotic Jaguar on display (our inherent Americanism), an American Idol pervades our senses as the developing world struggles to survive...

As the rich of the world celebrate Christmas Party on the Black Diamond in Genoa (25 Dec, 22:00 hours), the poor

of the world will die on the streets on these cold wintry nights...

The poor boy eyes the D'damas diamond collection on display..and farmers' suicides...

Rave parties, exotic Malibu and excess hoarding of wealth and material consumption..these are our notions of progress...

There is need for a universal language of peace and non-violence and equality..otherwise, there could be serious repercussions.

We have seen that in recent years, our polar ice caps are melting, temperatures have risen, Katrina struck and the Tsunami has grown fiercer.

Global warming has had the unprecedented impact of nuclear war. Climate change could have serious repercussions on global security unless nations change their lifestyles.

Climate change would hit crop yields and water availability everywhere, leading to greater human suffering and consequent regional strife. Scientists predict that global average temperatures will rise due to burning fossil fuels leading to rising sea levels, forced migration, freak storms, droughts, floods, wildfires, epidemics, famines and crop failures.

Inequality breeds inequality. Unless nations work to reduce the gap between the rich and the poor, the inevitable result would be issues such as deforestation (the poor would be forced by circumstances to cut down forests for a livelihood) and the burning of fossil fuels for power and transport both of which would exacerbate warming and rise in temperatures. As a result of rise in temperatures, there could be state collapses further increasing the rich-poor divide and heightening racial and ethnic tensions providing fertile breeding ground for more conflict.

Urban areas would not be exempt as falling crop yields due to reduced water availability and rising temperatures will push up food prices.

In brief, climate change will have serious implications for food, water and energy security issues and ultimately global security concerns.

Global inequality is a preventable cause of global warming.

The question arises: Which is the cause and which is the effect?

Such causes of poverty and inequality are no doubt real. But deeper and more global causes of poverty are often less discussed. The silent killers are poverty itself, easily preventable diseases and illnesses.

Climate change and global warming are the inevitable result of global issues that may be important. Like child hunger, which decimates on a daily basis. This daily tragedy, from poverty and other preventable causes like lack of information, rarely makes headline news. Many do feel that high levels of inequality will inevitably lead to changes in climate.

Extreme inequalities: There is a link between global warming and poverty, preventable diseases and neglect, causing a "tsunami every week".

Are global rules and institutions reducing global inequality and advancing development?

This is widely debated.

Over 11 million children die each year from preventable causes like malaria. On the other hand, there are claims that warming puts penguins and polar bears at risk. These are contentious issues. But priorities are priorities. I wish for once we could focus on social inequalities.

Or else, our polar ice caps will melt faster, our temperatures will rise faster and higher, another Katrina will strike and the Tsunami will grow even more fiercer...

61

What Aspects of Social Inequality Should we Focus on?

Globalization is not a new phenomenon. But it has come to engulf the whole world. This makes the meaning of justice so relevant in the contemporary era.

So, what are these our Global Questions?

The first global question is that of 'Linguistic Justice'. English is now the world's 'lingua franca'. This has come both as a boon and as a bane. As a common medium of communication, English has many benefits. But English comes with a price, not for native speakers of the language, but for those who must bear the costs of learning the language. For greater linguistic fairness, this second category of people has to be given increased free access to intellectual property. The world is dominated by English, and so it is our duty, the so-called enlightened 'elite' of the world, to show equal dignity and respect for those who do not speak the language, and enable such populace acquire skills in the language.

The second global question is that of 'Disabled' 'Diversity Justice'. It is now the fashion in our contemporary era to talk about 'diversity issues'. More and more, corporations are talking about the rights of the differently abled. But there's a slight hitch here, there is very little equality between the able and the disabled. We may talk about the disabled, but the truth is that we keep such people either in solitary confinement or institutional confinement throughout their lives. In the name of diversity, we are creating a class of

people who have no jobs, no homes or no social recognition either. This is a class without dignity. We must recognize that there are diverse people in all walks of life (diverse in terms of ability and mental/physical traits/attributes) just as there are diverse faiths, and start treating them in all fairness/ justice/dignity.

The third global question is that of enabling the poor. Talking about development aid and assistance, we often find that the rich are not sufficiently motivated to help the poor. There is enough money in the world but that does not induce sufficient giving. Let us now be concerned with the factors that will induce more giving, including creating institutions that will work to inform, assure and strengthen moral will to give.

One major global question that concerns us is that inequality is not just a 'within' states phenomenon, it exists across states as well.

Again, we must understand that in most of the world's poorest countries, development focuses too much on market access and foreign aid. There are other indices/factors in development, like relaxation of controls and a fairer trade agenda.

Labor Regulation can leave everyone worse off, therefore one has to be careful.

Another major global question is how to redistribute wealth at the national and global levels. Introduction of a 'Global Welfare Agency' to facilitate global redistributive transfers from rich to poor individuals is a highly welcome arrangement.

Trade fairness is a must. A condition under which a country offers subsidies to its people is a situation of unfairness.

What are the 'Principles of Justice' and how do they work? The question is of how our actions will affect those who will live in the future. Climate change provides us with policy problems whereby we must choose the degree to which

we are prepared to impose sacrifices on those that are alive, so as to benefit those that will live after us.

Also, another question that arises is whether we must exclude the world's poor from advanced medicines. Such medicines could, if they reached the poor in developing countries, be of invaluable help to them as they might need them. Pharmaceutical companies see more money in curing the diseases of the rich (indeed some diseases are the poor man's diseases while some are diseases of the rich only, modern medical science is also responsible for such discrimination), and much of clinical/pharmaceutical research aims at reaching the rich, often at the expense of research into alleviating the diseases that affect the world's poor. I see a strong need for greater health reform in the future.

One major global question is 'Gender Injustice'. More boys than girls go to school in the developing world, indeed a female child will be sexually assaulted at this moment as I write these words, and the girl child will inevitably be overburdened with household chores. It is obscene, the extent to which there is prevalent violence against women and girls in war, and obstacles to the progress of women seem to be rooted in customs and cultural norms (example FGM) and can be exacerbated by the subordinate social status of women in many societies.

We must try and achieve more Egalitarian societies. It would be difficult for the poor otherwise. Look at the debt crises in the Third World.

62

Las Vegas Lady Luck Casino

OBSCENE SPECULATION AND WEALTH ACCUMULATION DEBT CRISIS IN THE THIRD WORLD

"Let us seek new ways to break the stranglehold of debt, to redress its consequences, and ensure that debt crises will not occur. Can only be achieved through a new, just global order."

"As we forgive our debtors" (Unknown)

Contemporary globalized economy promotes wealth accumulation in the hands of a few through lending money or through speculation. This process is promoted by G-7 leaders through the Bretton Woods institutions, which have encouraged debtor countries to borrow on global financial markets, facilitated by the IMF's deregulation of capital movements around the world. But foreign debt can only be repaid in hard currency; therefore indebted nations are obliged to put all their attention on raising of these revenues from exports or new loans. This is why nations in debt are forced to concentrate on cash crops like coffee and cocoa as opposed to staple foods, and are caught up in endless cycles of borrowing.

Debt management is now a major challenge of our contemporary era. The Heavily Indebted Poor Countries, or 'HIPC' Initiative offers very little and to too few countries. Designed by creditors, their purpose is debt collection not debt relief. In addition, Western creditors, primarily the IMF, always impose difficult conditions on debtor nations making it more difficult for them. Debt management plans have to

be transformed into debt-release opportunities to bring relief from the scourge of debt to the suffering millions.

Debt bondage to Western governments and creditors in which the poorest countries find themselves is today's new slavery. There is increasing polarization of wealth in the richest nations of the world and a simultaneous terrible decline in living standards in the poorest nations. The social, political and environmental costs of the debt crisis must not be tolerated and must be redressed. Canceling the debt of poor nations and addressing the terrible cycle of debt accumulation are matters of urgency.

The policies of Bretton Woods institutions, particularly the rapid liberalization of capital flows, are increasingly being questioned. The Bretton Woods institutions have applied double standards to Western economies on the one hand and nations in debt on the other. Poverty eradication policies are the need of the hour. One must understand that basic human needs and human rights and ecological protection ought to take precedence over debt repayment.

Debt repayment must not take precedence over spending on education, health, sanitation, clean water and other social needs. This undermines accountability by debtor governments to their people, which in turn erode local democratic institutions.

Diverting resources from poor peoples in debtor nations to rich Western creditors amounts to violation of a morally accepted code of conduct and also one's human rights. This imposition of policies is in itself a travesty of justice. Women and children are forced to bear the entire costs of debt repayment through reductions in social sector spending. Too much emphasis on exports may lead to more deforestation leading in turn to climate change problems. Debt and with it economic degradation may also lead to social conflict and further disintegration finally to war.

Both parties must assume responsibility for the debt crisis. Creditors must not be allowed to dominate the debt

relief process. Full support must be extended to the poor of indebted nations which cannot service their debts and suffer sanctions as a consequence. The need of the hour is a new just process of arbitration for canceling international debt as well as an international insolvency law to ensure once and for all that losses and gains are equally shared.

Collective political will is needed, and civil society must be involved. We need mechanisms producing ethical, mutually responsible and transparent solutions for greater economic efficiency, respect for basic human needs and human rights and ecological sustainability. Civil society organizations must be enabled to determine how debt funds released may be optimally reallocated into social priorities. We must work to make global financial institutions more democratic, transparent and responsive to the needs of the world's most impoverished.

Let us appeal to the leaders of the G8 nations to recognize the urgent need for global economic reform, a more just distribution of wealth in the world and greater responsiveness to the basic human needs of the Third World.

63

Storms Shalls Rage and Oceans Roar

WILL OUR WORLD COME TO AN END? THE WORLD NEEDS A MESSIAH

This is a planet in peril. There are rivers of luxury surrounded by a sea of poverty. This is not a very welcome arrangement. A brief history of man suggests that economic slavery of all kinds has existed from the beginning of time. But it is only in recent years, in our so-called (contemporary) casino era, that man has become so material (it seems generations now carry the 'material gene') that he chooses to remain oblivious even when a child hunger death has been reported from another part of the world, the 'lost world'.

How can we as free nations ever afford to shut our eyes to the misery the Third World lives in? We are Church-goers, and we read the Holy Book. Every holy book prescribes certain codes of conduct, and we have chosen to write our own prescriptions. This is utterly unfair. That I choose to party atop the Fashion-TV diamond yacht with a billion-dollar splurge is as contrary to the laws of nature and as unfair as that malnutrition should take a child away in remote Sub-Saharan Africa or perhaps South Asia.

Man's materialism claims more lives than does anything else. Drought, famine, the cutting down of rainforests, forest fires, the tectonic shift, hurricanes and cyclones, rising temperatures, melting glaciers, rising ocean levels, the Tsunami-are but the result of man's greed and excessive material consumption and mindless consumerism and unprecedented levels of inequality.

And not only "storms shalls rage and oceans roar" but

lack of equality may disrupt the global order, leading to more chaos, more social ferment, more social disintegration and finally war.

The future can be changed; the future is in our hands. These are some futuristic notions of progress.

'The greatest period of danger is in September 2001', the prediction for America went thus. And 'The white man will battle people in other lands'. And the Twin Towers fell, and then Afghanistan and Iraq happened.

What did we get out of all this?

-A poor child eyed the exotic beach holidays on TV with disdain. The child was after all a child. This could have been the birth of social discontent.

-We interviewed some policy analysts from the John F. Kennedy School of Government. What was the point talking to some people from Harvard? There was a lot of display of glamour and opulence in America anyway. This could have led to more social ferment.

- We executed Saddam Hussein following a pre-emptive war. Freedom was an untidy business. Our mission was not accomplished.

-We interviewed some prominent individuals. "What were the instructions to the guards?" Could we put an end to Guantanamo and Abu Ghraib?

-We partied so extravagantly that it would be seen from space. The first world was now to become synonymous with wealth and excesses.

- We failed to feed the world's children. This was a serial incompetence and not just a lack of compassion.

64

Towards Greater Compassion

THE FUTURE IS IN OUR HANDS THE FUTURE CAN BE CHANGED

We are told that the world's most extravagant party will be seen from space. Hollywood stars, billionaire business moguls even heads of state will be attending the grand opening of the Atlantis. The final bill for the four-day long beachside celebrations is estimated to go beyond 15 million pound sterling. Invitations are to be sent out each studded with hundreds of pounds worth of Swarovski crystals. This is all in a part of the world synonymous with wealth, opulence, and extravagance and excess.

Lifestyles of the rich and the famous! We are all familiar with the unusually extravagant lifestyles of wealthy entertainers, sportspersons and business moguls, those wealthy opulent residences and glamorous lifestyles, also exotic resorts and tourist attractions.

Everyone wants a house in Malibu, a house by the beach. Movie stars live there after all. Malibu is 'A Way of Life'. Everyone wants a private jet. Sprawling, majestic, Tudor style mansions and estates. A private golf course, tennis centre, fitness facilities, club houses and one could feel like the 'King of the County'. And horseback riding, canoeing and a private yacht. One could choose to relax on the estate, cook like a French chef or take a trip down the ocean.

I would like to see famous people living on the streets! "I'd like to see them spend a week. Livin' life out on the street"- Good Charlotte has sung.

Is that the answer? Dragging the rich out of their palatial mansions and forcing them to live the same kind of existence that the poor are living. That would mean chaos, social ferment and still more bloodletting. I guess not, when there's a better way.

We know that there is something for every man's need, but not much for every man's greed. We have to promote more equitable distribution of resources, prevent the over utilization of resources by a class/classes/group(s) of people, build up a fora against mindless/limitless material consumption and dumping and get the rich to give more to the poor than they ordinarily would.

We have to move towards greater compassion. Only more and more compassion can heal the world.

First of all, we must promote arms control. This would involve discouraging the production of small arms, establishing fora for disarmament and diverting a part of global military spending to social sector spending, like health and education. We must also impose controls on the trade in arms. This will act to regulate conflicts.

Second, promote more equitable distribution of resources, set up a coalition to prevent the over utilization of resources by a class/classes/group(s) of people. This will work to check deforestation, protect biodiversity and reverse climate change and global warming.

Third, we have to exercise a check on the power of corporations. Build up fora against mindless/limitless material consumption and consumerism. Promote free and fair trade, and impose checks on mindless food dumping and promote just official development assistance (aid) patterns.

Fourth, since there is "enough food to go around" and food is often used for "fattening animals", producing enough food for the future population will require concerted efforts by both the public and the private sectors to increase agricultural yields while avoiding damage to the environment. Earth produces enough food for nearly all the

people alive today. In fact, if everyone adopted a vegetarian diet and no food were wasted; current production would theoretically feed 10 billion people, more than the projected population for the year 2050. We come to the question of "Genetically-modified" food.

This is also a question of policy. That innocent people should starve and nations should lose their children to malnutrition is as much a question of faulty policy as when people should get displaced when the gates of a dam are opened.

Who makes these policies? For whom are they made? What are the short-term and the long-term implications? Has the G8 been given too much power?

Then, there are questions of health, population and rights. The question of new and re-emerging diseases and health and health reform. The question of feeding the future world population. The question of leading a life of freedom, liberty and equality. Because of the fact of being 'born free'...

Sometimes, one can misuse one's freedom. The International Criminal Court (ICC) exists to deal with perpetrators of war crimes, genocide and crimes against humanity.

Wars and threat of war continue on a daily basis. Even today, a war rages daily on the West Bank/Gaza Strip. Israel and the Palestine are questions that have not recently emerged. The Iraq Crisis was a result of pre-emptive war in motion. The War on Terror vis-à-vis 9/11, the Middle East and Darfur were questions highlighted in the mainstream media. But there is still more bloodletting, and innocent lives continue to be lost in the process...

Natural disasters take away many lives each year too. How can we at this rate achieve our goals of sustainable development and eradication of world hunger and poverty?

Today, over 26,500 children died of hunger around the world. The tragedy is that poverty rarely makes headline

news. In most nations today, inequality-the gap between the rich and the poor-is often widening, the result of unequal distribution of resources, limitless consumerism and faulty government policy, and inequality will lead to problems such as increasing crime and violence and risks of social cohesion. Decreased global security may have important ecological implications such as climate change and global warming.

More than ever before, issues of food production are directly tied to national security, now in the post 9/11 era, we stand to confront greater malnutrition and hunger in the developing world..there could be no greater catastrophe.

On the same day (9/11), around 16000 children worldwide died from hunger-related causes. By the time I finish writing; a few children will have died.

Why should another child die of hunger? Why must a nation be allowed to lose her children to hunger? That a nation should go hungry; there cannot be a greater catastrophe...

A world situation in which children die daily is simply not acceptable...

ANOTHER WORLD IS NOT ONLY NECESSARY BUT POSSIBLE.

65

The Prosperity of Nations

THE RIGHT PATH TO PROGRESS

A NEW HUMANITY

"Justice and righteousness..Caring for the poor and needy..Is not this to know me? Says the Lord".

(Jer.22:15-16)

It's a world of stark injustices. Righteous indignation often focuses on issues like pornography, violence and sexual sins. Macro-ethical issues like poverty and hunger, injustice, race and war are rarely the subject.

Very often, we as the Free Nations of the World, thrust our own peculiar judgments on the world. We believe, for instance, that the poor are either lazy or stupid. If one nation can do it, why not another?

Then, there is the question of human dignity. We free nations often lack respect for the poor.

As a direct consequence, the income gap between the poor and the rich, everywhere, is widening. Since the Industrial Revolution, we have never learned to share it properly.

The earth was given to all, not just to the rich. There is enough food to go around-for our need, but not for our greed. It is not God's will that a quarter of us live in luxury while the rest struggle to survive.

DOING JUSTICE

"The really important teachings of the Law are justice and mercy and honesty. These you shall practice..." (Matthew 23:23)

Talk to the "poor". Who are the poor? The poor know who they are. These are the geographically "displaced" or emotionally, spiritually, materially deprived, within their communities, of the basic necessities, to "live decently".

Just why are they poor? Wherein lies their fault? The answer lies in Economics and the economic systems of the world. National and global systems revolve around greed and power. The global distribution system is faulty. This is "the international imperialism of money".

Each of the world's peoples has its own particular cultural, ethnic and political distinctive features. These must be respected. One model of development may not work in another environment.

ALBERT EINSTEIN once famously remarked: "The problems of the world cannot be solved with mechanisms, but only by changing the hearts and minds of man and speaking courageously." JESUS went on to change the hearts and minds of people. Disappointing the Zealots, he renounced violence, exploitation and apathy..they're all dehumanizing..His was the way of sacrificial LOVE.

PRAY

Pray for the poor, and then pray for their oppressors.

66

A More Tolerant, Democratic and Compassionate Generation

"We won't do this as well as Jesus did but we must try. We must not act for others merely through feelings of personal outrage, but when – and until – through caring friendship we earn the right to be invited to be their helper or advocate. Such feeling presence enables us to transcend narrow bigotries."

(UNKNOWN)

It matters really not much whether one should or should not be highly educated, but that (s) he ought to adhere to the faith principles of justice, mercy, pity, compassion, and non-violence and reconciliation as a matter of lifelong commitment in one's work and day-to-day living! Mahatma Gandhi and Martin Luther King Jr., are each a case in point!

An unknown author has said and I quote:

"A basketball in my hands is worth about $19.

A basketball in Michael Jordan's hands is worth about $33 million.

A tennis racket in my hands is useless.

A tennis racket in Roger Federer's hands is a Wimbledon championship.

A rod in my hands might keep away a small dog.

A rod in Moses' hands parted the Red Sea.

A slingshot in my hands is a kid's toy.

A slingshot in David's hand was a mighty weapon.

Two fish and five loaves of bread in my hands is a couple of fish sandwiches.

Two fish and five loaves of bread in Jesus' hands fed thousands.

Nails in my hands might produce a birdhouse.

Nails in Jesus Christ's hands produced salvation for the entire world..."

It is time for this salvation. Let us surrender to the Lord Almighty to give us strength in this time of turmoil, hope in this time of poverty and violence and solace when we the peoples of the world have lost our way. Lord Almighty, we need those soothing balms of compassion and sweet words to guide us on our journey. Let violence and war be things of the past; make me a channel of your peace, Lord, a sentinel of good times to come. Help me be part of a more tolerant, democratic and compassionate generation.

Lord, I have lost my way. Show me the path to progress, to the prosperity of nations, to a new humanity. Bring hope to the new world that is emerging. We are children of a lost generation, and we have sinned. The material has overpowered us, and we have shunned the spiritual. Lord, guide us and show us the way, Lord. And forgive us so that we may in turn learn to forgive...

Peace, Peace and More Peace...
Lord, Show us the Way.

Index

H

I

Q

R

S

W

Y

Z